Cornel West

Cornel West

The Politics of Redemption

Rosemary Cowan

Polity

First published in 2003 by Polity Press in association with Blackwell Publishers Ltd, a Blackwell Publishing Company.

Editorial office:
Polity Press
65 Bridge Street
Cambridge CB2 1UR, UK

Marketing and production:
Blackwell Publishers Ltd
108 Cowley Road
Oxford OX4 1JF, UK

Published in the USA by
Blackwell Publishers Inc.
350 Main Street
Malden MA 02148, USA

Library of Congress Cataloging-in-Publication Data
Cowan, Rosemary.
    Cornel West : the politics of redemption / Rosemary Cowan.
      p. cm. – (Key contemporary thinkers)
    Includes bibliographical references and index.
    ISBN 0-7456-2492-8 (alk. paper) – ISBN 0-7456-2493-6 (pbk.
    : alk., paper)
    1. West, Cornel–Political and social views. 2. African Americans–Intellectual life.
  3. African Americans–Politics and government. 4. African Americans–
Religion. 5. Religion and politics–United States. 6. Pragmatism. 7. United
States–Race relations. 8. United States–Politics and government–1989 – Philosophy.
I. Title. II. Series : Key contemporary thinkers (Cambridge, England)
    E185.86.C589 2003
    305.896'073 – dc21
2002007679

Typeset in 10.5 on 12 pt Palatino
by SNP Best-set Typesetter Ltd., Hong Kong
Printed in Great Britain by MPG Books, Bodmin, Cornwall

This book is printed on acid-free paper.

Key Contemporary Thinkers

Published

Wes Sharrock and Rupert Read, *Kuhn: Philosopher of Scientific Revolutions*

David Silverman, *Harvey Sacks: Social Science and Conversation Analysis*

Dennis Smith, *Zygmunt Bauman: Prophet of Postmodernity*

Nicholas H. Smith, *Charles Taylor: Meaning, Morals and Modernity*

Geoffrey Stokes, *Popper: Philosophy, Politics and Scientific Method*

Georgia Warnke, *Gadamer: Hermeneutics, Tradition and Reason*

James Williams, *Lyotard: Towards a Postmodern Philosophy*

Jonathan Wolff, *Robert Nozick: Property, Justice and the Minimal State*

Forthcoming

Maria Baghramian, *Hilary Putnam*

Sara Beardsworth, *Kristeva*

James Carey, *Innis and McLuhan*

George Crowder, *Isaiah Berlin: Liberty, Pluralism and Liberalism*

Thomas D'Andrea, *Alasdair MacIntyre*

Eric Dunning, *Norbert Elias*

Jocelyn Dunphy, *Paul Ricoeur*

Matthew Elton, *Daniel Dennett*

Chris Fleming, *René Girard: Violence and Mimesis*

Nigel Gibson, *Frantz Fanon*

Keith Hart, *C. L. R. James*

Sarah Kay, *Žižek: A Critical Introduction*

Paul Kelly, *Ronald Dworkin*

Carl Levy, *Antonio Gramsci*

Moya Lloyd, *Judith Butler*

Dermot Moran, *Edmund Husserl*

James O'Shea, *Wilfrid Sellars*

Kari Palonen, *Quentin Skinner*

Steve Redhead, *Paul Virilio: Theorist for an Accelerated Culture*

Nicholas Walker, *Heidegger*

Contents

Acknowledgments

I should like to thank the people whose perspectives and insights have helped me to shape this book. The book is based on doctoral research undertaken in the School of Politics at the Queen's University of Belfast between 1994 and 1998 and I am grateful to Vince Geoghegan and Jim Martin for their supervision of that research. Their support, suggestions, and criticisms strengthened my work considerably, as did the comments of my examiners, Michael Kenny and Iain MacKenzie. I also want to express deep gratitude to Cornel West for his support of my work and for the warmth and friendship he has displayed towards this "sister from Ireland." I know that he has a hectic schedule, yet he was more than generous with the time that he gave me for interviews. Thanks are also due to the anonymous readers for Polity Press for their helpful comments on my proposal and the penultimate draft of the book. They pushed me to clarify much that I had taken for granted. I hope they will be able to endure a second trip through my work in order to see just how helpful their remarks turned out to be. Of course, none of the above are in any way responsible for what follows.

Introduction

This book is a critical introduction to the eclectic and provocative thought of Cornel West. Although he has received limited attention in Europe, in the United States his best-selling books, television appearances, and popularity as a speaker on the lecture circuit have earned him a reputation as one of America's leading public intellectuals. A *New York Times* review of his best-known book, *Race Matters*, praised West's "compelling blend of philosophy, sociology and political commentary" and concluded "one can only applaud the ferocious moral vision and astute intellect on display on these pages."[1] It is the roots, nature, and outworking of this broad moral vision that lie at the heart of my evaluation of West. Central to his work is an exploration of what it means to be human when confronted by death, despair, and the absurdity of forces such as racism, and a corresponding search for liberation that draws upon the resources of Christianity, pragmatism, and Marxist analysis. He sums up his overall project as an attempt to wrestle "with the problem of evil in modernity . . . it has very much to do with the dark side, the underside of the human predicament. . . . How do you preserve some compassion in the face of the absurd?"[2] Thus West's work centers on the interplay between his apocalyptic language of crisis and despair and the utopianism of his emancipatory politics, and his vision is framed between the limits of human finitude and human capacity for self-transcendence. In short, he examines the tragic face of American civilization and seeks to disclose the democratic possibilities that lurk beneath the surface.

Biographical sketch

West was born in Tulsa, Oklahoma, in June 1953 and grew up in the segregated Glen Elder neighborhood on the outskirts of Sacramento, California. The GI Bill enabled his parents Cliff and Irene, a civilian Air Force administrator and a school principal, to buy a three-bedroom house in Glen Elder in 1958. West has warm memories of living in this predominately blue-collar community and recalls that most people felt upbeat about the future: "Even for black families with modest means in segregated neighborhoods, it was a land of pleasant single-family homes, of barbecues and baseball diamonds. All of us kids had dads, most with jobs – that, we took for granted."[3] The themes of love, community, and struggle that occupy a pivotal place in West's thought were imbued in him from an early age. Of particular importance in this regard was the unconditional love and affirmation he received from his family, together with the black church's emphasis upon community, black cultural distinctiveness, and its attempt to wrestle with despair. However, West's early school years were far from idyllic and were characterized by a sense of rage. He recalls being "kind of the bad boy in class. . . . I'd get in fights five or six times a week. I was full of energy and anger. I don't know where it came from, because my family was very loving."[4] In the third grade he was expelled from school for hitting a pregnant teacher after she slapped him for his refusal to salute the flag in class. For six months he was unable to get into any school and his mother taught him at home until he entered an integrated "enrichment" school. A fundamental change occurred when he became a Christian at the age of eight, and he went on to excel in both junior and high school where he successfully made the transition from bully to school president.[5]

In his early teens West developed a fascination with the work of Søren Kierkegaard which prompted him to study philosophy at university. He entered Harvard as a student in 1970, at a time when the Ivy League was starting to open up to African Americans, and graduated *magna cum laude* in 1973 with a degree in Near Eastern Languages and Literature. He then moved to Princeton where he received an MA and Ph.D. in Philosophy. His first teaching post was at Union Theological Seminary in New York (1977–83, 1988), followed by appointments at Williams College (1982), Yale University Divinity School (1984–87), the University of Paris (Spring 1987), Princeton University (1989–94) where he was director of the Afro-American Studies program, and most recently Harvard University

as Alphonse Fletcher Jr University Professor. In July 2002 he will
return to Princeton as the Class of 1943 University Professor of
Religion, following a highly publicized dispute with Harvard
President Lawrence Summers. West's first book was published in
1982, and to date he has written or edited over twenty books,
including best-sellers such as *Race Matters* and the two-volume
Beyond Eurocentrism and Multiculturalism, which was awarded the
1993 American Book Award. West has also contributed to a diverse
range of periodicals, such as *Monthly Review*, *The Yale Law Journal*,
and *Christianity and Crisis*. His work has drawn an impressive array
of accolades from fellow academics – for instance, Henry Louis
Gates described him as "the preeminent African-American intellectual of our generation."[6] West's work covers a diverse array of
themes, and this eclecticism is motivated by his genuine desire to
see fundamental transformation in the lives of the urban black
community. This desire prompts his engagement in a number of
progressive campaigns and organizations, such as the Democratic
Socialists of America, of which he is an honorary chair, and the 2000
presidential campaigns of Bill Bradley and Ralph Nader.

West is an exciting and provocative thinker who touches on a
host of issues at the heart of contemporary intellectual and political debate, such as race relations, the nature of American capitalism
and its impact on the poor, the importance of identity politics, the
need for connection rather than polarity between disparate groups,
the purpose of contemporary intellectuals, affirmative action,
family life, the meaning of democracy, corporate greed, and the role
of faith in public life. He offers a compelling vision of the way
in which moral values derived from spirituality can undergird a
movement for radical social transformation. This represents an
important alternative voice in contemporary America where public
religion has in recent years been dominated by the Christian Right.
West's political ethic seeks not only to reinvigorate leftist politics,
but also to reconcile American democratic practice with democratic theory. In this regard he seeks to construct alliances across the
lines of difference in order to fashion a pluralistic political culture
that sustains both difference and connection between diverse
groups in its population. Although West emphasizes the importance
of the highly visible racial question, he suggests that it is just one
facet of a broader crisis within American democracy. The threat
that continuing racism poses for the spirit of American democracy
is compounded by the fact that its democratic system has been
further undermined from within by the polarizing rhetoric of the

culture wars, the selfishness of market culture, a fractured social
ecology, and apathy about the political process. Here he concurs
with commentators such as Jean Elshtain and Robert Putnam who
have lamented the lack of civility and decline of intelligent public
debate in America, warning that anger and bipolarism threaten the
very roots of American democracy. The danger is that as a sense of
the "common good" disintegrates, with people being less inclined
to reach a compromise designed for the good of all, the very legitimacy of American democracy is challenged.

In West's view the "crisis" confronting America requires an
urgent and "prophetic" response, and a quick glance at the titles of
West's books will reveal his fixation with the term "prophetic." West
speaks of "prophetic Christianity" and "prophetic pragmatism," yet
"prophetic" is a slippery term that he does not fully define. There
are strong biblical overtones to the term – Old Testament prophets
such as Amos thundered at society's defection from godliness and
called people back to faithfulness. Stylistically, West often utilizes
the genre of the jeremiad and biblical overtones are also found in
the content of his prophetism, which tackles spiritual malnutrition
and calls for "conversion." According to West, the constitutive
elements of prophetism are discernment, connection, tracking
hypocrisy, and hope.[7] First, prophetic thinkers must identify and
analyze forms of evil. They must provide deep analysis of the
present in light of the past, but this historical sense must be counter-
balanced by empathy and close contact with the humanity of others.
In terms of tracking hypocrisy, they must draw attention to the gap
between rhetoric and reality. Finally, they must keep track of hope,
as without hope their work may remain reflective and sophisticated
analysis, but will lack engagement in struggle. Those who hope
must cling courageously to the idea that history is incomplete and
that in an open-ended future their actions can make a difference.
With these points in mind, he suggests that it is incumbent upon
the prophetic thinker to develop critiques of America's chronic
racism and obsession with big business. The prophetic task of
speaking the truth in love with courage troubles the nation's conscience by placing issues on the agenda that society would rather
ignore. Prophetism is a minority voice that challenges the mainstream values of society, scrutinizes accepted beliefs, and demythol-
ogizes accepted "truths." West's prophetism does not try to "predict
an outcome," but rather identifies "concrete evils" and tries to "generate enough faith, hope, and love to sustain the human possibility
for more freedom."[8] As such, he uses his prophetic imagination to

develop an alternative consciousness for our time. The alternative vision that he presents is based on the values of democracy and individuality in community as a way of doing justice and healing broken relationships. As a prophetic thinker, West attempts to challenge and unsettle, thus laying the foundations for a major rethinking of America and the American experiment that is concerned with how things ought to be.

Overview

With the exception of works on West by George Yancy and Mark Wood, there has been little substantial examination of West's work as a whole, and so this book aims not only to reconstruct and appraise West's thought but also to thematically order and unify his extensive oeuvre. Chapter 1, "Reading West," expounds the book's underlying thesis that West's work should be read and interpreted primarily as a theology of liberation as this is the perspective from which we can best "make sense" of his overall thought. In chapter 2, "Race and American Democracy," I consider the twin questions of what it means to be human and what it means to be black and thus "problematic" in America. West's work can be distinguished from fellow commentators of "crisis" in American democracy by the way in which he explicitly links arguments concerning racial justice to his vision of the American democratic ideal. We shall see that West's sublime expression of hope in the midst of adversity is written out of pain and tries to love in the face of hatred and struggle in the face of persistent defeat.

The next four chapters consider the key intellectual traditions with which West engages in addressing the crisis within American democracy. Specifically, we shall consider how he responds to crisis and suffering in existential, political, and intellectual terms. Chapter 3, "Jazz Philosophy: Westian Pragmatism," considers the way in which philosophy, in its attempt to understand the contingent and tragic in the human existence, can contribute to the expansion of democracy through an emphasis on innovation and possibility. Chapter 4, "Prophetic Christianity," outlines the central tenets of his liberationist theology and investigates the impact of Walter Rauschenbusch, Reinhold Niebuhr, Martin Luther King Jr, and James Cone on his thought. The next chapter, "Re-conceptualizing Marxism: West's Radicalism," discusses his uneasy relationship with the Marxist tradition. Attention will be focused on his affinity with the New Left and his understanding of Marxism as both indispensable and inadequate. In chapter 6, "The Multicontextual Public Intellectual," I consider West's location within the new tradition of black public intellectuals and assess how he balances intellectual substance with popular accessibility.

The final part of the book is concerned with interventions and with how West responds to the democratic crisis. Chapter 7, "The Politics of 'Conversion': West's 'Love Ethic'," addresses his political strategy of love which attempts to construct alliances across the lines of difference. We will see that he emphasizes recognition and self-love as well as commonality and love of others. The next chapter, "Achieving Democracy: Applying the Love Ethic," carries this analysis further by highlighting the tensions that accompany implementation of the love ethic. We will examine the difficulties surrounding his recent attempts to build a parents' movement and to build a black–Jewish alliance, as well as the deeper tensions that come into play when the vague and universal language of love is translated into concrete policy proposals. Finally, in the conclusion I consider the "creative tensions" at the heart of West's work. It will be argued that while a "coherent" West does lurk beneath the eclecticism, his work is shaped by the contradictory themes of realism and idealism. Thus West's work attempts to challenge the limitations, distortions, and exclusions of American society, aware that progress is possible but paradise is an impossible dream.

1

Reading West

Despite the praise West's work has received, its eclecticism has been condemned. He has turned his attention to a myriad of topics, from architecture and Marvin Gaye to Marxism and pragmatic philosophy – themes that at first glance appear unrelated. West also has a tendency to compile lengthy lists of diverse influences and then situate himself in proximity to those figures. Indeed, in his appropriation of a selection of themes from the work of Dewey, Foucault, and Nietzsche he has a propensity to act as an intellectual magpie, and consequently his work is dismissed by critics such as Adolph Reed and Leon Wieseltier as a thousand miles wide but two inches deep. Less hostile critics have also struggled to make sense of West's career, suspecting intellectual opportunism in his shift from philosopher to cultural critic and celebrity academic. Perhaps more problematic is the fact that once sympathetic readers of West are bothered by his perceived shift in emphasis from revolutionary to reformist politics and a new reluctance to attack "the system" of capitalism. Many have struggled to see how the style and focus of *Prophesy Deliverance* can be equated with that found in *The War Against Parents*. In *Prophesy Deliverance* West wanted to build a counter-hegemonic working-class movement to challenge global capitalism, yet his recent works accept capitalism as the framework within which to advance the struggle for democracy and seem preoccupied with rebuilding America. At face value this appears to be a radical shift, but is it? Is this simply the maturation of his perspective or is the mainstreaming of the critic an inevitable consequence of the quest for status?

This chapter will assess whether there is a coherent way to read West's assemblage of Christianity, pragmatism, and Marxist analysis. Is his thought simply a hotchpotch of unrelated ideas or is there a connecting thread that runs throughout his work? It is my contention that there are principled reasons why West's work covers so many divergent themes. His eclecticism is prompted by the inherently broad nature of his project to secure black liberation and surmount social fragmentation through the revitalization of American democracy, rather than some form of intellectual opportunism. Understanding West is not aided by his self-designation as a "cultural critic." I find this label to be too narrow, and its inability to explain his divergent interests gives credence to his critics' charge that his eclecticism spawns incoherence. Thus I replace the "cultural critic" label with the descriptions of "multicontextual public intellectual" and "liberation theologian." We shall see that while West embraces the former of these descriptions he rejects the latter. This chapter will probe why West disassociates himself from theology and why I see liberation theology as the most helpful hermeneutical approach to West's work.

Public intellectual and political theologian

A succession of articles in 1995 celebrated the development of the black public intellectual tradition, and articles by Michael Bérubé and Robert Boynton highlighted West as the tradition's shining star. Although West's "vocation" as a public intellectual will be considered in chapter 6, some preliminary remarks can be made here. West believes that intellectual work is not an end in itself; rather, intellectual debate must be linked to some form of political practice. Through his intellectual work West seeks to galvanize the oppressed to work for their liberation. In order to inspire this political activity West's work must be intelligible to a wide range of people; unless people understand *why* change is needed in American democracy there will be no sense of urgency concerning transformation. This prompts flexibility concerning the medium and specific content of his message so that it can be targeted to different groups. In his conscious attempt to address a variety of publics – those who inhabit the diverse realms of the academy, the church, prisons, grassroots political organizations, popular television talkshows, and so on – West can be identified as a *multicontextual* public intellectual. His work attempts to explore radical democracy and racial healing at as broad a level as possible in order to touch as many people as possible, and he is eager to address the particular interests of each of these publics. While some are drawn to his project of rejuvenating the Left, others are more interested in his discussion of rap music. Crucially, however, West frames his remarks to specific groups within the project of black emancipation. West wishes to create new space for intellectual work outside the academy where citizens can debate issues such as race and he associates the public intellectual enterprise with the attempt to reconstitute the public sphere in America.

The second label I ascribe to West's work is that of liberation theology. This is considerably more contentious than the public intellectual label as West explicitly disavows the description of his work as any form of theology. However, an understanding of West's work as liberation theology actually imbues it with more coherence than the public intellectual label does. Central to West's work is the "prophetic-Christianity" he espouses and the political ideas that follow from that faith. West's "love ethic" emanates from his Christian perspective and provides a key normative standard by which he judges American society and condemns its polarization. Before turning to consider the grounds upon which I base my conclusion that West's fusion of Christianity and politics fits best into the tradition of liberation theology, it should be noted that there is a close association between the identification of West as a public intellectual and as a theologian; for instance, as political theology is also public theology, it is a form of public intellectual work. More significant, however, is the intellectual legacy of liberal theologians such as Walter Rauschenbusch, Reinhold Niebuhr, and Martin Luther King, who exerted profound influence on American intellectual life. Rauschenbusch's Social Gospel, which asserted that "where religion and intellect combine, the foundation is laid for political democracy," had strong ties to the political progressivism of the early twentieth century.[1] Niebuhr fused politics and spirituality in a very public manner and attempted to shape public discourse on themes such as the immorality of American isolationism in the face of Nazism. King, like his two predecessors, co-joined intellectual, moral, and Christian commitment to public affairs. West suggests that King's struggle for democracy, freedom, and equality "embodies the best of American Christianity" and "exemplifies the best of the life of the mind involved in public affairs."[2] Rauschenbusch, Niebuhr, and King demonstrate that a religiously inspired social and political concern can contribute to serious intellectual engagement, not simply at the personal level but at a broad and "public" level. In viewing religion as a source of moral inspiration that can inspire civic discourse and political action in the pursuit of the revitalization of democracy, West is part of their intellectual tradition. While West's theological and intellectual concerns with the state of American democracy overlap, it is Christianity that provides the normative standard by which West is rendered dissatisfied with the present state of American democracy. In this sense, Christianity motivates his sense of intellectual engagement.

Political and liberation theologies

Within the landscape of twentieth-century theology a significant place is occupied by political theologies. Contemporary political theology emerged in the 1960s in a context of technological growth, welfare expansion, the questioning of traditional values (such as religion, but also a general scrutiny of liberal capitalism), and the growth of social protest movements challenging injustice. While classical political theology was an Enlightenment theology which supported the status quo, the political theology of figures such as Johann Metz marked a radical break from Constantinian assumptions which linked Christianity to the dominatory practices of the state, as well as from the individualistic and apolitical Christianity popularized by Karl Rahner and Rudolf Bultmann. Metzian political theology does not attempt to merely politicize theology or develop a theology of politics, but rather analyze and implement the practical, radical political implications of Christianity, and thereby transform society; as such it does not look for the revelation of God in a metaphysical sphere beyond history, but rather in history itself. This theology constitutes the most significant theological development of the last 35 years. It has produced a paradigm shift in theology from transcendentalist idealism to liberationism, and the two main schools of thought in debates over biblical hermeneutics have become the liberationists and their opponents.

"Political theology" operates as an umbrella category encompassing the multiplicity of contextual liberation theologies (Latin American, South African, Palestinian) and feminist, black, womanist, and poststructuralist theologies. Although any attempt to generalize about the parallels between these contextual theologies is an enterprise fraught with difficulty, certain broad themes do emerge making it possible to discern six central tenets of liberation theology. First, liberation theology is often referred to as "a new way of doing theology"; it places less of an emphasis on theology as imparted by clerics and more on dialogue and collective interpretation of the Bible. It has a strong democratic impulse that takes seriously the equal status of all individuals and seeks to open up the theological endeavor to all sections of the community, asserting that "minority" interpretations of the Bible must be given equal voice as the dominant white, male interpretations. It is thus a flexible form of theology that is open to dialogue and negotiation. Second, liberation theology develops a critique of both church and society. It constitutes a critical theory that attempts to demystify and uncover clichés and hidden truth; for instance it exposes the way in which capitalism appropriates religion in its quest to rule society. This criticism does not exist in a vacuum and strong visions of an alternative society are presented. Third, because liberation theologians believe theology must be practically lived rather than purely theoretical, action on behalf of the oppressed takes precedence over theologizing and theorizing. The fourth point is that liberation theologians view God as an active force who constantly identifies with his people in their sufferings. Humans must be agents of their own liberation and work with God to change their situation by becoming part of the revolutionary process if necessary. Fifth, liberation theology rises from the specific historical, cultural, social, and political circumstances of a particular country or cultural grouping. As the specific context in which theology is done determines its nature, one form of liberation theology cannot simply be lifted to another context; there can be no neutral or universal liberationist theology.

Finally, it is theology that draws upon extra-theological sources to reach conclusions about society. Its disregard for traditional intellectual disciplinary boundaries is evident in its appropriation of social and political theory, cultural studies, and theological ethics. Most notably, its socio-economic analysis is often, but not necessarily, Marxist in inspiration – for instance, in *A Theology of Liberation* Gustavo Gutiérrez asserted that true Christianity involves the overthrow of capitalism and its replacement by socialism. So, while Arthur McGovern asserts that liberation theology is not essentially *by nature* Marxist, he admits he has yet to find any liberation theologians who do not embrace some form of socialism that emanates from their Christian convictions.[3] Another recent emphasis of liberation theology has been participatory democracy. From the outset liberation theology was both a protest against capitalist domination and a demand for "true" populist democracy. In *Liberation Theology at the Crossroads*, Paul Sigmund suggests that in the late 1980s the radicalism of populist democracy became the dominant of the two strands in Latin America. This change was partly dictated by political events, but also by growing awareness of non-economic sources of oppression (race or gender), to which Marxism is often blind. An emphasis on democracy encouraged broader consideration of excesses of economic power as well as fresh consideration of issues such as government corruption.

West as liberation theologian

There are very strong continuities between West's thought and these central tenets of liberation theology. His democratic and non-dogmatic interpretation of Christianity persistently adopts a critical and questioning manner toward hierarchies in society and the church. Second, West repeatedly argues that American democracy is in a desperate state of crisis, characterized by racial oppression and the erosion of systems of care for others. He is thus critical of inadequate forms of democracy that fail to challenge racial stereotyping and dualistic and individualistic expressions of Christianity that fail to address this crisis. Third, West locates God on the side of society's victims and he stresses that the lens through which Christians should examine society is the perspective of the oppressed. He recognizes the urgency of the quest for African-American liberation from an oppressive location of second-class citizenship and asserts that emancipatory action must take precedence over the development of systematic theories about oppression. The fourth area of continuity concerns emphasis on history as open-ended and on humans working with God to change their circumstances. While West remains uncertain about how human action and divine action correspond, and believes that God cannot be limited by the actions of humans, his work actively encourages the oppressed to work for their own liberation. Fifth, contextualism is crucial to the historicism of West's spirituality. His work is experiential and concerned with the real life experiences of particular people (African Americans), in a particular place (the United States), at a particular time (the beginning of the twenty-first century). He draws on the insights of Latin American theologians concerning class oppression, and on African perspectives concerning racial oppression and the value of one's cultural heritage, in order to build a theology that is centered on the lives and experiences of black Americans in terms of its specific context and visions. Finally, in terms of extra-theological sources, Christianity provides the impetus for West's political engagement by providing existential empowerment and prompting him to critically accept elements of Marxism. As we shall see, his revisionist Marxism is essentially New Leftist and thus places an emphasis on radical participatory democracy. West regards himself as a radical democrat who questions hierarchies, being concerned with the interaction of power and oppression in democratic systems, and seeks the expansion of democracy.

Christianity occupies a pivotal position in West's thought. Given his overarching concern for the liberation of African Americans and his broader liberatory vision encompassed in the call for a "healing" of relationships across gender, class, and racial lines, it would seem easy to conclude that he is a liberation theologian. However, West resists easy assumptions and argues that while he has been *influenced* by political theology, he is not a theologian. He finished his paper at the 1998 "Black Theology as Public Discourse" conference at the University of Chicago by saying, "if you really want to see how this relates to Jesus, read some theology, read some James Cone – you can't read anything I've got!" Similarly, he was astonished at his inclusion in the *New Handbook of Christian Theologians* alongside Barth and Brummer, asserting, "I really don't belong in there . . . I'm no theologian *at all*."[4] Instead, he describes himself as "a cultural critic with philosophic training who works out of the Christian tradition."[5] West's rejection of the description of his work as "theological" stems from suspicion about the construct "theology"; it relates to his historicism and uncertainty about how God acts and his assertion that there are human limits to interpreting and understanding divine action. He views theology as "an attempt to engage in a constructive work that renders consistent and coherent its viewpoint." However, although he tries to "make sense of the narratives and the myths and the rituals of the community of the faithful," he concludes "I don't think they can be rendered consistent or coherent."[6] While Christians ought to *attempt* to make their faith credible to the outside world through lifestyle and argumentation, West believes that such an attempt can never be fully realized. For instance, if a person states that they "understand" God and find his actions coherent, that person's attempt to limit God within the confines of human understanding demonstrates just how little of God they actually understand. Not only does West maintain that church doctrines cannot be rendered consistent or coherent, but "if they were coherent and consistent I think it would be so empty because the faith is really about the tensions and frictions."[7]

Despite West's aversion to the label "theological," strong elements of theology can be found in his work. The crux of the matter lies in how one defines "theology." On the basis of a definition of theology as systematic analysis of Christian doctrine, he is no theologian; West does not examine specific claims about God nor write about doctrines such as sanctification or justification. In this regard liberation theologians such as James Cone and Gustavo Gutiérrez can be seen as more "theological" than West, in the sense that they are concerned with theological method and systematic theology. When we read their work we get a sense of the "nature" of God, yet West says little directly about God. But all this rests upon a narrow definition of theology that privileges doctrine *vis-à-vis* ethics within Christian theology; thinking theologically may entail trying to conceive the nature of God, but equally it may entail ethical thinking about the requirements of God, the latter of which West does. Indeed, we must remember that Reinhold Niebuhr – who is widely regarded as the most influential American theologian of the twentieth century – gave scant attention to questions of theological method, hermeneutics, or exegesis.

It is possible to claim that West is not a theologian in the sense of developing coherent and systematic theories about how God works, yet still does theology. Robert McAfee Brown suggests that theology is simply "God-talk" in which all Christians engage at some point or other. Undoubtedly there are different levels of this God-talk or theologizing; for instance, while someone might call God "the all-cohesive source of reality," another person might simply say "Jesus is like God, only more so." While the former may appear more impressive, Brown stresses that both constitute theological statements.[8] This looser reformulation of the term "theology" enables us to see that West's call for a general spiritual awakening in America to counter nihilism and materialism is theology in action. This is because it derives from his interpretation of who God is and what he desires of us as humans – for instance, that we treat each other with a certain amount of respect and dignity. However, a difficulty with Brown's definition of theology is the implication that it is not simply religious believers who engage in "God-talk"; when atheists engage in God-talking are they engaging in theology, and, if so, how does their "God-talk" differ from the "God-talk" of Christian theology? We might refine Brown's point by suggesting that when *Christians* think as Christians they are thinking theologically, or, as Hendrik Kraemer put it, "Every bit of coherent Christian thinking on the meaning and scope of Christian Revelation and faith is theological."[9] This loose redefinition of theology is central to liberation theology which stresses that the task of theology should not be left to the professional theologians, namely the clergy and theology professors; in this regard West is not a professional theologian, yet he does theology. The difficulty is that West is familiar with this loose redefinition via the work of John Cobb, yet remains unconvinced by it. He recalls, "Cobb used to say 'a theologian is a Christian thinking.' Now in that sense I'm a theologian – I'm a Christian and I try to think."[10] West continues to believe that there is more to theology than simply thinking about God and although he accepts that political theology is distinct from theology *per se* in that it "is a *certain* kind of theological reflection that has to do with public life, that has to do with dynamics of power," he maintains that because he does not call himself a theologian, he could not then call himself a political theologian.[11]

However, no matter how much West insists that he is not a liberation theologian, it is impossible to fully understand his work without grounding it in a liberationist theological perspective. What West labels as non-theological "prophetic Christianity" is simply another name for his African-American liberation theology. In his review of Juan Luis Segundo's *Faith and Ideologies*, West suggests that liberation theology has two primary objectives: (i) a reshaping of Christian doctrines in light of current contextual concerns; and (ii) engagement in serious social theory and cultural criticism which is committed to and immersed in social struggle.[12] As this is what West seeks to do in his own work, it is misleading for him to say that he does not do political theology. Moreover, his rejection of the description of his work as liberation theology devalues his work, as liberation theology constitutes the key unifying thread of coherence in it. Returning to the concerns raised at the start of this chapter about West's shift in focus from revolution to reform, we can say that while this may appear incoherent when approached from the perspective of political theory, it is not incoherent when viewed from the perspective of liberation theology. West's politics are explained and guided by his Christianity; both revolution and reform can be consistent with Christianity and can in their own ways further Christian expansion of democratic values.

Liberation theology resuscitates and radicalizes the utopianism
and leftist politics of the Social Gospel and chastens this with a
Niebuhrian realist perspective grounded in the crisis and despair of
ongoing oppression. It is the foundation for West's entire body of
work; from it stems his interest in overcoming black oppression, his
vision of radical democracy, and his political engagement. West's
liberationist response to the crisis in American democracy is a call
for a healing of relationships, recognition of the humanity of all,
recovery of civility, and reconstitution of the public sphere that will
facilitate alliance building. Liberation theology not only provides
the theoretical grounding to his Christianity, but to his leftist politics and his sense of vocation as a public intellectual, and thus
demonstrates that his eclecticism is not simply intellectual opportunism. Rather, his eclectic multicontextualism is concerned with
liberating African Americans from their oppression under the
democratic façade that he believes is the United States. It is these
themes of crisis, hope, and liberatory redemption that will be developed throughout this book.

Terms of analysis

Political theology reads the Christian story with a hermeneutic
that makes the primary horizon emancipatory politics. It thus relies
heavily upon the debates of contemporary politics and political
theory. While political theology and political theory are two distinct
traditions, in *The Political Theory of Liberation Theology* John
Pottenger demonstrates that liberation theology offers a political
theory as it engages in normative social critique, incorporates
Marxist analysis, and its social theories (concerning the legitimate
use of violence, for instance) are influenced by political-ethical con-
siderations. An important issue to clarify at this point concerns what
difference there is between the work of a political theologian and
the work of a political theorist who is a Christian, such as Charles
Taylor. Although Taylor's arguments are primarily philosophical
and ontological, like West his concerns overlap with themes of political theory such as communitarianism, recognition, and identity.
Moreover, in terms of practical political arguments concerning
Quebec, he has written on charters of rights, citizen participation in
politics, nationalism, and federalism. Unlike many philosophers,
Taylor has been engaged in the politics of his country – in the 1960s
he was involved in the establishment of the New Democratic Party

in Quebec and stood as a candidate in four federal elections. Since 1971 his concerns have been primarily centered on developing philosophical arguments, but he continues to write about the constitutional politics of Quebec. It could thus be argued that Taylor's engagement in what could be seen as a liberation struggle for Quebecois means that he is a political theologian. However, while his work may match some of the criteria of liberation theology as outlined in this chapter, there are two reasons why he is not a political theologian. First, by definition some form of theological endeavor must lie at the center of a liberation theologian's work. However, Taylor's work is devoid of the explicit Christian references we find in West and his religious concerns are of a privatistic nature. Because he does not attempt to co-join radical expressions of both Christianity and politics in the way that liberation theologians do, we could say that while Taylor's idiom is secular political, West's is Christian. Second, liberation theology places more emphasis upon action than theory; despite Taylor's engagement in the politics of Quebec his more substantial works, such as *Sources of the Self*, remain more theoretical than the work of liberation theologians who relate all their work back to questions of oppression and liberation.

Political theology embraces systems of thought such as communitarianism and socialism, and the concerns of political theology and political theory coalesce in areas such as justice, power, freedom, utopia, and democracy. Thinking specifically of West, the political themes of justice, identity and difference, coalition building, democracy, socialism, and the common good are all important for his liberation theology. He also generalizes about human capacities, attempts to define the nature of their shared obligations, and offers a critique of prevailing forms of unjust power. While his basis for this is Christian rather than secular principles, his work attempts to fulfill the same function as other political theories. However, we must also remember that political theology is multicontextual and committed to breaking traditional disciplinary boundaries. It is just as reliant upon cultural studies and sociology as on political theory, and so to identify it too narrowly with political theory deprives the term of much of its meaning. Therefore, while I will use specific terms of analysis such as political theory and theories of race relations when considering specific elements of West's thought, the primary standard which will be used to analyze West's overall thought is political theology as it is sufficiently broad to embrace his multicontextual concerns.

2

Race and American Democracy

At the core of West's thought is a political struggle for freedom that is tied to an existential quest for meaning. Following the assertion of Camus that the first question of philosophy is the question of suicide, West is deeply concerned with what it means to be human when confronted by evil and suffering, and he asks how can a person cope and muster the courage to keep living when their humanity is undermined or deemed worthless? How are we to live compassionately in a world of tragedy, suffering, and injustice? West states that he is "fundamentally concerned with how we confront death, dread, despair, disappointment, and disease" and his prophetic vision "looks the inescapable facts of death and despair in the face."[1] His work tries to plumb the depths of human anguish and discern possibilities for hope and for a liberation that will broaden the scope of human dignity. These existential concerns are of vital importance to West's freedom struggle because, he argues, without a positive sense of the self political struggle will achieve little.

Although West's work points to the many faces of evil evident in the twentieth century, from Nazism to homophobia, his primary focus is the painful legacy of racism. In the case of his family, his grandmother died in Louisiana at the age of 30 when, due to her skin color, she was refused treatment at her local hospital for an infected tooth.[2] Despite West's position as an Ivy League professor, in the introductions to *Race Matters* and *Keeping Faith* he recounts the impact racism continues to have on his life – ranging from his inability to get a taxicab in Manhattan or being mistaken for a janitor, through to police harassment and the suspicion that he was a cocaine trafficker. Although he admits that such examples are negligible when placed beside the experiences of Rodney King or Amadou Diallo, they remain the everyday experiences of many African Americans that must be taken seriously. West moves beyond this experiential level of racism to raise fundamental questions about the implications of race for American democracy and states in no uncertain terms that African-American subordination is integral to American democratic practice: "It is the suffering which constitutes the precondition for the flowering of American democracy."[3] In the first part of this chapter we shall see that West is not simply referring to the slavery and segregation of earlier generations, but to the stereotyping and problematization at work today. He insists that race is not a marginal issue, but rather a litmus test that takes us to the heart of the American democratic promise. The second part of the chapter will consider West's response to suffering found in the motifs of hope and struggle. While later chapters will examine how these themes are played out in his intellectual engagement with Christianity, leftist politics, and pragmatism, these themes are introduced here through consideration of the strength he draws from the attempts of modernist writers and musicians – particularly Anton Chekhov and John Coltrane – to wrestle with despair. The final section will consider the implications this blues sensibility has for West's view of American democracy. Our concern here is whether white supremacy is an intrinsic part of American life that is irrevocably ingrained in the nation's collective psyche. Is it possible to imagine an America where whiteness, as an aesthetic and ontological category, is no longer the essence of normativity?

Race matters

West's attempt to understand the complexities of racism can be traced to the radical historicist investigation of the emergence, development, and persistence of white racism in modern Western discourse found in *Prophesy Deliverance*. Since then his work has continued to unearth the economic, political, cultural, and psychological forces that express racism and to analyze the mechanisms that maintain the logic of white supremacy. Although racial oppression has been a persistent theme throughout American history, there is a widespread belief that the Civil Rights movement overturned the legacies of segregation and subordination and made racism a

thing of the past. Moreover, it is often argued that African
Americans have been given a fair chance with the removal of discrimination and the establishment of affirmative action programs in
employment and college admissions. Following from this logic,
racial tension persists only because African Americans choose
to wallow in self-pity that points to past injustices, rather than
embrace the advances that have been made; thus the plight of the
black underclass has little to do with racial discrimination, as any
person, black or white, who works hard will succeed in American
society. Therefore conservatives such as Thomas Sowell and Shelby
Steele attribute the ghetto problems of joblessness and crime not to
race but to the failure of the underclass to acquire the values and
skills necessary for success in a market economy. Indeed the
overwhelming success and popularity of many African-American
musical and sporting stars seems to vindicate this position and
thereby imply that all African Americans are accepted. However, an
alternative explanation is that Michael Jordan can be viewed as an
American icon of athletic excellence because his blackness is never
referenced in a way that threatens whites; outside the worlds of
sports and entertainment the black male is often a menacing figure
associated with crime.

While the meaning of racial discrimination was once clear for all
to see in the presence of white and colored signs, we now live in a
racially murky era where racial antipathy is harder to prove. But
America remains a racialized society where race is engraved on
individual identities and sewn into the seams of the social fabric,
no matter how seductive the illusion that racial equality has been
achieved. Although Jim Crow segregation is now an anachronism
and vitriolic expressions of racism have been forced underground,
West contends that racism persists and echoes Malcolm X by asserting that one cannot stab a person six inches in the back and then
pull the knife out two inches and conclude that progress has been
made. West suggests that the legacy of explicit racism as condoned
by state and federal laws has been replaced by the subtler but no
less insidious racism of stereotyping, problematization, and exclusion of the black community. Such expressions of racism, entwined
with a general feeling of paranoia, continue to undermine African-
American humanity and demonstrate that race still matters. He also
suggests that the consequences of racism are apparent in the state
of crisis found in the black ghettos.

According to West, this crisis is most visibly apparent in poverty,
a growing underclass, and soaring suicide and homicide rates.

African Americans comprise a large percentage of poor Americans, and West suggests that this economic desperation is occasioned by unemployment and more specifically by deindustrialization, downsizing, labor-replacing technology, government cutbacks, career ceilings, and the modernization of southern agriculture that pushed the black tenant labor force into the urban centers. Although the civil rights legislation of the 1960s enabled black professionals to escape the ghettos and pursue upward social mobility, the result was that as black neighborhoods became less diverse in terms of socio-economic composure, the levels of investment and opportunity within them declined sharply; indeed the urban underclass is disproportionately black. Moreover, economic deprivation contributes to social problems such as inadequate health provision, which is in turn manifest in high levels of infant mortality and low life-expectancy levels. Economic anxiety also facilitates the growth of informal economies of prostitution and drug dealing, which in turn feeds the prison population. A 1995 report by the Sentencing Project found that while African Americans comprise 13 percent of the total American population, they make up 43 percent of the prison population. More tellingly, one in three black men in their twenties are either in prison, on probation, or on parole, compared to 7 percent of their white counterparts.[4] West concludes that if the state of siege in black America is allowed to fester, "there may not even be a black America in 50 years . . . because we will be so scattered and dispersed, in prisons and coffins."[5] All this breeds a sense of nihilistic despair – a form of "collective clinical depression" that is rooted in an absence of a felt sense of meaning.[6] This is compounded, West argues, by the dominance of market mentalities and the subsequent erosion of community, and by the fact that the church now stands at such a distance from the young that it is unable to present its message of love and affirmation.

The debate concerning responses to the crisis of poverty and crime stretches far beyond the ghettos, and racially charged debates about welfare, crime, and affirmative action rely on stereotypical images of African Americans to manipulate racial anxieties. In one sense African Americans represent hyper-visible "problems" evident, for instance, in debates about misogynist and demeaning imagery in gangsta rap and in the stigmatizing of African Americans in debates about crime. The national obsession with the black male as dreaded criminal feeds the paranoia that every black man is a potential Willie Horton. For instance, in Boston in 1989 Charles Stuart used the image of a fictitious black man to deflect attention from the fact that he had murdered his wife. It was the *perception* of black criminal proclivity that made his story believable. However, David Goldberg has demonstrated that although black criminality is associated with murder and rape, these crimes contribute less than 1 percent of African-American criminal arrests. The most common black arrests are for victimless crimes such as drunkenness, disorderly conduct, and drug abuse violations, and in violent categories robbery and aggravated assault.[7] Following from this, while West admits that black men are more likely to end up in prison than in college, he suggests that this is due in part to the differential treatment of African Americans by the police and the courts. Here Barbara Ransby points to the disparity in sentencing for the possession of crack and powder cocaine, when the only real difference between the two forms of the drug is the racial breakdown of users.[8] Moreover, a number of police departments continue to be permeated by racism. Most obvious in this regard is Detective Sergeant Mark Fuhrman's remarks during the O. J. Simpson trial about "giving blacks a good beating" and the beating of Rodney King. What is interesting about the amateur video showing the 56 blows King received is that it illustrates Richard Rorty's argument that anything can be redescribed to tell a different story. So while from one ideological viewpoint we read a story of police brutality against a black man, from another we read of a criminal suspect who threatened officers and where the beating was a justified response. By claiming self-defense the law enforcement authorities reinforced the image of the threat to law and order posed by the dangerous black man.

West suggests that the racist symbolism of images such as the black criminal, the welfare queen, and the sexual stereotypes of the Jezebel or the Bigger Thomas have played a crucial role in black subjugation by suggesting that these people are not like "us." He draws upon the work of Ralph Ellison and James Baldwin to argue that when viewed through stereotypical lenses a person is invisible and nameless in the sense that he or she is not a bona fide member of the community. The inferiority and anonymity denoted by invisibility mean that all African Americans can be treated alike, rather than as real, complex, and individual human beings. In this sense one negative stereotype can be applied to all. Thus West suggests that the concept of "double-consciousness," of looking at oneself through the eyes of others, outlined by W. E. B. Du Bois in the first chapter of *The Souls of Black Folk*, remains a significant phenomenon that accounts for the position of African Americans. From the unpaid exploitation of slavery that was essential to the nation's construction, through to contemporary figures like Michael Jordan, African Americans have contributed to making America what it is, to the degree that America is unimaginable without their presence. Yet while they live *in* America they are not made to feel part *of* America and are treated as outsiders.[9] Whiteness has always been closely associated with America's cultural identity and so while white people need only live within their own world, African Americans are forced to live in two worlds in order to survive: their own world of personal concerns and interests and the white world into which they must assimilate in order to gain societal acceptance. African Americans have had to constantly remake themselves to blend with white expectations, yet despite this remaking are unable to advance beyond the margins of American society, being simultaneously marginalized and included.

The stereotypical demonization of African Americans contributes to their problematization. If a group of people is considered *en masse* to be deviant from societal norms, the reaction is to view such people as "a problem" who threaten the quality of life for other citizens. However, West suggests that when race is portrayed as a problem that affects non-white Americans, rather than the nation as a whole, it is marginalized as an issue. Much "race" talk starts from the premise of black problematization and tends to imply that whites are somehow not part of this racialized discourse; indeed, part of the power of whiteness is to conceal itself as somehow non-raciated and beyond racial categories. As long as blacks are considered the problematic group the onus falls on them alone to improve race relations by assimilating the values of white society: "The implication is that only certain Americans can define what it means to be American – and the rest must simply fit in."[10] Here West notes that both liberal and conservative approaches to the question of race are built on problematization; both demand that African Americans should conform to the standards of white America, either through liberal integration or conservative behaviorism.

West attempts to turn the issue of problematization around, and asserts that any meaningful discussion about race in America must take as its starting point the flaws in American society rather than the problems of black people. Far from being marginal, race is central to America; it is everyone's problem because African-American experience and possibility is a litmus test for the viability of American democracy. Instead of examining the implications of poor race relations for white people, Americans must take a different starting point that asks what viewing a certain group within society as "problems" tells them about the nature of America. Stereotypes of African Americans as welfare recipients not only overlook the fact that blacks as well as whites pay taxes, but by portraying blacks as dependent on government handouts it becomes easier to view them as a problematic appendage to America. Thus West argues that while poverty afflicts many African Americans, it is essentially a flaw in American society caused by maldistribution of wealth that can confront all people, regardless of their skin color. To associate it narrowly with the black community as "their" problem is not only unhelpful in terms of assessment, but also adds to the problematization of African Americans. So while the black urban underclass has many problems, their plight cannot be detached from the state of the rest of the nation, as African Americans do not live in a vacuum separate from other Americans. Here West utilizes a striking metaphor of America as a ship with a huge leak: "In the end we go up together or we go down together, no matter where we are on that ship."[11] He insists that if America is to weather the storm there must be recognition that there are certain aspects of life that tie all Americans together, with the result that if one group falters then all society will falter with it. Thus African Americans on the poverty line should not be seen as problems but as people *with* problems, and as "citizens who need more of a chance for us all to be able to survive on the boat together."[12]

As a cultural critic West focuses on the meaning of democracy and the abuse of that term in practice. He suggests that although America upholds formal democratic procedural rules, it fails to hold up democracy in terms of class, race, and gender interactions. In other words, the distance between the American ideals of justice and equality and anti-democratic practices of stereotyping point to the disintegration of the American Dream. He warns that America is headed toward the Armageddon of race war if the operation of democracy as a façade is not called into question, and suggests that America may be at its last chance to confront the issue of race. If the issue "continues to fester, you'll have a third generation of gangster mentality. I can't see this country surviving that intact."[13] This theme recurs in his recent essay on James Cone where West the prophet asserts, "America can no longer deny the fact that either it comes to terms with the vicious legacy of white supremacy, or the curtain will fall on the precious experiment in democracy called America."[14] America cannot continue to marginalize the dark realities of its situation and hope to survive; if action is not taken to preserve democracy and engender mutual respect, American civilization will disintegrate. West stresses that this is not politically correct chitchat but a serious observation about the future of American democracy, as "race is crucial to any discussion about regenerating American democracy."[15] He is concerned with the duties and obligations of living in a democratic society, and asserts that a democratic society is obliged to keep raising and pushing the biblical question, what are we to do with the least of these? His point is not that white people are "cruel and callous," but that they are "indifferent" as they "lack exposure" to black suffering and hence are "subject to the dominant attitude toward race in America which historically has been that of denial."[16] Thus it is crucial that suffering be allowed to speak.

West's blues sensibility

President Clinton suggested that the 1990s were "good times" for America, and repeatedly pointed to American global political, economic, and cultural successes. West's conception of what "good times" might constitute is markedly different from Clinton's conception, for West maintains that a nation's soul and maturity is more important than its economic and military might. He claims that Clinton's approach evades struggle by undermining the continued prevalence of racism and poverty in America; it is part of a broader phenomenon in which America attempts to avoid and ignore pain. In this regard West suggests that "America is a hotel civilization . . . obsessed with comfort and convenience and contentment." A hotel is "a fusion of the home and the market" that "makes you feel at home if you have the cash to pay." When you leave the room everything is dirty, yet when you return it is clean. In a hotel you are shielded from the evil and the unjustified suffering in the world and do not hear the lament and the cries. "That's precisely why America doesn't like to talk about evil [and] the legacy of white supremacy."[17] In contrast to this optimism, West stresses that sunshine is unintelligible without the night. Because America tries to evade pain, truth-tellers are needed who will force difficult issues into the American consciousness and force the nation to confront pain. West attempts to shatter melodramatic and sentimental conceptions of the American past and present and he offers an apocalyptic image of America as "a twilight civilization – an American Empire adrift on turbulent seas in a dark fog." The challenge facing

America is "whether it will continue to deny, evade, and avoid various forms of evil in its midst" and this challenge will test the nation's maturity; immaturity denies pain and focuses on comfort whereas a mature approach wrestles with the nightside.[18] West acknowledges that "we want to remember our shining moments as a country. Race relations isn't one of them." He thus recognizes the difficulty in forcing America to grapple with suffering, as "trying to force a country that romanticizes its history into dealing with its underside . . . is like asking Peter Pan to deal with Dante's inferno."[19] However, following from his assertion that the problems of the black urban ghettos are not marginal but rather impact all Americans, the nation can no longer dodge consideration of suicide rates and poverty by pointing to American successes. This is because if people are suffering and dying in your midst, and if their humanity and citizenship is constantly undermined, then a nation that claims to be democratic must have something to say about it. West wants to inject a blues sensibility based on a sense of the tragic into American discourse; this entails facing up to the American past, in the form of subversive remembrance rather than sentimental nostalgia. Evil must be named and unmasked if it is to be overcome, and so West's response to the tragic is to *wrestle* with evil rather than simply accept it as the destiny of the way things are. He is influenced in this regard by the attempts of blues musicians and modernist poets and philosophers to find meaning to life in the midst of suffering.

Along with the church, music is one of two major traditions forged by African Americans and it occupies a position of profound importance as a means by which black creativity could be articulated. From the spirituals of the slavery era, music has been a powerful expression that depicts human joy and suffering and assumes without question the full humanity of African Americans. It thus performs a vital preservative function by helping to maintain human vitality of life in the face of storms of oppression, and by emphasizing creativity and dignity rather than self-pity. Music is a rich response to the "psychic wounds and social scars of a despised people" that "enacts in dramatic form the creativity, dignity, grace and elegance of African Americans without wallowing in self-pity or wading in white put-down."[20] Thus West suggests that artists such as Sarah Vaughan and Marvin Gaye provide sanity for their listeners; by grappling with issues of identity, death, and despair, and through an ability to transform the absurd into the tragic, their music provides cultural buffers that preserve African-American humanity. In short, music "convinces you not to kill yourself, at least for a while."[21] West suggests that his intellectual lineage reaches its highest expression in music, which he describes as "the grand archaeology into and transfiguration of our guttural cry, the great human effort to grasp in time our deepest passions and yearnings. . . . Profound music leads us – beyond language – to the dark roots of our scream and the celestial heights of our silence."[22]

West ascribes particular importance to the subversive and oppositional resources found within blues music and the blues-based music of jazz. Like the earlier spirituals, the blues captures the cry of the oppressed; it recognizes human possibility and human frailty and thus has a tragic base that rejects sentimentality. The blues is written out of pain and keeps details of one's painful experiences alive, yet attempts to transcend the pain; it expresses the agony of life as well as the possibility of overcoming evil through endurance. This quest for transcendence is distinct from escapism, as the blues does not blank out pain, but rather expresses it. The artistry of a "cultural worker" such as Billie Holliday presents a moral vision that highlights personal dignity and existential hope and provides political promise. However, West suggests that this moral substance is absent in much rap music, and so, rather than nurturing listeners and working to alleviate despair and meaninglessness, rap accentuates it. Although black rap music is "grounded in the Afro-American spiritual-blues impulse" certain expressions of rap "radically call into question the roots of this impulse, the roots of transcendence and opposition." Unlike the blues, some rap lacks a transcendent element and remains stagnant amidst angst; in place of opposition to evil there is lyrical hopelessness, and hence no sense of struggle.[23] However, he also recognizes that "the best of gangster rap constitutes a form of truth-telling that includes ugly elements but also challenges us."[24] In this sense, rap linguistically enacts the violence that is a constant reality of the African-American plight within oppressive America. So when Tupac Shakur raps in "Dear Momma" that everyday it's a struggle and that you've got to hold on, he is not talking about giving in to nihilism; he is talking about staying alive and living through the struggle of everyday oppression and urban reality. This is essentially a blues ontology of survival, self-empowerment, and transcendence.

Not only is West profoundly inspired by the music of John Coltrane and Charlie Parker, but on another level the electric artistic exchange of jazz music provides a powerful metaphor for West's ruminations on American democracy. He suggests that jazz constitutes "the middle road between invisibility and anger . . . where self-confident creativity resides."[25] Jazz celebrates individual invention, resiliency, agency, spontaneity, reinterpretation, and a capacity to make the music in the pressure of the moment. It is many-voiced and is a frame through which multiple expressions can be projected. Jazz relies on individual assertion and improvisation, on creative unity and group coordination, and so while it tells an individual story it arrives at an overall coherence; in fact, full-throated individuality of expression *enhances* the collectivity. These notions are central to West's attempt to work for the heroic expansion of democracy, an expansion that is dependent upon keeping faith and having the courage to hope and to overcome. He suggests that America needs to adopt a jazz-like flexibility and resilience that takes the form of heroic engagement against social limitations. To go against the way in which African Americans have been conditioned in America as inferior requires improvisation and reimagination of what an American is.

A similar sense of blues-tempered lyricism is found in the attempts of certain modernist philosophers and poets to wrestle with the question of what it means to be human in the face of despair. Dramatic poets of death, courage, and compassion, such as Fyodor Dostoyevsky, Franz Kafka, Herman Melville, Tennessee Williams, and Arthur Schopenhauer, profoundly influence West because of the way in which they address the struggles of life and survival. Specific works that he repeatedly cites as having influenced his intellectual development are Voltaire's *Candide*, Schelling's *Of Human Freedom*, Dostoyevsky's "The Grand Inquisitor" in *The Brothers Karamazov*, Cone's *Black Theology and Black Power*, and Kant's *On the Failure of all Modern Theodicies*. Although Kant is primarily associated with rationality and autonomy, West points to another side to Kant that deals with coping and which looks to the book of Job. Kant asserted that evil cannot be resolved and that one must learn to cope with it or, in other words, wrestle with it.[26] In West's most recent work it is Anton Chekhov who has emerged as the heroic figure. Chekhov portrayed the daily struggles of human beings against the circumscription of fate and history, and West applauds the fact that Chekhov refused to escape from life's pain and misery by indulging in dogma, abstract philosophy, or political utopia. West suggests that, like the best jazz artists, Chekhov "enacts *melancholic* yet *melioristic* indictments of misery without concealing the wounds inflicted or promising permanent victory."[27] West is obsessed with confronting the pervasive evil of unjustified and unnecessary suffering and social misery and his "Chekhovian Christian conception of what it means to be human puts a premium on death and courage." From Chekhov he learns that to be human is to "encounter honestly the inescapable circumstances that constrain us, yet muster the courage to struggle compassionately for our own unique individualities and for more democratic and free societies."[28] Thus West insists that we need courage and vision to confront death and despair; we must look terror and horror in the face and refuse to shy away.

Is there hope for change?

West provides us with an apocalyptic characterization of American democracy. Echoing Langston Hughes, West believes that the black search for democracy in America is "a dream deferred" and he warns of the perils if a genuine multiracial democracy is not created. The question we must now address is whether democracy can hope to prevail? Does American political culture possess the conceptual resources needed to grapple intelligently with issues of race and end racism? How much faith can be placed in the promise of American democracy? West knows that the evidence is not good, and in *Keeping Faith* he admitted "the extent to which race still so fundamentally matters in nearly every sphere of American life is . . . depressing and debilitating."[29] Time and again he concludes that he is in no way optimistic about America; he rejects utopian idealism as evil shatters any sense of idealism. Given his apocalyptic imagery, one might expect West to adopt a position similar to the pessimism of Derrick Bell in *Faces at the Bottom of the Well*. Bell asserts that African Americans will never gain full equality in America, and although resistance to racism is worthwhile in moral and spiritual terms, we should accept the inevitability of racism and work to mitigate its effects, as neither time nor goodwill can erase racism. West does not believe racism will be completely eradicated in America given fallen human nature, but he diverges from Bell in his assertion that forces of evil can be pushed back. Although West's apocalyptic picture acknowledges the depths of the racial chasm, he retains hope that one day the chasm will be bridged in spite of evidence to the contrary. Ultimately West emphasizes energy and courage rather than despair or complacency, and insists that a sense of possibility must be retained so that the death that is being wrestled is not allowed to have the final say. He refuses to surrender to the fate of racism – hence his quest for liberation and redemption that clings to the hope, no matter how slight, of the possibility of a reversal in fortunes. This kind of hope is not a sunshine optimism, but rather a blood-drenched hope that his love-inspired struggle is not in vain. He is concerned with both the dynamics of suffering and with how heroic energy can be enacted despite limits and constraints, and his hope is illuminated by the mystery of the cross and the revolutionary Christian patience of waiting for God on Easter Saturday.

West believes that hope is a vital ingredient for the well-being of society; he regards hopelessness as responsible for the despair, cynicism, and apathy that is prevalent in contemporary society. Hope is an elusive term. While it is a universal idea, it is always expressed in particularist terms. Thus while some find hope in the status quo, others locate it in radical change. Crucially, West's conception of hope means something deeper than facile positive thinking or President Clinton's description of America as "a place called hope," which made hope sound like an ideal that could be easily achieved and which is available to everyone. Instead West views struggle, sacrifice, and longevity as essential components of hope, likening it to long-distance running.[30] He rejects vague projections of a better future, and rather insists that hope must be grounded in the concrete and specific realities of present struggle. Of course, the specific nature of his hope increases the possibility that the precise goals will not be realized, thus creating a place for hopelessness in his thought.

West is concerned with the possibilities for America and so challenges the limitations, distortions, and exclusions of American society. He argues that it is a "betrayal" of America to accept its standing as "a chronically racist society, whose very conception of itself as a nation . . . is rooted in a discourse of negatively charged blackness and positively valued whiteness."[31] Rather, we must love America "for that in it which shows what it might become" as America "needs citizens who love America enough to reimagine and remake it."[32] West's re-imagination of America stresses that a vision of genuine democracy must take as its starting point recognition of the full humanity of all; this respect must be applied not only to relationships between blacks and whites, but also to those on opposing sides in the culture wars. The racial crisis cannot be resolved until citizens surmount polarization by attempting to form bonds of trust with each other; to do this there must be open acknowledgment of racial prejudices on both sides, rather than a glib assumption that racism is a thing of the past. Although it may appear that America lacks the conceptual resources required to grapple with the issue of race, as a "prisoner of hope" West maintains that, if Americans are willing to be experimental in their approach to democracy, new languages of empathy and compassion can be generated that will contribute to the creation of a genuine multiracial democracy. He suggests that some of the resources required for this transformation already exist in American culture, such as the American Dream's belief that limitations will not last as anyone can succeed against the odds. He calls upon Americans to apply their rich tradition of innovation and creativity to the crisis in public life. American "exceptionalism" must be sacrificed to American experimentalism and there must be an attempt to do things that do not come naturally or easily, such as being open and honest about pain. One must preserve "dangerous" memories of resistance that keep alive the reality of evil rather than explaining it away or covering it with silence. Racial healing requires dialogue and willingness to confront candidly past evils and oppressions; it also requires willingness to listen to and attempt to understand the perspective of others, despite the inevitable disagreements that will surface. This process requires the rejuvenation of the public sphere as a place for dialogue and where some sense of a common good can be located in order to counter polarization.

West suggests that democracy has a tragicomic nature evident in "a sad yet sweet dialectic of courageous agency and historical constraints, a melancholic yet melioristic interplay of freedom and limitations that identifies and confronts social misery only to see its efforts to overcome such misery often fall short of the mark."[33] He admits to often feeling pessimistic about the prospects for change in America. Yet, although he recognizes his dreams for invigorating democracy may not be entirely realized, the very act of contesting the limits of the "what-is" creates liberating possibilities that could not otherwise have been imagined. The *act* of contestation is crucial because "there's a species of winning that has little to do with being able to push back what you think needs to be pushed back. It has to do with the integrity of your soul [and] the integrity of your commitment. And in the end the larger consequences may flow."[34] Therefore, despite his lack of optimism about the status of democracy in America, he manages to cling to what he describes as "an audacious hope" that attempts to energize others to *create new evidence*.[35] West believes that a distinction can be drawn between optimism and hope. Optimism is based either on empirical possibilities or on blind ignorance of unfavorable evidence, whereas hope moves beyond questions of probability, utilizing a different orientation that is reliant upon courage to work to change the evidence. Hope is based on a sense of struggle; it knows that triumph is unlikely to be waiting just around the corner and so calls "good times" optimism into question. Hope is deep and enduring and provides an intent for pursuing the quest for justice in society, against what may at times appear insurmountable odds. West's hope is built on a deep and tragic sense of history and so does not seek a quick overnight solution. He strives to walk a path between idealism and pessimism, aware of both "the possibility of human progress *and* the impossibility of human paradise" and thus speaks of despair being "not eliminated but attenuated."[36] West recognizes that the world cannot be ridded of *all* evil, and so rejects utopian perfectionism as utopian schemes cannot escape the inherent limitations of human beings. Yet if we are unable to *imagine* a better world how can we work to create one? Thus he argues that if there is no hope, there can be no mobilization and pessimism will be a self-fulfilling prophecy. Because the world is incomplete and history is unfinished what we think and do makes a difference; even in an absurd situation our actions are always worthwhile.

Conclusion

West suggests that democracy is all about struggling with evil and unjustified misery, and with the question of what it means to be human. He is concerned with the night side of the human predicament and with how individuals confront their inevitable doom. His emphasis on the tragic is not a pessimistic wallowing in and acceptance of the status quo; on the contrary, he asserts that it is only when the absurdity of the human condition is confronted that struggles for justice can be enabled. In this regard West displays an ambivalent attitude toward modernity. He highlights the dark side to modernity found in the experiences of New World Africans regarding white supremacy and is critical of Eurocentrism – the imposition of Euro-American ideas of rationality and objectivity on other peoples – and stresses that African Americans must look beyond Eurocentric cultural traditions that are infected by the idea of white supremacy. Yet he also tries to illustrate the significance of modern thought for African Americans and so builds on what he considers the "best" features of Euro-American modernity, namely the critique of illegitimate authority, the dignity ascribed to ordinary people, and admiration of the experimental forces of curiosity and improvisation. Within the tragedies of the modern period West finds compelling accounts of how assaults on one's dignity have been resisted. In the preface to *Keeping Faith* he describes a "New World African modernity" that emerges when "degraded and exploited Africans in American circumstances" use "European languages and instruments to make sense of tragic predicaments." He suggests that "if modernity is measured in terms of newness and novelty, innovation and improvisation – and not simply in terms of science, technology, markets, bureaucracies and nation states – then New World African modernity is more thoroughly *modern* than any American novel, painting, dance or even skyscraper."[37] Thus African Americans are the most modern people of all, as they have constantly reinvented themselves to preserve meaning by fighting against persistent claims of deficiency or inferiority, exclusion, and double-consciousness. West concludes that to be "modern" means to have "the courage to use one's critical intelligence to question and challenge the prevailing authorities, powers and hierarchies of the world."[38]

West suggests that to be human and modern is to encounter honestly the inescapable circumstances that constrain us, while mustering the courage to struggle compassionately for one's own individuality and for a more democratic and free society. The reality, absurdity, and incongruity of evil must be confronted, and pain must be named if it is to be overcome; one cannot hide behind a sentimental picture of nostalgia. West recognizes that while evil cannot be destroyed, it can be pushed back and held at bay. Jazz and blues present a role model for this struggle, as in this music we see "a profound sense of the tragic linked to human agency. . . . It does not wallow in a cynicism or a paralyzing pessimism, but it also is realistic enough not to project excessive utopia."[39] A central aim of his work is to examine honestly American civilization and disclose its democratic possibilities and push back the limits of oppression. So alongside the Chekhovian emphasis on incongruity and absurdity he retains an Emersonian sense of possibility. West presents us with a tragic optimism that is aware of grim realities and does not expect to rid the world of evil, yet is not defeatist and manages to maintain hope that evil can be held back as a result of human agency. He wrestles with how to respond intellectually, existentially, and politically to suffering, and the fragmented intellectual resources that help him persevere include prophetic

Christianity, pragmatism, and radical democracy. Through these he tries to find a way to overcome, a way to transcend evil, and crucial to his task of reinvigorating American democracy is concrete politics guided by the strong ethical framework that stems from his Christian sensibilities.

In the next chapter we will consider pragmatism as the philosophical space that West's Chekhovian Christian perspective occupies. West highlights pragmatism's distinctive preoccupation with prospects for democracy that tries "to conceive of knowledge, reality, and truth in such a way that it promotes the flowering and flourishing of individuality under conditions of democracy."[40] His pragmatist spirit likens democratic experimentalism to jazz music and wishes American democracy to be as unpredictable as a Charlie Parker quintet. He also points to the jazz-like themes of improvisation and experimentation found in the work of Emerson, and concludes, "To talk about America is to talk about improvisation and experimentation, and therefore to talk about Emerson and Louis Armstrong in the same breath."[41] In other words, prophetic pragmatism can be described as jazz philosophy.

3

Jazz Philosophy: Westian Pragmatism

Unlike most of the prominent figures in African-American Studies, West's background lies in philosophy and he has appropriated a refashioned pragmatism to consolidate his multiculturalist vision of Left-Christian critique. His engagement with philosophy began at the age of 13 when he starting borrowing works by Søren Kierkegaard from the local bookmobile. West claims that by this stage he had found sorrow to be at the core of the human condition, and was thus drawn to Kierkegaard's attempt to wrestle seriously with despair and to how his philosophy illuminated the question of what it means to be human. Indeed it is from Kierkegaard that West acquired his fundamental sensibility that philosophizing should be linked to "existentially concrete situations, wrestling with decision, commitment, actualized possibility and realized potential."[1] Given this early Kierkegaardian engagement it is unsurprising that West proceeded to study philosophy at university. Although he took a course on pragmatism at Harvard, he did not seriously study that tradition until he encountered the work of Richard Rorty at Princeton. West approached Rorty from a perspective of contextualist and historicist anti-foundationalism, gained from reading Kierkegaard and Martin Heidegger, and found that Rorty couched this perspective in pragmatism. From that point, identification with the pragmatist tradition is easily discerned throughout West's work. *Prophesy Deliverance* recognized pragmatism as a key source of African-American critical thought, a position that he amplified in *The American Evasion of Philosophy*.

Pragmatism is not a philosophy or a school of thought, but rather a way of doing philosophy. While the term "pragmatism" holds together a contentious family, some familial traits can be located in the realm of method and approach, such as anti-foundationalism, rejection of Truth, and a practical perspective. First, pragmatism breaks with the traditional Cartesian quest of philosophy to guarantee knowledge by basing it on fixed grounds and rejects Enlightenment metaphysics' fixed world of essences, natural rights, and inalienable truths. It rejects universal conceptions of truth and reality that hint at some notion of a "God's eye-view" and thus is contextualist, seeking to expose the absolutes of the rationalist attitude and cast doubt on certainty. The second point we can make is that, as pragmatism dispenses with foundations, it follows that the pursuit of objectively true knowledge – truth utterly independent of human experience and interest – is futile. Pragmatists thus reject philosophy's traditional obsession with finding Truth and focus instead on a proliferation of truths that are in the making by humanity; truths are human products arising from experience. Although pragmatists reject the notion of final Truth, they maintain that there are better or worse ideas in which to believe, or, in other words, truths. We do not discover these truths through theorizing but by trying out ideas in our individual and common lives. Once discovered, truth proves its worth by "working." Thus what is true is simply the best interpretation we have to date, and potentially better truths may be established in the future on the basis of new and unforeseeable social practices. Third, we can highlight pragmatism's practical perspective. The purpose of inquiry, from a pragmatist perspective, is not an attempt to embody the True or the Good but an effort to solve problems and shape a satisfactory world. Thus the point of imaginative thinking is to help us shape the world, so seeking not simply to explain reality but to improve it. The ultimate philosophical goal of pragmatism is thus improved experience.

In this chapter we shall consider what the black liberation project can glean from philosophy's attempt to understand the contingent and tragic in the human existence. We will thus examine West's accentuation of the role pragmatism's "jazz-like" qualities of experimentation and improvisation can play in the progressive project of re-imagining America. The chapter will also consider West's attempt to balance pragmatist anti-foundationalism with certain truth claims. We shall begin by examining the categorical question of whether West is a philosopher or a cultural critic, and then recount West's genealogy of pragmatism as outlined in *The American Evasion of Philosophy*.

The pragmatist as cultural critic

Despite his background in Ivy League philosophy departments, West has an ambivalent relationship with philosophy. He is widely viewed as one of the most prominent African-American philosophers, and by demonstrating how philosophy can connect with matters of human suffering he has been instrumental in shaping African-American interest in philosophy. Yet not only has West never held a position in a philosophy department, but he has been vocal in his critique of moribund academic philosophy that is detached from pressing socio-political concerns and that ignores the relationship between knowledge and power. In particular, although he appreciates the intellectual intensity of the analytic philosophy of Bertrand Russell, Rudolf Carnap, and Gottlob Frege, he perceives their work as too detached from his Kierkegaardian concerns of how one responds to evil and suffering. So, while he acknowledges the wisdom that can be found in professionalized and analytic philosophy, he condemns analytic philosophy for a failure to relate its sharpness to themes of struggle, misery, and suffering.[2] In short, he rejects analytic philosophy's stress on formal logic, argument, and analysis, rather than overarching vision. West wants to see professional philosophy stripped of its "pretense" and thereby transform philosophy into a public conversation that is based on lived experiences, with the purpose of leading America away from chaos towards community.

West's ambivalence toward professional philosophy has encouraged the widely held assumption that he has radically shifted from the position of philosopher to that of cultural critic wherein his prophetic role has overtaken theoretical pursuits and where he has shunned the narrow and limiting label of "philosopher." Indeed, such a view is given added weight by West's assertion that he has "been a cultural critic since 1989."[3] Talk of such a shift can erroneously be construed to mean that philosophy is now a peripheral rather than central influence on West's work. Such a view is mistaken because there is a close correlation in West's mind between pragmatism and cultural criticism. In fact he claims that American pragmatists *are* cultural critics whose work has political consequences; they are concerned with the meaning of America in response to specific social and cultural crises and strive to present new interpretations of the world. West sees pragmatism's evasion of epistemology as a form of emancipation, in that the rejection of absolute standards of knowledge releases intellectual action for cultural criticism and political action. This correlation of pragmatism and cultural criticism is by no means unique to West, as most neo-pragmatists present their work as an evasion of philosophy in favor of social, cultural, or literary criticism. However, West is adamant that his cultural criticism is distinct from that of Rorty, because while Rorty's is "critical of the academy and primarily literarily engaged" West's takes the form of the politically engaged public intellectual.[4] In *Prophesy Deliverance* West sums up his own inter-pretation of philosophizing as "cultural expression generated from and existentially grounded in the moods and sensibilities of a writer entrenched in the life-worlds of a people."[5] West has never viewed himself as a philosopher in the narrow sense of the word and instead views philosophy as simply a means to the end of understanding the world in order to change it. As a social critic of American life West is not concerned with foundationalist notions of knowledge and truth, but rather with philosophy as a mode of inquiry that can address issues of power and that is linked to con-crete problems and embedded in experience.[6] Although West feels best able to articulate his pragmatist vision from outside the confines of academic philosophy, he considers his philosophical training to be a vital aid in making his political-cultural reflections subtle and nuanced.

The genealogy: Emerson to prophetism

The difficulties in offering a definitive definition of pragmatism are well rehearsed, given that any two pragmatists may share a theory of truth and yet diverge sharply on political matters. Moreover, while some pragmatists consider pragmatism to be a theory of meaning, others view it as an epistemology stressing action, and still others as a skeptical anti-essentialism. The definitional diffi-culty is compounded by the fresh concerns of neo-pragmatism and by the fact that central pragmatist concepts can be found in other approaches such as deconstruction. Indeed pragmatism's now voguish status inspires loose usage of the term. In contemporary lit-erature we can find Michael Walzer, Benjamin Barber, Stanley Fish, Richard Bernstein, and even Jacques Derrida labeled as pragmatists along with James and Dewey, yet one struggles to build any salient or meaningful connection between such diverse figures. Nevertheless, in *The American Evasion*, West attempts to offer a cohesive definition of pragmatism as seen through the work of its main exponents. His survey begins with Ralph Waldo Emerson's "pre-history" of the genre that prefigures what he regards as pragmatism's dominant themes, namely optimism, moralism, individualism, and an emphasis on human agency. West suggests that a clear sense of moral and political continuity can be discerned from Emerson via Dewey to his own brand of "prophetic pragmatism."

In West's lexicon "evasion" is inferred in a positive sense, meaning the abandonment of abstract philosophical speculations about the nature of truth and reality in favor of a more experimental approach that West commends. West claims that although Emerson considered modern philosophy to be anachronistic and outdated, he chose to *evade* it rather than deny it. In other words, he rejected philosophy's search for foundations and certainty and argued against Descartes that knowledge is guided by human interest rather than a set of representations to be justified or privileged. In place of philosophy Emerson pursued cultural criticism that offered both a legitimation and critique of America; he sought to enhance his *ideal* of America through critique of the selfishness and low moral standards found in "actually existing" America. He thus viewed the world as incomplete and in flux, highlighting the need for contingency and human experimental power to overcome the limitations of the world. But while Emerson was concerned with the empowerment and flourishing of human personality, he devoted little attention to concerted political involvement. Thus the human activity that he sought to provoke was not social revolution but moral transgression based on individual integrity. He considered all morality to be experimental; no vice or virtue is final but rather initial, and so we must learn to abandon our present moral standards in the light of better ones. This is a crucial concept for later pragmatists who point with Emerson to the futility of a search for the certainty of enduring truths, emphasizing instead the value and necessity of continual reassessment of one's beliefs.

If Emerson's evasion of epistemology-centered philosophy represents pragmatism's pre-history, West suggests its actual emergence is found in the work of William James and Charles Sanders Peirce and their elaboration of the Emersonian evasion within the context of academic philosophy. James emphasized that pragmatism does not offer dogmas or systems, but rather an attitude or orientation that serves as a method of conducting discussions. He also rejected the notion that truth corresponds to some non-experienced or preconstituted reality and instead suggested that ideas are true in so far as they help one relate with other parts of the human experience. James dismissed as futile attempts to derive truth from general first principles and instead urged philosophers to ask, as the scientist would, what practical effects result from choosing one view over another, as the meaningful is discerned in practical behavior and experience. Similarly, Peirce stressed that no truth or idea can be considered final, as it is impossible to be certain of what humans will know several hundred years later. While Peirce's interest in technical issues of semiotics, mathematical logic, and scientific technique is widely recognized, West also calls attention to his more speculative views concerning ethics, politics, and religion. So although Peirce argued that we arrive at beliefs through scientific method, West reminds us that Peirce saw "scientific method as a value-laden and normative social activity."[7] West concludes that ultimately Peirce, like Emerson, was concerned with fulfilling human potential.

The third and highest point of West's genealogy is located in John Dewey – whom he calls the American Hegel *and* Marx. Although the influence of Peirce and James was crucial to Dewey's journey from neo-Hegelianism, he supplemented their interest in individuality and personality with a consideration of social structures, political systems, and economic institutions. Like them he rejected the notion of infallible knowledge and stressed the need to revise norms in light of experience, but he saw this reworking as a social or communal process. Dewey's vision of individual growth and self-realization was to occur through participation in collective forms of life, where achieving one's individual potential and shaping the broader social and political context go hand in hand. In other words, he regarded community and political engagement as central to self-construction, and his emphasis on collective collaboration is evident in his conception of communicative democracy and in the pedagogical approach of his Laboratory School in Chicago. Dewey believed that philosophy should be transformational rather than foundational, directing its critical acumen and imaginative energy to the resolution of concrete social and political problems. Thus it was unsurprising that he became increasingly alienated not only from academic philosophy's narrow epistemological concerns, but also from the discipline's scholastic professionalism. His emphasis on the need for critical intervention in the world was evident in his intellectual pursuits outside the university, such as his presence in the popular press and attempt to launch *Thought News*, his trip to Mexico to chair the Trotsky inquiry, and his role in the creation of the New School for Social Research and the American Civil Liberties Union. This political engagement coupled with what West regards as Dewey's strong moral dimension is a crucial model for West. West thus strongly rejects, along with Matthew Festenstein and Robert Westbrook, traditional readings of Dewey as an ethically unreflective ideologue who eschewed substantive moral claims in favor of articulation of "technique."

West suggests that Dewey inspired latter pragmatists to be social, cultural, or literary critics, and he locates the fourth phase of the genealogy in a loose assemblage of mid-twentieth-century critical intellectuals. His primary concern here is with how Sidney Hook, C. Wright Mills, W. E. B. Du Bois, Reinhold Niebuhr, and Lionel Trilling struggled with the pragmatist legacy in a time when political catastrophes and national uncertainty imposed a sense of limits on the optimism of Emerson and Dewey. West observes that war and Depression disillusioned middle-class notions of perfection and progress, and so this era of diminished expectations questioned the very survival of pragmatism. It was in this era that pragmatism began to acquire "a sense of the tragic, a need for irony, a recognition of limits and constraints, and a stress on paradox, ambiguity and difficulty."[8] These thinkers were less genteel than their pragmatist predecessors and lacked their associations with northeastern highbrow culture. As cultural critics they questioned the realities of American life and sought to enlarge the basis for a tradition of native American thought. To give two examples, while Niebuhr confronted the liberal establishment with the reality of sin and a sense of the tragic, Du Bois highlighted the silences in pragmatist reflections on individuality and democracy. As will be discussed later, this part of the genealogy is problematic, as it would appear that many modern intellectuals, and not just self-professed pragmatists, could fit into it. It thus begs the question of whether West is attempting to be too inclusive and lax with his terminology.

The fifth part of West's genealogy is located in neo-pragmatism's blend of classical pragmatism and the European philosophy of Derrida, Heidegger, and Ludwig Wittgenstein, as personified in the work of Richard Rorty. Whereas pragmatism's original mandate was to present an alternative to systematic philosophy, essentialism, and transcendental positivism, neo-pragmatism urges the

American critical community to move from an emphasis on theory and methodology to historicism and interventionism, and is thus evident in the turn from "theory" into cultural studies and identity politics. Rortian neo-pragmatism reintroduces the classical opposition between rhetoric and philosophy, where rhetoric stands for contingency and persuasion as opposed to universality and Truth, and is strongly influenced by the reversal of Platonism found in the linguistic turn of continental philosophy since Nietzsche. In reinterpreting pragmatism along linguistic lines Rorty replaces the original emphasis on ideas and experience with an emphasis on language and alternative vocabularies as the medium through which desires are fulfilled. Like earlier pragmatists, Rorty asserts that truth and knowledge are simply tools for coping with the world rather than a foundation or ultimate definition of reality. He refuses to engage in any attempt to explain or analyze truth, as truth is not an explanatory notion but simply a compliment paid to sentences that seem to be useful. Thus the pursuit of Truth is absurd, as truth is not a reflection of logic but a product of language games where "anything can be made to look good or bad, important or unimportant . . . by being redescribed."[9] Rorty thus dismisses attempts by philosophers to adjudicate knowledge as presumptuous and unwarranted, and instead proposes a post-philosophical approach of ironism or strong textualism. His claim that this liberal ironism is continuous with Dewey is the starting point for West's critique of Rorty.

Although West credits Rorty with almost single-handedly reviving pragmatism's intellectual currency and affirms Rorty's historicism and emphasis on contingency, he is deeply dissatisfied with the moral and political consequences of Rorty's work and concludes that Rorty's pragmatism actually points to the *demise* of the pragmatist tradition. West appreciates Rorty's anti-foundational epistemological critique, but disagrees strongly with his liberal political position and his militant secularism. As we shall see, the main thrust of his critique centers on Rorty's strident anti-theoretical position and his egocentrism. He suggests that Rorty strives for a society infused with public solidarity and private irony – a position that is distinct from that of Dewey. West thus locates pragmatism's demise in the way Rorty replaces the communal concerns of Dewey with a negative liberty and egocentric concerns about what works best for the individual. So although Rorty claims to develop Dewey's liberalism in a cultural context, his continuity lies not with Dewey but with Emerson's libertarian ethos of self-realization.

West's "prophetic pragmatism" constitutes the final phase of the genealogy and is essentially an attempt to unite what he considers the "best" features of earlier pragmatism, namely Emersonian democracy, Deweyan historicism, and Niebuhr's religious inspiration. In particular, he suggests that a retrieval of Deweyan pragmatism will enlarge the terms of debate about freedom, democracy, and self-transformation within contemporary pragmatism. Like Dewey, West emphasizes social commitment and democratic activism, and appeals to intellectuals to join in popular struggle. West sees little merit in abstract philosophical debates concerning the nature of knowledge and the foundations of belief, rejecting excessively obscure speculation and philosophy that eschews political involvement. Instead he strives to present a practical, politically engaged philosophy that offers "a continuous cultural commentary or set of interpretations that attempt to explain America to itself at a particular historical moment."[10] The remainder of this chapter will focus on specific aspects of this prophetic pragmatism. West is critical of Rorty's "silences" and largely defines his own pragmatism in contrast to that of Rorty, and so we will consider their divergence in terms of theory, politics, and existential matters. In particular we will consider West's emphasis on political consequences and his accentuation of the oppositional and emancipatory possibilities of theory. West suggests that pragmatism promises the transformation of society and the self, while its sense of invention and innovation serves the purpose of socio-cultural critique. The goal of his pragmatism is to inspire political action to achieve profoundly moral ends. Prophetic pragmatism is sensitive to matters of race and class and West believes it can contribute to a regeneration of social forces that empower the disadvantaged and degraded. He thus attempts to *extend* the insights of pragmatism so as to resonate with African-American experiences. However, this raises the pertinent question of whether, given West's revisions and extensions of the tradition, prophetic pragmatism is really pragmatism at all.

Theory and prophetic pragmatism

We have seen that Westian pragmatism evades academic philosophy in favor of cultural criticism. This does not mean that West evades theory, and in fact he is critical of Rorty's "distrust of theory and preoccupation with transient vocabularies."[11] West notes the importance of Rorty's attempt to *demythologize* modern philosophy by rendering contingent and provisional things considered neces-sary and permanent. However, he insists that it is insufficient to simply demythologize, as there must also be an attempt to *demys-tify*. This latter project aims to "lay bare the complex ways in which meaning is produced and mobilized for the maintenance of rela-tions of domination," and it is a "*theoretical* activity" that attempts to explain the functions and ideological roles of specific social prac-tices.[12] West thus rejects the widely held view that pragmatism's anti-foundationalism entails the renunciation of, or at least resis-tance toward, theory. So although pragmatist literary critics such as Steven Knapp and Walter Benn Michaels see the theoretical enter-prise as a cover for new forms of epistemic foundationalism, West claims that the reason they take an anti-theory stance is because they mistakenly view all theory as *grand theory*, which of course all pragmatists reject. In dismissing the extreme anti-theory position of some pragmatists, West insists that pragmatists need not be opposed to theory *per se*, and points appreciatively to the work of "ultratheorists" such as Frank Lentricchia and Jonathan Arac who shun grand theory and yet consider Marxist and feminist theoreti-cal insights indispensable. West resists dogmatic theories and sees no use for Marxism as a grand theory applied to everything, yet claims that his allegiance to Marxist theory, "is not for its polemi-cal force but for its theoretical acuity regarding the power of capital and the rule of power elites."[13] He insists that there are no genuine theories of society as a whole, but rather there are tentative, provi-sional, and revisable theories that function as analyses of particular people and specific societies.

One reason theory is important for West is that it is the specialized conversation of the academy that must be linked to other sites of rhetorical exchange. West wants to converse with those inside and outside the academy and so he must be able to speak the specialized languages of the academy as well as the languages of the grassroots. However, he recognizes that while theory can be liberating, too often it is encased in inaccessible elitist language. For instance, West sug-gests that Fredric Jameson's work lacks political consequences, and attributes this partly to his work being "too theoretical . . . too far removed from the heat of political battles, too little reflective on and about the prevailing political strife." Here West claims not to be articulating an anti-intellectual or anti-theoretical argument, but rather "a call for more sophisticated theory aware of and rooted in the present historical and political conjuncture in American capital-ist civilization."[14] It is thus a redefined role for theory that follows

Dewey in breaking from the earlier ivory tower pragmatism of Peirce. West suggests that theory has an important role to play in his quest to see democracy and freedom flourish, and he aims to "deploy thought as a weapon to enable more effective action."[15] He is conscious that theory need not necessarily prioritize thought over action or impose on practice, nor need it be abstract and totalizing. In a loose sense, theory is simply the set of assumptions that underlie one's conduct and thus all of human existence is in some sense theoretical. So when West speaks of the merits of theory he is not referring to abstract logic, but to theory that is concerned with concrete social and political events. This sort of theory helps to illuminate our present political position and so prophetic pragmatism recognizes the potency of thought as a means of social empowerment. West insists on the necessity of theory for understanding experience, analyzing differences, and effecting change, and reminds us that a progressive movement cannot be built without progressive theory. For theory to be "liberating" it is essential that it be developed out of one's experiences and context; as such it must be communally and historically grounded, as there is no community-neutral way of understanding anything. In short, it is possible to theorize and yet resist abstract theory.

Liberatory politics

A typical view of pragmatism is that it has no necessary, logical connection to any particular ideology, and so can be a justification of either radical democratic reform or a reactionary defense of traditional institutions. On the one hand, it can lead to political quietism as it provides no objective basis for ethical choice, or, on the other, to social anarchy as it provides justification for *any* political choice. However, in *The American Evasion* West not only constructs an evolutionary history of American pragmatism, but also reinterprets that tradition to address the crisis of the American Left, pointing to the radicalism and inbred rebelliousness of pragmatism as an indigenous progressive tradition that can inspire leftist attempts to reform America. West calls for a re-examination of pragmatism whereby the non-radical caricature presented by neo-pragmatism's dilution of Dewey will be stripped away and the transformational power of pragmatism unveiled.

The emphasis of West's pragmatism is on democracy, social critique, and recognition of difference, and so he offers a scathing

critique of the way in which Rorty's demythologizing project
"retreats into the philosophical arena as soon as pertinent socio-
political issues are raised."[16] That is not to say Rorty is disinterested
in politics, for he does in fact chide fellow intellectuals for aban-
doning "real politics."[17] Rather, West is unhappy with the moral and
political consequences of Rorty's work because Rorty appears to be
content with the institutions of liberal bourgeois capitalist society.
As such, "Rorty's neo-pragmatism only kicks the philosophic props
from under liberal bourgeois capitalist societies; it requires no
change in our cultural and political practices."[18] Rorty's liberalism
urges the politics of tolerance rather than emancipation and defines
liberalism negatively as the desire to avoid pain or cruelty. His negative liberty separates the private and public spheres, insisting that
any public preoccupation with an individual's self-realization
intrudes on individual liberty. This is because his ideal of a free
society is one where opportunities for self-creation are equalized,
after which people should be left alone to either use or neglect those
opportunities. West claims that Rorty's liberal ironism demands no
change in political and cultural practices and simply combines reformist tinkering in the public realm with aesthetic self-fashioning
in the private. Moreover, Rorty displays too little concern with the
multileveled operations of power. West suggests that the power dif-
ferentials of the social order determine who has access to various
discourse sites with the result that everyone cannot participate in
discourse equally, yet he feels that Rorty's political liberalism
ignores questions about how conversation is structured. Instead,
Rorty's envisioned conversation is genteel "smooth and witty Attic
prose" that fails to speak to specific social differences, and his "eth-
nocentric posthumanism" provides no critique of the culture or
politics of Western civilization.[19] Indeed, West suggests that pragmatism as a whole has paid insufficient attention to the operations
of structural and institutional power and has failed to grasp the role
of power in democratic and dialogical practices.

West is particularly bothered by the fact that Rorty's prominence
has led a number of commentators to take Rortian liberalism to be
the Deweyan position. The pragmatist revival has obscured the
radical emancipatory potential of Deweyan pragmatism, with the
result that radical democrats falsely assume they must look elsewhere than pragmatism for their predecessors. We have seen that
West presents Dewey as a morally and politically engaged figure
who emphasizes communal democracy as a means of individual
self-fulfillment. Although he is aware that there is no uniform prag-

matist political position, his own reading of pragmatism, to which Dewey is central, finds a strong democratic impulse where the people deliberate and shape their creative democracy. Dewey's notion of social intelligence was inextricably linked with the case for participatory democracy, and he presents a model for West's desire for broad public participation in cultural criticism and inclusiveness in decision-making. Thus West urges the American Left to look to pragmatic sources such as Dewey and Emerson rather than to European sources such as the Frankfurt School, stressing that the Emersonian aspirations to self-creation and self-realization are themes the Left must draw upon. West's radical pragmatism attempts to be both critical and constructive in an effort at social reform. He concludes that the insights of pragmatism and its emancipatory social experimentalism are of crucial importance for the rebuilding of the Left, and offer the Left a way out of its current epistemological obsession with deconstruction and poststructuralism.

Despair and hope

In addition to the political critique of Rortian neo-pragmatism, West offers an existential critique. Although West commends the sense of the tragic developed by mid-twentieth-century pragmatists, he suggests that both neo-pragmatism and even the heroic Dewey lack an adequate conception of the tragic. West engages most forcefully with this theme in "Pragmatism and the Sense of the Tragic" in *Keeping Faith*, where he suggests that pragmatism needs to be supplemented by the tragic temperament of Josiah Royce. West characterizes prophetic pragmatism as "a form of tragic thought" that "confronts candidly individual and collective experiences of evil in individuals and institutions."[20] West's philosophy of struggle emanates from an African-American legacy of suffering and resistance, and his blues sensibility accentuates hope and agency in the face of the tragic. Although he has no illusions about the difficulty of the challenge of remaking America, he retains hope, recognizing both the possibility of progress and the impossibility of paradise. West is aware that history offers little hope for the possibility of future transformation yet maintains that human progress and growth are possible.

The pragmatist spirit of remaking sits at the center of his blues sensibility, and this sensibility is all about "the making and remaking of one's self, the centrality of agency, heroic human agency in the face of death as well as in the face of social misery."[21] Thus prophetic pragmatism looks both backwards and forwards: it recognizes past difficulty and struggle and yet clings to a sense of utopian possibility. Retention of hope in the midst of pessimistic experience promotes agency and recognition of the contingency of the self and society. Given prophetic pragmatism's emphasis on human agency, West presents it as a form of third-wave Left romanticism located in a historical lineage of the American and French Revolutions, Marxism, and Emersonian nineteenth-century theories of social experimentation and their twentieth-century reformulations by Dewey and Gramsci. He defines romanticism as a hope-filled belief in the possibility of human achievement that has profound faith in the capacity of human beings to remake themselves and society in more free and democratic ways. West displays confidence in human creative potential and ingenuity, and is concerned with what can be brought into being. He balances this optimism with a sense of the pessimism and insatiable appetite for anguish found in Henry Adams's despair at the moral and intellectual disorder of society. This attempt to balance a utopian vision with the tragic reality of life, and the notion that love and resistance lead to human flourishing, flows throughout the entirety of West's work.

Merits of West's genealogy

West is highly critical of pragmatist silences and shortcomings – particularly Rorty's inadequate sense of the tragic and lack of social analysis of the rule of capital or white male supremacy – and uses Left politics and Christianity to plug these gaps. But is West's rejection and revision of Rortian neo-pragmatism a convincing attempt to drive pragmatism back to its Emersonian and Deweyan roots? Does his genealogy illuminate our understanding of pragmatism? To support his claim that prophetism is continuous with the "best" pragmatism found in Emerson and Dewey, West's genealogy presents a contorted selection of pragmatists. He excludes consideration of figures such as George Herbert Mead and C. I. Lewis, offers a selective account of those pragmatists he does include, and yet also broadens the term to include other figures such as Niebuhr and Du Bois whose first identity is not pragmatist. Therefore the first difficulty is that he is selective rather than exhaustive; for instance, he emphasizes Peirce's deconstructive anti-Cartesianism and yet excludes Peircian themes such as concrete reasonableness in the world or metaphysics of evolving Thirdness. West openly states that he focuses more on Dewey than on Peirce and James because Dewey's historical consciousness and socio-political emphasis speak more to his concerns than the preoccupations with logic in Peirce or with individuality in James.[22] This admission that Dewey is more useful to his purposes immediately undermines any sense in which the genealogy could offer a comprehensive overview of pragmatism. However, it should also be noted that his omissions from the genealogy should not be taken as a suggestion that certain figures are not "true" pragmatists or that they are charlatans.

Omissions can certainly be excused on the basis that no one can be fully exhaustive. However, the second difficulty with the genealogy is that, despite this selectivity, West claims to favor a broad definition of pragmatism that not only includes Emerson and Dewey but also Du Bois and Niebuhr. As is true with much of his work, West engages in an exhaustive drive to incorporate and in this case seems to paint everyone he admires, from Emerson to King, as a pragmatist. The difficulty is that if you say everything is something, it loses its meaning and so nothing is. Thus, although it serves West's purposes to suggest that Emerson contributes to the pragmatic reconception of philosophy as cultural criticism, it is debatable whether this was Emerson's intention. Also contentious is the inclusion of Du Bois. Robert Gooding-Williams asserts that it is "psychological conjecture" rather than marshalling textual evidence that justifies the inclusion of Du Bois in a narrative history of pragmatism.[23] West is vague about how Du Bois's turn from philosophy to the social sciences was an *evasion* of philosophy in the Emersonian sense, and one wonders why he felt the need to include Du Bois in the genealogy in the first place. The answer to this lies in the way Westian pragmatism connects with feminist, black, and third-world social movements; as such, the inclusion of Du Bois is an attempt to demonstrate that there is more to pragmatism than simply the concerns of white man, which lends support to West's suggestion that concerns of race and gender are continuous with the general pragmatist tradition. However, the difficulty is that without Du Bois pragmatism appears to say little to such concerns and is largely silent regarding difference. Clearly, West wants to extend the insights of pragmatism so as to resonate with African-American experiences, and we have observed his sharp divergence from Rortian neo-pragmatism in terms of theory and political and

existential concerns. However, it is not just an aspect of Rortian pragmatism that he rejects, as he finds flaws in much of the pragmatist
tradition and none of the heroic figures are entirely absolved of criticism. Indeed, we could argue that what he really embraces is a
more specific Deweyan philosophy as opposed to a broad pragmatist philosophy. This begs the question of why he wants to be a
pragmatist. If he finds so much of pragmatism lacking in terms of
theory, politics, and tragedy, can he really claim continuity with that
tradition?

West admits that his genealogy is selective and self-serving and
does not purport to be a comprehensive account of pragmatism. But
he makes two divergent moves when locating prophetic pragmatism within that genealogy by pointing to both organicism and
rupture. As such, he seems to suggest that his work fits organically
into a developing tradition while simultaneously breaking sharply
with that tradition. On the one hand, West emphasizes his continuities with Emerson and Dewey and talks of pragmatism as an
evolving tradition of which he is a part. He relies on organic
metaphors such as "growth," "reaches maturity," "decline," and
"resurgence" to argue that pragmatism is a developing organism,
albeit with distinct parts, whose most recent stage is found in his
prophetism. This enables him not only to claim that his prophetism
is continuous with earlier expressions of pragmatism, but also to
justify his attempt to develop and invigorate the ideas of earlier
heroes such as Dewey. However, on the other hand, we have
seen that West is quick to point out what he considers the major
deficiencies of the pragmatist tradition. Alongside his organic
metaphors West stresses how pragmatists (himself included) *revise*
the pragmatist tradition. The sharp breaks that West identifies
between Rorty and himself are much more radical than an organic
model would allow. But how can West reconcile the conscious
intentionality of revision and rupture with unconscious organic
processes? How can he embrace both an organic and genealogical
view of history? Of course it is true that, in itself, the concept of
genealogy need not be problematic, as West could utilize it in an
unphilosophic sense of providing a deed of origin and legitimation
for the cultural Left; indeed, in one sense this is precisely what he
does do. However, the difficulty is that he also associates his conception of genealogy with Foucault and Nietzsche and states explicitly that his pragmatism "incorporates the genealogical mode of
inquiry initiated by the later phase of Foucault's work."[24] The contradiction here is that both Foucault and Nietzsche used their

conception of genealogy as a critique of organic models of history and as a signifier of rupture and the radical reconstruction of meaning. So, although West rejects the anti-romanticism of Foucauldian genealogy and places the emphasis instead on human agency and moral discourse, tensions remain in his use of even a revised Foucauldian genealogy and his organic genealogical rhetoric. In effect he wants to have it both ways; the organic model is self-serving for West as it enables him to highlight the continuities between his thought and Dewey, yet he also recognizes that the history of pragmatism is not as simple as an organic model might suggest. This of course raises the question of just what is so valuable about the pragmatist tradition that he goes through such convolutions to reinherit for his own purposes.

Liberation and reimagination

Given what he outlines as the political and existential flaws of the pragmatist tradition, why is West so keen to be a pragmatist? What are the strengths and resources of pragmatism that he draws upon for his liberatory project? In *Prophesy Deliverance* West identifies pragmatism as a key source of African-American critical thought, second only in importance to prophetic Christianity, and portrays pragmatism as an approach concerned with creating "a mode of discourse that interprets, describes, and evaluates Afro-American life in order comprehensively to understand it and effectively to transform it."[25] West builds a distinctive discourse that aims to be a "material force" for black liberation from pragmatism's assertion that history must be interpreted from a specific vantage point. He sees profound liberating and empowering possibilities within the pragmatist quest for better experience and improved self-realization. Pragmatism promises the transformation of the self and of society and is thus a term for the creative and often-unexpected way American ingenuity has articulated itself.

The Westian vision of pragmatism has a strong moral and political thrust, and at its heart are themes of democracy and freedom with strong continuities to leftist politics. West wants his pragmatism to be more than just an interesting academic fad or conversation piece, but rather a material force for changing the world, and suggests that the distinctive feature of pragmatism *vis-à-vis* other philosophical traditions is its emphasis on the "ethical significance" of the future and a belief that human beings can make a difference in the world.[26] In pragmatism West sees an approach that aids his quest for a better description of America, with a radical transformation of society that will force actuality to match the ideal, and finds liberatory possibility in pragmatism's uncertainty, plurality, and suspicion of authority. He also appreciates the way in which pragmatism honors the past yet recognizes that past traditions have changed and will continue to change. West is preoccupied with the meaning of "Americanness" and wants America to come to terms with its turbulent history. This involves trying to incorporate the political struggle of blacks and women into the story of America, and creating a discourse about what America has been and what it aspires to be in order to forge a national moral identity. Thus West says we need a conversation about differences in order to broaden a sense of community, and he engages in a democratic quest to thicken rather than deplete public culture. He suggests that pragmatism is a discursive space that is not concerned with foundations or transcendental grounds, but rather with building a public language that inspires a drive for freedom. Pragmatism attaches importance to dialogue, recognizing that it is through public discussion that the validity of claims can be established. West's interpretative imagination stresses the need for both a critical consciousness and a historical consciousness; in other words, if social change is to be achieved critique and self-critique are vital, as is an awareness of human finitude and conditionedness. Although West is cognizant of the constraints to efforts at reform, he retains a sense of national hope and recognizes that something other than resigned pessimism is needed. As a pragmatist he attempts to use his imagination to understand the actual in light of the possible, and so try to make the actuality of America match its self-image.

Liberation as truth claim?

West's work offers both a critique of present inadequacies in America and alternative scenarios that he seeks to construct. One difficulty is that his liberatory quest could be construed as a quest for truth. Such a claim is hugely problematic as it implies that, although he rejects foundational conceptions of rationality, he continues to justify his critical conclusions with some notion of rationality. We have seen that pragmatism rejects foundational grounding and definitional certainty, instead striving to be experimental and open to revision. But is pragmatism's rejection of fixed foundations just another form of relativism and, if so, is it possible to talk of human solidarity while rejecting truth and all universal ethical norms? In other words, is it possible for a pragmatist to say flatly that something is wrong, unjust, or untrue? These questions represent a problem for someone with a liberationist perspective, because if there is no Truth how can there be injustice? Moreover, if no belief can transcend one's limited perspective, how can we work together for a better world, and on what grounds can unjust social relations be critiqued?

Like other pragmatists, West rejects philosophy's traditional search for Truth, and he replaces foundationalism with an emphasis on conversation and continuous inquiry. However, along with Frank Lentricchia, West is critical of the relativist overtones of much neo-pragmatism, which he views as vulnerable to self-refutation and political quietism. Following Rorty's assertion that there is nothing within moral law or written in the skies to back up human values, standards, or justificatory strategies, pragmatism can be taken to mean that there can be no appeal to anything beyond our practices. But West claims that although foundationalism and objectivism are now widely considered to have failed, skepticism and relativism are not the sole alternatives; absolutes may have dissolved, but one can still prefer some beliefs and ways of knowing to others. Pragmatists are not interested in what makes claims "true" or in how truth is discovered, insisting that there is no objectively true knowledge to be found; but this does not circumvent a pragmatist from making positive claims, as there are still better and worse ideas in which to believe. Thus pragmatism does not deny that we can make intelligent, adjudicable claims about the world; indeed, to manage in daily life, individuals need to advance claims about the world as it is based on these understandings that we orient and justify our actions. The point then is that interpretive conflicts ought not to be settled by trying to elaborate some general theory of Truth or social knowledge, as one's vantage point is local. In short, there is a proliferation of truths rather than one final Truth.

Although West challenges certainty, he does not undermine attempts to resist injustice and he claims that it is possible to say something is truer and less partial than its alternatives. According to West, it is impossible to make final Truth claims because history and therefore knowledge are incomplete. But precisely because history is incomplete, the possibility persists that a better argument and a richer narrative could be constructed in the future in light of new knowledge. Until then, certain provisional and revisable truths exist, and certain cultures are morally preferable to others because of the degree to which they conform to his radical democratic principles. Thus West cannot be viewed as an "anything goes" relativist. He recognizes that in order to promote debate and cultural exchange, rather than mere partisanship, it is important to cling to threadbare notions of objectivity and universalism. So, although he does not believe that we have access to a God's eye-view of objectivity that allows us to jump out of our skin, he does believe in "a certain threadbare notion of objectivity that has to do with acknowledging we can get some critical distance from an issue in order to be more balanced and keep track of its complexity."[27] For this reason, although the context from which West seeks liberation is African-American experiences, he suggests that such particularity need not be pursued at the expense of a loose universality. In this sense he maintains that his contextualism is distinct from relativism. Although West rejects absolutes he takes and defends certain positions and makes discriminations, stressing "I'm not a relativist, I'm a fallibist. I think that I'm right, but I recognize I could be wrong."[28] Historicist premises do not lead inexorably from a naïve objectivism in ethics to ethical relativism, and a modest pragmatism is able to support meaningful discussions of truth while avoiding relativism and skepticism. In this sense, it is possible for West to embrace both pragmatism and the truth claims of Christianity.

As a theological pragmatist West rejects metaphysical foundationalism, yet strives for truthfulness and searches constantly for evidence to support truth claims. He articulates and defends theological beliefs, yet does not appeal to an ahistorical rationality as the basis of such beliefs. This is because he sees no "neutral" ground on which believers and non-believers can stand in order to evaluate theological truth claims. So, although West is steeped in the tradition of a particular interpretive community, he attempts to be truthful in every situation, regardless of whether a particular idea is in agreement with the opinions of that community. He thus refutes the assumption that there is an essential theological core of untouchable doctrines exempt from revision. In other words, truth demands that faith, like other parts of one's make-up, must be continually revised in light of new experience, evidence, and arguments. While a religious sectarian is certain that their faith will be vindicated, a religious pragmatist must wait and see. Therefore West acknowledges the difficulty he faces when trying to mount a defense of his faith:

I do not think it possible to put forward rational defenses of one's faith that verify its veracity or even persuade one's critics. . . . The fundamental philosophical question remains whether the Christian gospel is ultimately true. And, as a Christian prophetic pragmatist whose focus is on coping with transient and provisional penultimate matters yet whose hope goes beyond them, I reply in the affirmative, bank my all on it, yet am willing to entertain the possibility in low moments that I may be deluded.[29]

He recognizes that it is impossible to "prove" the Truth of the Christian faith, and it is thus faith intertwined with doubt.

Conclusion

As a philosophy, pragmatism is critical, progressive, creative, and destabilizing, and we have seen that West's pragmatism evades philosophical concerns with the nature of knowledge and the foundations of belief, instead offering a practical, politically engaged philosophy and a cultural commentary that attempts to explain America to itself. In so doing he offers a strong political and existential critique of Rortian neo-pragmatism and looks behind Rorty to earlier pragmatists. Like jazz music, West considers pragmatism to be part of American New World modernity that affirms creative unpredictability. The vital legacy of pragmatism for West is the moral, political, and prophetic thrust evident in the themes of democracy, social criticism, and freedom that lie at its normative core. Thus he portrays pragmatism as a form of indigenous American oppositional thought that can be utilized in the quest for reinventing and expanding American democracy. His perspective acknowledges that history offers little hope for future transformation, and yet maintains that human progress and growth can be achieved through struggle and resistance.

4

"Prophetic" Christianity

West's prophetic spirituality "combines Christian themes of deliverance and salvation with political ideals of democracy, freedom and equality" and is an explicit part of his broader socio-political agenda.[1] Thus themes such as dignity and social critique, to be considered in this chapter, provide the foundations to his political arguments concerning community, integrity, and social activism, and the manner of truthfulness and humility in which those arguments should be presented. I have already asserted that liberation theology is the foundation for West's entire body of work, and so this chapter attempts to examine the central tenets of his liberationist theology and locate it in the Christian tradition. We shall see that West's thought is a creative synthesis of several perspectives. Most notably, his upbringing in the black church has had a profound impact on his intellectual development. The critique of nihilism, cynicism, exploitation, and dogmatism that is so crucial within his work presupposes the "prophetic" Christian values of hope and love in the face of suffering, exemplified in the black church and in the black theology of James Cone. Additionally, it will be demonstrated that although West barely mentions Social Gospelers such as Walter Rauschenbusch in his thought, and makes only passing references to Reinhold Niebuhr, his spirituality fits into a framework of Rauschenbuschian social concern tempered by a Niebuhrian "realist" perspective. Thus Howland Sanks's emphasis on the continuities between the Social Gospel and liberation theology is crucial to an understanding of West, as his work ebbs between these two traditions. While they are two distinct perspectives, both reject a purely spiritualized understanding of the Gospel, seeing salvation as social and as achieved in and through human history. Both also reject excessive individualism and equate God's Kingdom with the quest for social justice.[2]

The black church, King, and Cone

West suggests that African-American culture has historically had a profound preoccupation with Christianity to the degree that black culture would be unimaginable without the church. West is the grandson of a Baptist preacher and he notes that despite the wane in the church's influence among the young, levels of religious affiliation remain high. Testimony to the strength and importance of the church in black America is that it constitutes the source from which key leaders such as Martin Luther King Jr, Jesse Jackson, Benjamin Hooks, and Joseph Lowery emerged and developed their support bases, often leapfrogging over potential leaders from other black groupings. West identifies three reasons – institutional, political, and existential – why African Americans historically turned to the church.[3] First, he suggests that the church stands as "the major institution created, sustained and controlled by black people themselves."[4] African Americans were drawn towards the democratically structured nature of the "dissenting" denominations such as Baptists and Methodists. They found resonance in the themes stressed by these denominations, such as conversion, the egalitarian and personal nature of God, and institutional autonomy. In these churches preachers were answerable to the congregation who themselves had access to church leadership. The freedom and control enjoyed in church was unique within the African-American experience, and the church also functioned as a center for debates and public discussion of ideas within the black community. West suggests that the church's provision of cultural solidarity is as important as the type of theology it expounds, and he admits that many African Americans do not attend church as part of an individual spiritual quest for God, but rather to participate in the cultural heritage of the church and experience the sociality provided therein. The political implication of institutional freedom has been the opportunity to develop political opposition to the social order. African Americans found that the church offered them the means and encouragement to engage in a critique of slavery and oppression. In *Prophesy Deliverance* West highlights the socio-political critiques that the black church has offered, from the critique of slavery that inspired the slave revolts led by Nat Turner and Denmark Vessey in the nineteenth century through to black theology's critique of white North American theology in the late twentieth century.

Third, at the existential level, the love ethic of the church provides affirmation and a sense of meaning in the midst of despair and white supremacist bombardment; like music, it provides mechanisms to enable people to survive the absurdity of being black in America. For West, the Christian narratives are empowering and enabling and provide sustenance against meaningless and emptiness. He suggests that the "christocentric language of the black church – of Jesus as the bright morning star against the backdrop of the pitch darkness of the night, as water in dry places . . . a rock in a wearied land" exemplifies the close relationship between God and a seemingly world-forsaken people.[5] The notion that God sides with the oppressed and affirms their humanity is incredibly powerful, and the black church has attempted to transform the *absurd* into the *tragic* through empathy with the crucified and risen Christ. The black church strives to understand and overcome tragic predicaments in the same way that Jesus overcame death, and thus articulates a sense of the tragic that does not preclude the possibility of ultimate triumph. The church provides cultural solidarity in the form of a community that sustains its members by holding despair at bay and striving to find means of empowerment to struggle against the darkness of oppression. West suggests that in terms of visibility and salience the church is of greater cultural significance than Black Nationalism, and he claims that it stressed black cultural distinctiveness, self-love, and self-affirmation long before nationalists did.[6]

The most famous son of the black church and greatest single influence on West is Martin Luther King Jr. Not only is his language of hope, freedom, and justice crucial to West, but so too is the way he grounded these values in the Christian tradition. Indeed, Michael Dyson views West's work as a development and extension of King's moral vision in relation to contemporary struggles.[7] It was because of the Christian Gospel that King rejected the "triple threat" of materialism, militarism, and racism, thereby explicitly combining Christian values and political actions. In praising King as both a prophetic Christian and an organic intellectual, West sees King as more radical than popular iconography suggests. King's call for freedom and justice was not simply a call for "civil rights," but a call for a fundamental change in the very foundations of America. He called America to adopt a new system of values based on love, freedom, and compassion, one that rejects the goals of self-centeredness and seeks to cross boundaries of race, nationality, and ideology, actively demonstrating love even to one's enemies. King believed that the Christian Gospel demanded identification with the poor and underprivileged, and so he sought empowerment of the powerless and committed himself to struggle against poverty.

King is remembered as a moderate integrationist whose oratory offered gentle inspiration to all Americans, yet his vision was deeper than a call for rights and equal opportunity. While the 1963 March on Washington and its "free at last" language is often viewed as the culmination of King's vision, it was in fact a rallying call to the next stage of struggle – a stage when King posed a sufficient political threat to the American government to be under constant covert surveillance by the FBI. Following the Selma marches of 1965, King's criticism of the dominant values of American life deepened as he exposed systemic rather than superficial flaws, questioned American capitalism and militarism, and was strongly critical of the war in Vietnam, stressing that peace and justice are interconnected. The period between 1964–8 also saw King place more focus on the plight of the urban black community, condemning slums in the West Side of Chicago and attempting to mobilize and organize black ghetto dwellers for self-liberating action. Indeed, his final trip to Memphis in April 1968 was in support of striking black sanitation workers and their struggle for justice. While most King biographers detect a change from the time of Selma to a less optimistic and more radical King, Douglas Sturm insists that this discernible change is not a transformation but simply a refinement of his basic orientation: from the time of his student days, King's thought was democratic socialism informed by his Christianity.[8] It is this radical King, whose democratic socialist call for the radical reconstruction of American society was grounded in the values of the black church, with whom West identifies.

In West's thought, King operates as a bridge between the social Christianity of Walter Rauschenbusch and Reinhold Niebuhr and the black theology of James Cone. Through his theological training at Crozer Seminary and Boston University King embraced the Social Gospel and its central concepts of love and justice, and admitted that Rauschenbusch's thought left an indelible imprint on his thought, giving a theological base to his social concern. Indeed, two books that

King constantly referred to explicitly were Rauschenbusch's *Christianity and the Social Crisis* and Niebuhr's *Moral Man and Immoral Society.*[9] Through reading Niebuhr, King concluded that theological liberalism lacked an adequate conception of human sinfulness, but subsequently Mahatma Gandhi's concept of *satyagraha* transformed King's Niebuhrian skepticism concerning the power of love. Through his emphasis on the love-force of non-violent protest, King used Christianity as a resource for struggle and emancipation, and in so doing reinvigorated the Social Gospel. As we shall see, one can discern a strong line of continuity in the way Rauschenbusch, King, and West collapse prophetic religion into social ethics. All three engage in a moral quest to radically transform society and, as part of this process, weave together democratic and Christian themes with deep political awareness. This line of succession attempts to "redeem" the soul of America, and King in particular brought talk of social redemption to center-stage in American culture.

King's vision and thought can be understood only in light of the strong black church tradition of which he was a part, and his southern Christian base was an important starting point for the development of black theology and the revolution which James Cone wrought within theology. Cone's early groundbreaking works, such as *Black Theology and Black Power*, upheld Malcolm X rather than King as the authentic voice of blackness, and he saw the Black Power movement as an attempt to make King's dream a reality. Nevertheless, it was around the radical ideas that King derived from his Christianity that Cone developed a systematic theology pertaining to black liberation, and this theological revolution gained momentum with the assassination of King. In wrestling with the question of what it means to be both black and Christian, Cone attempted to develop a liberation theology that was both fully black *and* fully Christian. So, while he defended historic Christianity from Black Nationalist critiques (which rejected Christianity as "the white man's religion"), he also attacked the theological bankruptcy of white Christianity by placing an emphasis on the affirmation of blackness as a gift of God. He sought to relate Christianity to the practical struggle for black freedom and maintained that this liberation required the Black Power perspective. Because he believed that Jesus and Black Power share a concern with freedom and humanity and seek liberation for the oppressed, it followed that God's liberating power in history must be evident in the activity of Black Power. Given the urgency of the need for liberation, Cone was intolerant of appeals to non-violence and racial reconciliation.

The premise for Cone's work is his belief that faithful Christianity must renounce allegiance to the status quo and work for fundamental changes in the oppressive structures of society. In this sense, any theology indifferent to the liberation of the poor and oppressed is not Christian theology. However, he viewed much American Christianity as indifferent to the question of racial oppression. While he criticized the black church for its social irrelevance and for operating oblivious to the growing momentum of Black Power, his main target was white Christianity. Most white churches preached about God as if racism was non-existent and displayed more interest in debating issues such as the Sunday opening of shops. Moreover, he suggested that the theological tokenism of liberal Christians was as bad as the open religious segregationism of conservative Christians. Cone felt it was crucial "to expose white theology for what it was: a racist, theological justification of the status quo."[10] White theologians did not view racism as a theological problem, but as a political issue unrelated to the Gospel, and Cone was angry that white theologians were more concerned with the "Death of God" debate than with black suffering. Cone viewed this silence of white theologians on racial oppression as collaboration in that oppression. Crucially, while he denounced the racism of much white theology, he maintained that Christianity does not necessitate racism and domination and that it could indeed be a source of liberation. He stressed that God is seen in the face of the oppressed and that God helps the oppressed to survive.

To Cone the issue was clear: black people are oppressed because of their blackness; the Bible shows that God identifies with and seeks to liberate the oppressed; thus it is necessary to think of God's blackness in America. He asserted, "There is no place in black theology for a colorless God in a society where human beings suffer precisely because of their color. . . . Either God is identified with the oppressed to the point that their experience becomes God's experience, or God is a God of racism."[11] It followed for Cone that because white is the color of the oppressor in America, God could not be seen as white in that context – hence his claim that "Christ is black."[12] Unlike Albert Cleage, Cone's primary concern was not with the literal color of the historical Jesus but with how the symbol of blackness can further one's understanding of God. So, while concerned with the black community's quest for liberation, he does not see blackness as a restrictive term; rather, blackness encompasses all who are oppressed or who join with the oppressed in their liberation struggle. Like West, Cone acknowledges that race is a social construct and that "black" and "white" possess cultural rather than metaphysical meanings. Although these terms are metaphors for the dialectic of oppression, they do not signify different types of human beings.

Despite Cone's assertion that black theology is not academic theology, James Harris suggests that black theology is foreign to the black church, as most churchgoers are not interested in arguments about the existence or nature of God but rather in what God has done and can do to help with their practical concerns. Moreover, many black churches still display prominent pictures of a white Jesus and sexism remains prevalent in terms of leadership positions.[13] Thus it seems that black theology is not a mass movement but rather is largely confined to the academy. Gayraud Wilmore argues that this should not be considered a major problem. He suggests that black theology was not destined to be a mass movement; rather it should seek to impact other institutions and create an educational program and ethos to talk about power, social change, and liberation. As such, the aim of black theology is to articulate ideas that *others* can transform into practical action and movement building.[14] In this regard, Cone's creative theology is of crucial significance to West's attempt to develop an African-American theology of liberation, and West draws upon the methodology black theology offers for changing social, economic, and political conditions. Certainly West has not been uncritical of Cone, suggesting that his "Barthian christocentrism was too thick" and viewing his liberation perspective as "theologically groundbreaking yet lacking in serious philosophical substance."[15] So, while Cone's work is politically engaging and culturally enlightening, West feels it would benefit from adopting the historicism of Rorty or Bernstein. Nevertheless, West admits that *Black Theology and Black Power* has been pivotal in his life as it wrestled with the question "what does it mean to be human in the face of death?" He admires the way in which Cone's intellectual work comes from the heart and soul as well as the mind, discerning in Cone's work a deep love ethic and a blues sensibility which attempt to envisage ways that heroic efforts can be enacted against limits to thereby shatter melodramatic visions of America.[16] Moreover, it was Cone who first voiced within Christian systematic theology the issue of African-American oppression, stressing the importance to theology of developing economic and political analysis of oppression. He called on Christians to fight injustice, and his work stresses the eschatological hope that is so important to West. While this does not diminish what West sees as the deficiencies of Cone's method, it is on the foundation of Cone's work that West develops his own liberation theology with his call for an alliance between prophetic Christianity and progressive Marxism.

Christianity as a social critique

Given that West's fundamental theological perspective is liberationist – asserting that God is just, liberating, and concerned with the plight of the oppressed – it follows that he should stress that Christian beliefs necessitate social and political critique and engagement. Indeed, one reason he is wary of the metaphysical aspect of much theology is that it distracts Christians from the real burdens of social and political life toward a transcendent being in whose hands all is well. West's quest for social transformation is derived from his application of biblical values and norms, and in *Prophesy Deliverance* he points to the biblical roots of radical egalitarianism as the source of appeal for his social ethics. He believes that Christianity makes a statement about the way the world ought to be, which constitutes a radical social theory in which justice is the standard by which society can be measured and evaluated. Thus he strongly rejects the reductionist assumption of pietism that salvation is fundamentally about one's narcissistic desires for getting oneself straight with God, and in this regard he concurs with Jim Wallis that "any idea of conversion that is removed from the social and political realities of the day is simply not biblical. . . . The goal of biblical conversion is not to save souls apart from history."[17] Rather than being simply a compendium of moral teaching that applies only to an individual's life, West believes that the Bible possesses a clear social dimension, demonstrated by the Bible's repeated condemnation of structural evil and the velocity of biblical calls for justice. West suggests that it is the ethical obligation of Christians to engage in the alleviation of oppression by fighting for the expansion of democracy, freedom, and equality by being at the forefront of struggles against imperialism, multicorporate domination of economy and government, racism, sexism, and homophobia.[18] Christians should not only seek to interpret the world, but to envisage ways to participate in the struggle for change.

West recognizes that this critical dimension to Christianity has been frequently overshadowed, particularly by skepticism about involvement in "the world" in tandem with a strong otherworldly dimension. Moreover, because the personal definition of sin is predominant in modern expressions of Christianity, the capacity to relate the Bible to collective social and structural sins has been lost. In contrast, prophetic Christianity accents both this and other-worldly liberation and salvation – indeed, he suggests that to emphasize one at the expense of the other is a truncated under-standing of the Gospel. West thus attempts to develop a holistic approach that maintains a balance between the personal and the social, and he does so partly by recasting the typical interpretation of the individual side and rejecting the simplistic moralism so often associated with it. He suggests that many Christians, particularly those on the Right, fail to draw the connection between personal moral behavior (piety) and moral action (justice) in society, with the result that piety becomes an end in itself rather than a means to build a just society. His response is to distinguish between moral-ism and morality, viewing the former as resting upon "a narrow, parochial anti-intellectualism that sees only pitiful individuals," whereas, in contrast, morality or moral action is based on "a broad, robust prophetism that highlights systemic social analysis of the cir-cumstances under which tragic persons struggle."[19] So morality, as West presents it, is able to encompass both the personal and the social dimension to spirituality. As such, it is a fuller and biblically more faithful interpretation. In calling for Christian thought and reflection to incorporate social analysis, West is attempting to recap-ture the idea of Christianity as a social critique: a critique that is not triumphalistic, but presents alternative visions.

West calls on Christians to be imaginative enough to develop an alternative consciousness for our time, and his prophetic Christian-ity presents an alternative vision based on the values of democracy and individuality within community as a way of doing justice and healing broken relationships. Prophetic Christianity is thus critical of sections of the church that promote or condone domination in what-ever form it takes (be it racial or sexual), and of certain mainstream expressions of Christianity that he characterizes as blindly accom-modationalist to modern culture, particularly in terms of indi-vidualism, privatism, and materialism. He suggests that such accommodation to the cultural status quo "is at bottom idolatrous – it worships the gods created by American society and kneels before the altars erected by American culture."[20] West thus points critically to "market religion" where "sermons become melodramatic com-mercials for Jesus, and the prayers become let's make a deal with God." This "consumer religion" is centered on "What do you want done? A car, a girlfriend, new clothes – and that becomes the measure of God's blessings." In this scenario the church has succumbed to the influence of the mass media, the preacher is simply another sales-person, and the result is that the message of the cross is diluted. Moreover, instead of living "dangerously against the grain of the world" market religion "identifies with the world's winners based on health and wealth."[21] It is thus far removed from West's under-standing of Christianity: "For me, to be a Christian is not to opt for some cheap grace, trite comfort, or childish consolation but rather to confront the darker sides, and the human plights, of societies" with "compassion and justice."[22] West attributes the strength of these materialistic and individualist trends to the growth of Christian con-servatism in political, social, and cultural terms, seeing the religious Right's discussion of politics and religion as characterized by the dogma of "ideological narrowness and intellectual naiveté" that has replaced Jesus's condemnation of piety that excludes social justice with adherence to the cultural values of middle America.[23] It ties an otherworldly spirituality to a materiality that is very much this worldly. While West does not suggest that conservatives should take full responsibility for these developments, and indeed stresses that prophetic thinkers should guard against demonizing the majority, he believes they stem from that particular worldview.

Human dignity and depravity

Dignity is a linchpin of West's thought. From his earliest work he has attempted to demonstrate the oppositional potential of prophetic Christianity, seeing its basic stance as being that "every individual regardless of class, country, race or sex should have the opportunity to fulfill his or her potentialities."[24] This claim is based on his belief that all individuals are made in the image of God and thus possess inherent dignity and are entitled to a respectful treat-ment. It is because African Americans possess inherent dignity that justice must be done to them, and central to West's work is the asser-tion that a peasant in Alabama has the same right to human flour-ishing as the President of the United States because justice entails the recognition of the humanity of all people.[25] One's self-worth is not dependent on white society but is bestowed by God; in the eyes of God all people are equal, regardless of gender, race, or religion, and so while individuals may not share the same natural capacities, they should at least have the same opportunities and be treated with dignity. In order to maintain human dignity, oppression and cor-ruption must be denounced.

Parallel to this emphasis on dignity is West's understanding that human nature is fallen. Because of the individual and collective sins that emanate from the Fall, the prophetic Christian conception of democracy is two-sided, recognizing both the dignity and depravity of individuals. In *Prophesy Deliverance* West argues, "The Christian dialectic of human nature and human history makes the norm of democracy necessary and possible; yet only the praxis of imperfect human beings renders it desirable and realizable."[26] In other words, accountability mechanisms are required to insure that fallen human beings do not abuse their power and to prevent institutional corruption. West possesses no naïve optimism regarding human attainability of perfection and, as we shall see, this has implications for the form of politics he espouses, setting him apart from some Social Gospelers who overlook the reality and depth of human evil.

These values of dignity and depravity provide the basis for West's emphasis on democracy and individuality in community. The stress on human dignity incorporates elements of individualism, but it is an individualism that only makes sense in the context of a community who strive to preserve the dignity of each other. This requires concern for others, particularly those on the fringes of society, on the basis that love of God is inseparable from love for one's neighbor. In short, the strength of a community can be judged by how the weakest members within it fare. West suggests that these radical egalitarian ideas of democracy and community are inextricably linked, in that while the self-realization of individuality in community represents the moral core of the Christian Gospel, democracy is its historical realism.[27] West's interpretation of democracy is fundamentally grounded in the dialectical relation between tragedy and romanticism. His prophetism acknowledges the deep sense of evil in the world that can never be eradicated yet simultaneously posits that much evil is not inevitable, but is rather the result of human action and so humans possess the possibility within themselves to eliminate some evil in the world. Thus his prophetism accents "the possibility of human progress and the human impossibility of paradise."[28]

Kingdom talk: despair and hope

West has a deep Pascalian and Kierkegaardian sensibility and running throughout prophetic Christianity is a liberationist perspective grounded in "darkness." West's spirituality is inextricably bound to the forces of darkness and despair, together with the question of how one can muster the courage to resist the threat of "non-being" that accompanies those forces. His faith wrestles with both darkness and with God, and he asserts that humans have a right to question God and ask him why he allows the darkness to persist.[29] He draws strength from Jesus's confidence in the sustenance of God's sovereignty, despite "his blues-question on the cross about God forsaking him."[30] West's spirituality is thoroughly christocentric in that it garners empowerment from Jesus's stance as both "an agent of deliverance, but also a human exemplar of pain and agony" who signifies the conquest and abolition of evil.[31] Thus the lens of the cross provides empowerment and insight into how to address despair. Despite the apparent hopelessness and tragedy of present circumstances, the cross reminds us that we are not forsaken: God "came into this filthy, fallen world in the form of a common peasant in order to commence a new epoch . . . in which Easter focuses our attention on the decisive victory of Jesus Christ and hence the possibility of our victory over our creaturehood."[32]

West's "combative spirituality" attempts to preserve meaning by fighting against claims of inferiority; it focuses on political struggle but also transcends it by looking death and despair in the face and asserting that there is hope beyond these. Linked to this emphasis on struggle is "subversive joy" that attempts to transform despair into laughter; it confronts overwhelming levels of misery face on and recognizes just how difficult it is to persevere, yet refuses to yield to forces of despair.[33] West believes that this is a courageous response that will leave deep scars, because it is grounded in the ideas of sacrifice, service, and risk. He stresses that hope is a crucial means of perseverance in contexts of oppression, because once hope is lost so too is the willingness to continue the struggle for change. Hope has to be grounded in some concept of human dignity and worth, and this entails encouraging people to believe that their lives matter. West claims it is the love ethic of Christianity that enables him to sustain hope and prevents him from succumbing to paralyzing pessimism or misanthropy. Furthermore, it is because of hope that Christians should be open to creative and imaginative possibilities regarding social change. He suggests that if prophetic thinkers lose track of hope their work may remain reflective and sophisticated analysis, but will lack engagement in struggle.

The idea of the coming kingdom of God is important because West believes this sustains a sense of meaning in a meaningless situation, which provides empowerment in the face of evil.[34] The kingdom is not simply an otherworldly ideal at the end of history (heaven), but a new community-making social order within history; the biblical call for the kingdom and its values to come "on earth as it is in heaven" is a call for the ushering in of a rule of justice. Thus although West looks forward to a family reunion in heaven, where there will be no more suffering and evil will end,[35] he also seeks to advance that kingdom on earth by promoting its values of justice, love, and care. The coming kingdom can be seen as the fulfillment of history, and this eschatology generates a sense of hope, providing the prospect of a better time to come that one can strive towards. While the reality of the human condition generates pessimism the idea of Kingdom Come stands in contrast to human fallenness and, although the pervasiveness of sin places limits on the extent to which any reform amounts to genuine change, the politics of redemption and of the coming kingdom of God creates hope for the Christian thinker. As such, "kingdom-talk" is essentially Christians acknowledging "there is always something *beyond* the evidence, there's something more, [and] that something more helps keep us going."[36] Although West points to a better time ahead in heaven, he does not suggest that people should meekly accept their lot in life until that time comes; rather they must work to bring that kingdom of justice to earth, which entails fighting forces such as racism and sexism. His thought is melioristic in the sense that he imagines a better future and strives for another order of existence. He believes that history is open and that we can create an increasingly better society.

Historicism

West believes that human knowledge is not universal, but fallible, and so views the human quest for absolute certainty and objectivity as futile. This leads him to reject triumphalist, dogmatic, and over-confident expressions of Christianity that give the impression of being sure of all the answers to everything, thus leaving no room for doubts. Indeed, he questions the way in which some Christians can claim to be certain of precisely what God is doing in the world at present, and suggests that the certainty of such "airproof claims that you *know* exactly what God is doing . . . has to do with our own conceptions of God's self-limitation *vis-à-vis* our free will." He believes that those Christians who claim they "understand" God, rather than possessing impressive intellectual acumen, are actually limiting God by making such a claim and they lose sight of the claim that "there is a power working greater than us, that in some ways is inscrutable, that in some ways is almost *mystical*."[37] Prophetism holds to a form of skepticism, even agnosticism, concerning human certainty about what God is doing. However, this agnosticism about God's actions is an entirely different claim from saying "God does nothing"; historicist prophetism believes that God acts, but that there are severe limitations to human understanding of those actions. In terms of making faith claims, the prophetic Christian acknowledges the limitations to interpreting divine action that their humanness provides. Because such faith claims are just one person's *interpretation* of divine action, they will always be found to be lacking in some respect.

This raises questions concerning West's orthodoxy. Perhaps the greatest difficulty with his Christianity concerns religious truth. While some idea of eternal Truth as manifest in God is essential to most mainstream Christianity, West is wary of the term "Truth" and also of the idea that God has a providential plan designed for each individual.[38] He believes that both notions are open to manipulation by unaccountable elites who claim they know "the Truth" and the way in which history is going. Instead West asserts that history goes only where we take it, and human beings are responsible for working with God to create their own history. In being wary of traditional Christian conceptions of Truth, West does not go so far as to reject truth altogether, nor does he lapse into relativism. What he does reject is the epistemological certainty that some Christians ascribe to their interpretation of the Bible, whereby they claim to *know* the Truth and reject interpretations that differ from theirs as, quite simply, wrong. Here some might detect a paradox, as West himself states unequivocally that the Christian Right are *mistaken* in their interpretation of the Bible. When I asked him if the Right's interpretation of the Bible is as valid as any interpretation he replied "No. There are still *ways* of making better arguments, better interpretations, richer narratives."[39] Clearly West has no difficulty saying that his moral position is better than others, but crucially he does not claim *vis-à-vis* the Christian Right that his position is somehow ahistorically True. He simply suggests that some positions are "better" than others. In so doing West opts for a more open and flexible approach towards biblical truth – an approach with more vulnerability and modesty than the expressions of triumphalism displayed by certain Christians. West makes no claim to absolute moral superiority, nor does he claim to know the answers to everything. Truth-talk for West is not ahistorical but rather local; instead of the universal he adopts a historically situated perspective. West does not suggest that all positions are equally true or equally false, and so it is possible for him to deny foundations and yet claim that a contrary position is erroneous.

In "A Philosophical View of Easter," West uses historicist analysis to support the "truth" of the Christian resurrection claim yet confines religious "truth-talk" to specific communities of discourse construction:

> When we say we 'know' that a particular scientific or religious description . . . of the self, world and God is true, we are actually identifying ourselves with a particular group of people, community of believers, or tradition of social practices. . . . There is no true description, version of theory of the self, world and God which all must and should acknowledge as inescapably true, but rather particular descriptions, versions or theories put forward by various peoples, groups, communities and traditions in order (usually) to make such views attractive to us.[40]

Of course West wants to convince his partners in dialogue that his particular views are correct and hence worthy of adoption by others, but there is no ahistorical basis to this claim. According to West, the truth claims of a particular religion cannot be adjudicated by transhistorical criteria and there is no metanarrative by which to weigh up the "truth" or accuracy of the various religious narratives that exist. Rather, the truth of one's religious beliefs is discerned in the framework of one's specific religious worldview. In their essays in *Cornel West: A Critical Reader*, George Yancy and Victor Anderson correctly observe that there are serious difficulties with this view, not least that it empties Christianity of any ontological explanatory role by suggesting that religious narratives are unable to "explain" anything outside their own narrative framework of intelligibility. For West, there is no way to *know* or to establish outside of Christian social and historical practices "whether one's Christian beliefs correspond to some given metaphysical, transcendent, or ahistorical divine referent" or if the Christian narrative has "gotten the world right."[41] Many religious believers would find this a rather empty conception of faith and of God. For instance, most believers in the resurrection maintain that it is true because it is an actual historical event rather than a contextual affair. Similarly, when most Christians claim "God exists," they refer to a transcendent Being who exists beyond the grid of a specific religious community. West appears to suggest that God's "reality" is relative to a religious discursive field; yet for many Christians faith requires a God whose being is not reducible to the valuations of any particular person or denomination. Moreover, as West is unable to declare that his particular worldview is True, why worship a God about which nothing can be known, as opposed to worshiping nothing at all? West clearly thinks that it does matter which religious tradition one embraces; he states unequivocally in countless places that he is a Christian, and as such has chosen Christianity over, say, Hinduism. But why choose *Christianity*? His reply would no doubt center on the love ethic of the Christian Gospel. This love ethic is of course absolutely central to the Christian faith, yet "love" does not constitute a *distinctive* belief of Christians, as many non-Christians hold it too. So here one is left wishing that West would go further with his theology. He should at least be able to tell us what he finds true in Christianity without undermining his historicist perspective. Yet, as Yancy claims, "concerning questions about the 'truth' of Christianity ... West is left with a Wittgensteinian response, 'This is simply what I do.'"[42] The demand that West tell us more about his religious beliefs is reasonable given his claim that he is not a Marxist because he is a Christian, and that he finds the Christian faith probes the meaning of death, suffering, and love more deeply than Marxism. One wishes that West would develop this point by addressing, for instance, the way in which divine grace and judgment interact with the human struggle. However, although West's lack of commentary on God adversely impacts his theology, it does not make him any less of a theologian.

Echoes of Rauschenbusch and Niebuhr

West develops his prophetic Christianity in a manner that does not simply critique both mainstream Christianity and general socio-political life, but which explicitly utilizes spiritual metaphors when calling for social change. When West calls for a spiritual awakening in America, he is not calling upon all Americans to convert to Christianity but rather to adopt values such as love, concern, and humility, which although constituting part of Christianity are not exclusive to Christianity. It is thus a broad understanding of conversion, and its call to moral regeneration is far removed from the evangelical Christian's call to personal conversion; instead it collapses the traditional meaning of spirituality into a broad ethical stance that calls for compassion and justice. In chapter 7 we shall consider the "love ethic" that stems from this social spirituality. One obvious influence West cites in this regard is Martin Luther King and his moral vision of compassion, love, courage, and alliance. But here I want to focus on two equally notable influences that he fails to acknowledge adequately, namely Walter Rauschenbusch and Reinhold Niebuhr. The references made to Rauschenbusch are considerably sparser than those to Niebuhr. For instance, while he devotes considerable attention to Niebuhr in *The American Evasion of Philosophy* and in an address reprinted in *Prophetic Fragments* from a 1987 Niebuhr symposium, Rauschenbusch receives only cursory mention in a handful of sentences from various articles. The references that are made to Rauschenbusch tell us that West attaches high value to a Rauschenbuschian perspective: he sees Rauschenbusch's work as similar in motivation to that of Gustavo Gutiérrez; praises *Christianity and the Social Crisis* as an "exemplary" Christian socialist text; and upholds Rauschenbusch (along with Emerson and the Niebuhrs) as exemplifiers of a rare trend in American theology to probe into their own indigenous circumstances in order to meet new theological challenges.[43] While it is true that, taken alone, these references provide insufficient justification for the emphasis I ascribe to Rauschenbusch's influence on West, I intend to demonstrate that Rauschenbusch's emphasis on the assertion of the moral values of Christianity (especially love) in the public sphere and his concern with the democratization of America occupy a position of profound implicit importance in West's thought. In other words, West's failure to explicitly acknowledge the influence of Rauschenbusch is a notable omission, given that his spirituality is essentially a continuance of Rauschenbusch's Social Gospel with added insights and chastening from Niebuhr. West blends the idealism of Rauschenbusch with Niebuhr's realism about fallen human nature and the limitations this places on human progress.

Walter Rauschenbusch was Richard Rorty's maternal grandfather, and he occupies a pivotal, though frequently forgotten, place in the development of radical Christian politics. As Gary Dorrien observes, "It was Rauschenbusch who conceptualized the Christian social revolution in Christian thought, who defined its social vision, who epitomized its spiritual character, and who legitimized Christian support for radical democratic politics."[44] Although the early twentieth-century Social Gospel, of which Rauschenbusch was the leading exponent, has been castigated for its superficial moralism and over-optimistic emphasis on progress, it left an enduring theological legacy and decisively shaped modern religious thought in the United States. The Social Gospel's emphasis on the social mission of the church as mediated through its themes of the social message of the Old Testament prophets, the social aims of Jesus, the insistence that religion and ethics are inseparable, and the rejection of piety have assumed tremendous importance within Christianity. In particular, there are strong affinities between the Social Gospel and the liberationist theological tradition of which West is a part. Both traditions take socialism seriously as a framework for stating the Christian faith, and further affinities lie in the rejection of individualistic Christianity, a deep commitment to the oppressed, recognition of the systemic nature of evil, and an emphasis on praxis. This has prompted John Bennett to assert that today's liberation theology "is in a line of succession from such representatives of the Social Gospel as Walter Rauschenbusch. The Social Gospel was a theology of liberation for the industrial workers of this country."[45] Moreover, Jürgen Moltmann and Gustavo Gutiérrez have both asserted that Rauschenbusch's work represents the most instructive precedent for a liberationist theology of praxis in the United States.[46]

Despite the obvious anticipation of liberation theology that we find in Rauschenbusch, his significance tends to be overlooked. There are two reasons for this. First, the work of Rauschenbusch and contemporaries like Washington Gladden was dependent on the turn-of-the-century spirit of confidence and hope, and these Protestant liberals were part of a like-minded progressive generation. However, the credibility of the context-dependent optimism of the Social Gospel was so convincingly demolished by Niebuhrian realists as being naïve and simplistic that individuals since the 1930s have been reluctant to claim allegiance to the tradition. Second, although the movement itself has been discredited, its social goals have not been rejected – indeed if anything they have increased in importance. However, these social goals are not unique to the Social Gospel: for instance the prophetic zeal of abolitionists such as Elijah Lovejoy was a clear prelude to the Social Gospel. The Social Gospel movement was also heavily reliant on the British Christian socialism of Charles Kingsley and John Ruskin and the German liberal theology of Albrecht Ritschl. So, because the Social Gospel is simply one facet of a broader expression of social Christianity, the temptation is to focus upon other exponents of social Christianity who have not been tainted by the criticisms referred to in point one. However, Rauschenbusch remains crucial to an understanding of

West. This importance lies not merely in his social concerns or his development of a powerful religious argument for socialism – indeed if it did we could pick any number of Christian socialists with whom to draw parallels to West. Rather, the importance of Rauschenbusch is that he stands as an explicit precursor to West's love ethic in his assertion of the moral values of Christianity in the public sphere, and there are profound continuities between Rauschenbusch's *Christianizing the Social Order* and West's politics of conversion.

Rauschenbusch attempted to build a bridge between Christian theology and social analysis of contemporary problems. He was frustrated with the dominant expressions of Christianity as personalistic and otherworldly, emphasizing instead that Jesus was most concerned with bringing about the kingdom of God or, in other words, bringing about the reign of justice. Rauschenbusch saw an emphasis on the kingdom of God as a basis for the work of social regeneration and argued that the advancement of God's kingdom is simultaneous with the expansion of peace, justice, democracy, and freedom in society. He suggested that much socialism was flawed in that it attempted to bring about the kingdom of God, with God left out, and thereby grasped only a fraction of the full meaning of the biblical kingdom of justice. Nevertheless, he saw socialism as the moral conclusion that emanated from his Christianity, and his 1907 work *Christianity and the Social Crisis* linked political democracy and Christian morality through the common ideal of equality. By equating the realization of the kingdom with the growth of democracy, he stressed that the Christian movement for justice had to be viewed as a struggle that would not realize its goals simply through goodwill. Although less moralistic than some of his Social Gospel peers, Rauschenbusch remained a moralist. He attached supreme value to the concept of love, and both King and West echo his suggestion that love could be a working principle in society.

Rauschenbusch believed that his form of social Christianity could constitute the soul of a worldwide movement for democracy, and in so doing he prefigures West's attempt to use a Christian-derived morality to attack social evil and call for liberation and justice. Dorrien notes that Rauschenbusch had a tendency to use words such as "Christianize," "moralize," "democratize," and "humanize" interchangeably, seeing Christianity as the highest form of humanizing, thereby enabling him to promote a politics of common morality.[47] For instance, in *Christianity and the Social Crisis* he insisted on "the fundamental truth that religion and ethics are inseparable, and that ethical conduct is the supreme and sufficient religious act."[48] When he called for the Christianizing of American society he was not calling on Christianity to be adopted as a state religion, but rather was attempting to build a more just and democratic society, believing that those normative values emanated from the Christian faith but were also shared by all people of "good will." There is thus a strong element of Rauschenbusch's "Christianizing" mission in West. However, neither West nor Rauschenbusch call for the Christianization of America in the sense that the religious Right do. West does not seek the enshrinement of anti-abortion legislation or the restoration of prayer in public schools, but rather speaks of general ethical principles which although common to all people in his thought emanate from Christianity.

Rauschenbusch was much more optimistic than West about the prospects for democracy in America and he believed that America was constantly democratizing (thus demonstrating just how much he underestimated the depth of racism). While Rauschenbusch admitted that there was no guarantee of progress, he could see no structural impediment to the spiral of improvement in society. It is here that Niebuhr's critique of the Social Gospel's utopian moralism proves to be of importance to West. In saying this we must also observe that Rauschenbusch's optimism is often mistakenly overemphasized and simplified. Thus, while Niebuhr characterized Rauschenbusch as an idealist who did not take the realities of evil seriously enough, Rauschenbusch was actually profoundly aware of what he called "the kingdom of evil" – for instance, his 1917 work, *A Theology for the Social Gospel*, contained six consecutive chapters on sin. Thus in one sense the corrective to Rauschenbusch's over-optimism can be found in his own later work as he became disillusioned and dispirited by World War I.

Niebuhr adopted Rauschenbusch's socialist politics in his early thought, but rejected his style and emphasis, considering Rauschenbusch's liberal Protestantism too moralistic and placing too much hope in the concepts of community and love. Niebuhr's active political engagement has been a deep source of inspiration to West. He joined the Socialist Party and ran for state senate in 1930 and for Congress in 1931, then in 1941 helped to found the Union for Democratic Action that aimed to gain American support for the Allied effort to save democracy from the German threat. West believes that Niebuhr's *Moral Man and Immoral Society* "remains today the best Christian defense of an American democratic socialism."[49] So although neo-conservatives make much use of Niebuhr's realism, they tend to overlook the fact that his critique of idealism came from *within* the Social Gospel wing of Protestantism; this realism-idealism debate was between Christians at the center and the left of the political spectrum. Indeed, Niebuhr's views of social sin and his denouncement of injustice and American imperialism can be seen as anticipating the approach of the liberation theologians, despite the fact that his realism stands in fundamental opposition to liber-ationist utopianism. In this regard neo-conservatives do Niebuhr a disservice by presenting him as the defender of the status quo against hotheaded utopians. Although it is true that Niebuhr moved away from socialism to embrace political liberalism in the 1940s, his work prior to that has been of enormous influence to West. This is because it was grounded in a tragic perspective yet believed spirituality could work as an impetus for social transfor-mation.

Having lived through the disillusionment of two world wars, the Great Depression, and the tyranny of Soviet Communism, Niebuhr's language emphasized crisis and pessimism rather than love and cooperation. His Christian realism stressed the all-pervasiveness of human sin and made him deeply pessimistic about what humans can achieve in the socio-political realm. Because of sin, he argued, human history is not on an inevitable upward scale of progress. Niebuhr regarded much liberal Christianity as being too attached to the myth of progress to confront evil in the world and as being too naïve about human nature. In contrast Niebuhr insisted that, while occasionally individuals are capable of altruism, human groups never overcome their collective group egotism, and so consequently arguments pertaining to morality possess little power. He thus saw it as unrealistic to envisage a society charac-terized by cooperation where selfless humans seek the common good. While he held a firm belief in the necessity of democracy, this was in a realist rather than moral sense: democracy is necessary because human nature is selfish. West, on the other hand, agrees that democracy is needed because of fallen human nature, but also stresses the importance of democracy as a moral norm. Of course, Niebuhr believed that a moral perspective emanates from the Bible and saw Christianity as the basis from which to provoke meaning-ful human struggle and moral action. He called on Christians to struggle for justice and so did not discount moralism *per se*. In this sense Niebuhr's perspective is an impetus for West's moral argu-ments. However, in contrast to West, Niebuhr rejected the language of Christian moralism *when applied to the realm of politics*. Niebuhr stressed that politics is not about morality but the distribution of power and so he saw Christians as mistaken when they sought to justify political actions by appealing to moralistic arguments. In this regard he distinguished between the church's moral identity and its social mission. Because he regarded politics as an interest-driven struggle for power, it was futile for churches to waste their influence by attempting to moralize the public arena; it was not the church's mission to transform the social order to a realm of peace and justice, but rather to provide religious support for the secular agents who struggled for these norms. In contrast, West calls for a new social ecology of community based upon moral concern and religiously inspired good, one that will work to advance the common good. It is precisely such moralism that Niebuhr sought to discredit with his arguments that power can only be challenged by power.

In terms of moral and liberatory arguments Niebuhr and West diverge sharply. Niebuhr used no language of liberation, emphasizing instead ideas of sovereignty, repentance, and submission. He saw salvation not as a message of liberation, but as God enabling individuals to surrender their egoistic attempts to master their experience. While Niebuhr did not suggest that liberation is unimportant, he stressed that the public political sphere is not the appropriate context for such language; concepts such as liberation and kingdom language provide only confusion in the public sphere, as they cannot constitute specific policy goals. Certainly, despite his personal socio-political engagement, Niebuhr could be accused of discouraging struggles for justice by creating resignation rather than hope, and of unintentionally undermining the church's vocation in the public sphere by denying that sphere ethical language. It is into this realm of the public that West seeks to reintroduce the language of moral values. While he shares Niebuhr's belief that the Fall creates limits to the potential for liberation and moral action, West maintains that this does not entirely discredit such arguments, and he chooses to ground his progressive political arguments of economic justice and social equality in the moral values of his Christian beliefs, such as the dignity derived from being created in God's image.

Despite fundamental differences, the influence of Niebuhr on West remains profound, particularly in terms of a fusion of politics and Christianity in a very public manner. West sees part of his prophetic Christian task as being to speak truth to those in power

concerning production of wealth, distribution of power, and accrue-
ment of status. Itabari Njeri draws an explicit parallel between the
two, observing that Niebuhr sought to shape public discourse about
the immorality of US isolationism in the face of Nazism, articulating the concerns of working people at a time when politicians were
indifferent to them.[50] However, it is primarily in terms of chastening his Rauschenbuschian leanings that Niebuhr's influence is significant in West's thought; his is thus a corrective rather than a
self-sufficient perspective. It is with a Niebuhrian wariness that
West adopts the early Social Gospelers' desire for a cooperative
commonwealth, aware, like Niebuhr, of the difficulty of seeing such
a commonwealth as being literally achievable. West acknowledges
that the inevitability of social evil means that human perfection
cannot be achieved, yet stresses the necessity of struggling for
attainable gains toward a good and just society. In his struggle to
locate hope in the midst of darkness West uses both Rauschenbusch
and Niebuhr, while rejecting what he sees as the excesses of both.
In other words, Niebuhr's pessimism tempers Rauschenbusch's
optimism and points to the dialectic of hope and despair, idealism
and pessimism, which flows throughout West's work.

Conclusion

West's prophetic Christianity wrestles with crisis and darkness,
attempting to present a "love ethic" in a dark, blood-drenched
world. In contrast to dominant interpretations of Christianity, he
suggests that the Gospel is not about the market or convenience but
rather struggle and depth. We have seen that his perspective is
strongly influenced by a fusion of the perspectives of Niebuhr,
Rauschenbusch, and black theology. West tempers Rauschenbusch's
optimism concerning social change with the realism of Niebuhr's
emphasis on the limits the Fall creates for change. This dialectic of
hope and despair is also present in Cone's attempt to address the
question of what it means to be human in the face of death.
Throughout his work West seeks to respond to the crisis of being
black in America, and Christianity equips him with vital existential
resources to respond to suffering. Central to his perspective is the
dialectical interplay between crisis and the hope for liberation.

5

Re-conceptualizing Marxism: West's Radicalism

We have seen that West's prophetic Christianity stresses the necessity of political engagement, and his struggle for democracy and freedom leads him to embrace progressive politics. Our concern in this chapter is to consider the theoretical political ideas that underpin this struggle. This is no easy task as West tends towards ambivalence on the specific labeling of his politics. In *The Ethical Dimensions of Marxist Thought*, one finds a bewildering array of self-descriptions, including "Hegelian Marxist," "Gramscian democratic socialist," and "non-Marxist socialist."[1] Elsewhere he describes his thought as "undogmatic Marxist social analysis"[2] and adopts the New Left's language of democracy and community. Furthermore, in addition to strong elements of communitarianism in his thought, he is happy to adopt the label of "market socialist" in the mold of Alec Nove. The difficulty of defining his politics is compounded by the fact that he constantly seeks to modify and rework his political stance in light of present realities. This reworking is particularly evident in the shift from the suggestion in *Prophesy Deliverance* that Marxism "is the most penetrating social criticism" and an indispensable weapon for advancing the goal of human liberation to the claim in *The Future of American Progressivism* that Marxism is "paralyzing."[3]

At a basic level West's thought can be viewed as emancipatory politics that addresses the tragic character of life, but an attempt will be made in this chapter to provide a more rigorous categorization of his political thought. In essence, his thought is a form of American radicalism that draws upon Marx's ideas, but is open to all progressive insights no matter what their origin. In probing his radicalism particular attention will be devoted to his location within the American Left and to his understanding and reconceptualization of Marxism, whereby he claims that Marxism is both indispensable and inadequate. Crucially, we must note that his Christianity has a profound influence on his political thought. Although the debates of the 1960s between Christians and Marxists concerning atheism and violent revolution are less pronounced today, West feels that deep existential tensions centering on tragedy and possibility remain. Hence his unambiguous assertion, "I am a non-Marxist socialist in that as a Christian, I recognize certain irreconcilable differences between Marxists of whatever sort and Christians of whatever sort."[4]

West has an uneasy relationship with the leftist tradition. On the one hand he believes his work requires the insights of both leftist politics and Christian beliefs, and maintains that both progressive Marxism and prophetic Christianity have values of self-fulfillment and self-realization with concern for the liberation of the oppressed at their heart; both focus on the plight of the oppressed and their possible empowerment. West views Marxism as "one of the essential components in a Christian understanding of institutional forms of evil" and so is highly critical of the rejection of Marxism by many Christians.[5] He also suggests the society Christians strive toward should be "a distinctive version of democratic and libertarian socialism," which co-joins Christianity with neo-Marxist, feminist, anti-homophobic, anti-racist and ecological perspectives.[6] Unlike readings of Marx that stress a historical determinism that severely attenuates human agency, West detects an emphasis on human powers in Marxism's origins in the Enlightenment's assertion of human capacity. In this context of autonomy West points to the arrogance of Marxism *vis-à-vis* the humility of Christianity. Although both traditions are concerned with human betterment and the changing of existing realities, Marxism anticipates the eventual perfectibility of individuals within history while Christianity stresses the dialectical relation between human dignity and depravity. Marxists believe that human betterment is possible, while Christians suggest that the fallen nature of humanity seriously curtails the possibility of betterment – evil can be alleviated but not eliminated. West suggests that the tendency in Christianity is "to view the intelligence as just as fallen as any other faculty or capacity we humans have. . . . We *do* have a relative autonomy, but you've got to be thoroughly humble in terms of our capacities."[7] Thus he concludes, "my own Christian skepticism regarding human totalistic schemes for change chastens my deep socialist sentiments regarding radically democratic and libertarian socio-economic and cultural arrangements."[8] The key word here is "chastens," because the disputes that West as a Christian has with Marxist-socialist interpretations of human nature do not lead him to abandon socialism. Rather, he believes that these disputes help him to think more clearly and realistically about the possibilities for change in the world. It is through Christian lenses that West looks at Marxism, and so his Christianity exerts a profound impact on the type of politics to which he is attracted. This explains his willingness to adapt or dispense with certain aspects of Marxist theory.

The American Left

Unlike Europeans who had to struggle for political liberty, Alexis de Tocqueville observed that Americans are "born free." The development of American democracy simultaneously with capitalism meant there was no strong idea of a democratic class war against capitalism and property in America, as was the case in Europe. Moreover, the ideals of liberty, equality, and fraternity are implicit to the American ideal that all people are created equal and are endowed with inalienable rights. So, although the American Left uses the rhetoric of justice and democracy, these nebulous concepts are inherent to the American ideal and have a usage that extends beyond the Left; for instance, neither leftists nor conservatives would claim to be opposed to "justice," as such, and so the difference lies in the vision behind the rhetoric. Marxist ideas that arrived in America with German immigrants in the post-1848 years were used to support the radical movement that was already present in America, and so crucially the American Left is just as concerned with Jefferson, Thoreau, and Whitman as with Marx, and is also inspired by the tradition of dissent in American culture, evident for instance in the Puritans and Abolitionists. Thus when compared to the European Left, it seems that the concerns and influences of the American Left are better described using the broader term "radical" rather than simply "leftist," as radical is a term that incorporates not just Marxism and democratic socialism but also grassroots populism and radical liberalism. In the case of West, his radicalism is an American interpretation of Marxism that is reliant on insights from pragmatic philosophy, prophetic Christianity, and liberalism. His major concern is with freedom struggles of oppressed peoples, particularly African Americans, and he believes this necessitates attention to Marxist analysis of economics and class divisions; for instance, he focuses on how existential concerns are shaped by the processes of capital accumulation and the constraints the rule of capital places on the life chances of black people. But while some form of Marxism is crucial to him, he displays a deep ambivalence towards Marxism, considering it both indispensable and inadequate. West is opposed to dogmatic forms of Marxism that are closed to the insights offered by non-leftist progressives, and so reaches beyond the confines of Marxism to embrace the radical potential of all ideologies. In this sense it is more fitting to describe his political thought as American radicalism, albeit a form of radicalism with revisionist Marxism at its core.

In terms of specific concepts utilized and critical use of Marxism, West displays a particular continuity with the rhetoric of the New Left. The New Left of the 1960s was born as a reaction against the paralyzing dogma and pessimism of the "Old Left" of the 1930s–50s. The New Left was concerned with revising Marxist ideas yet was never a Marxist movement *per se*. While particularly drawn to the early Marx and syndicalist Marxism, it also drew extensively on anarchism, Gandhian philosophy, Weberian sociology, and the writers of the Beat Generation, such as Jack Kerouac, who challenged American ideals and repudiated wealth. Hostile to ideological orthodoxy, the New Left was quick to dispense with elements of Marxism it saw as irrelevant, such as the philosophical understanding of dialectical materialism, communist state socialism and the disciplined vanguard party, and the prediction of the impending collapse of capitalism. Marxist language of the role of the proletariat and bourgeoisie was rejected and replaced with an emphasis on the increasing diversification of social classes. They argued that not only was there a numerical decline in industrial workers but these workers were increasingly integrated into the system through the process of "embourgeoisement" and were drifting to the right. Moreover, the New Left's ties to the new social movements and the Civil Rights movement meant that they placed more emphasis on the identity politics of gender and race than on class relations.

Although the New Left rejected doctrinaire social theory, there was a clear New Left perspective on society that centered on participatory democracy, community, agency, decentralization, dialogue, and social and sexual equality. New Leftists offered a critique of alienation, militarism, imperialism, and the artificiality of capitalist culture, pointed to the irrationality of advanced capitalist society, and questioned material progress on the basis that it did not lead to human fulfillment. As a radical alternative to bourgeois culture and possessive individualism, the New Left called for the creation of decentralized communities of democratic self-regulation. They also stressed the need for building alliances with groups such as feminists and ecologists who shared their revulsion of capitalist values. In their arguments about community, decentralization, and suspicion of established institutions there was an obvious debt to anarchism and syndicalism, yet at the same time Marx's vision of equality, liberty, and community remained vital. Although anarchism provided the goals of New Left thinking, it grounded its critique of society in Marxist arguments concerning the negative effects of capitalism, such as alienation and lack of freedom, and the assertion that "community" must replace capitalism; also important were Marx's ideas of revolution and praxis. They saw Marxism as a way of thinking that is intended to produce action, and stressed that theory must be constantly tested and redefined in light of present reality and personal experience. The assertion that a theory was worthless if not strategically effective was their premise for rejecting blind orthodoxy.

There are strong continuities between the New Left's rhetoric and legacy and West's political language. Of greatest importance are the corresponding ideas of praxis, engagement, and the primacy of action (which are central to liberation theology); the attempt to rework Marxism in light of present reality; and the critique of capitalism and the alienating effects of modern industrial society. West's critique of "market morality" attacks modern civilization in a manner similar to Herbert Marcuse for the way it destructs basic human values. Also crucial is the New Left's legacy, which lies not only in the women's movement and in suspicion of institutions, but more crucially lies beyond conventional left–right political categories. So, for instance, a New Left adherent will stress the "liberal" ideas of cultural tolerance, civil rights, and a clean environment, but may also stress the "conservative" agenda of reduced inflation, safe neighborhoods, and less bureaucracy. This helps to explain why West can be hard to pin down ideologically and is related to the fact that he is primarily a radical rather than simply a leftist. Of course, there are also strong differences between the New Left and West. For instance, while both desire individualism to be replaced by community, the New Left took this idea further than West does in their aspiration for decentralized communes to replace the nuclear family. A second difference is that West stresses the need for the

organizational grounding that the New Left lacked. Third, he rejects
the anarchist tendencies of the New Left and remains more deeply
influenced by earlier theorists of the Left than members of the New
Left were. So while many of West's ideas and language are derived
from the New Left, he adds the theoretical grounding and realism of
the Old Left of the 1930s–50s and attempts to build leftist politics out
of despair rather than optimism. In terms of icons, while the New
Left held up Che Guevara and Mao Tse-Tung, West adopts icons of
the Old Left such as Gramsci, Marx, and Lukács. Thus Michael Harrington is crucial to West not only in his emphasis that politics must
have an ethical content, but also in the way he forms a bridge
between the Old and New Lefts. The Democratic Socialists of
America (DSA), founded by Harrington and of which West is an honorary chair, can be viewed as a merger between the New American
Movement branch of Students for a Democratic Society (SDS) and
the Old Left's Democratic Socialist Organizing Committee.

The New Left's lack of a mass base and organizational grounding contributed to its demise in the late 1960s. It fragmented into
disarray, pressured by Black Panther militancy and embarrassed by
some aspects of the hippy culture. On the one side there was pressure from the Progressive Labor Party, who wished to establish
close relations between students and industrial workers and
defined class in terms of relation to the means of production, and,
on the other, the liberation movements who expressed the newly
unleashed radical energies of women, gays, and blacks. Since then,
notwithstanding the continued presence of community organizing
for social justice issues, the Left has retreated from national politics
and shifted toward academic issues and audiences. Consequently,
the Left's strongest basis in American society now lies in the
academy where its concern since the 1970s has been cultural hegemony rather than class war. This Left has no basis in the working
class, has no social constituency beyond the campus, and places no
hope in the Enlightenment. Instead it embraces perspectives such
as postmodernism and poststructuralism. The attempt to "unread"
old texts in order to breathe new meaning into them has resulted in
a shift from labor to language (obscure jargon at that) and an
attempt to explain the problems of modern society by reference not
to the mode of production but to modes of discourse. West is
ambivalent toward these academic trends. The dominant language
of the academic Left is power, domination, and discourse, yet West
continues to emphasize the more traditional Left language of emancipation. Because he views the active pursuit of liberation as more

important than the study of theories such as power, he seeks to break the academic Left's rigid adherence to theory (be it post-structuralist, deconstructionist, or critical theory) and so bring politics back into the public sphere. He does not discount the Left's basis in the academy, as it is an important premise on which the Left can be rebuilt. However, he sees it as an insufficient premise.

West draws on both the redistributive economic concerns of the Old Left and the academic Left's concerns with deconstruction and identity politics, thus relying on Nancy Fraser's analysis in *Justice Interruptus* of how the Left is trapped between a politics of recognition and a politics of redistribution. The politics of recognition is concerned with cultural injustice and promotes the interests of identity politics. The more traditional politics of redistribution is concerned with economic injustice that affects social classes and so cuts across the lines of identity-group categories. Fraser suggests that to find a way forward the Left must look beyond the narrow concerns of redistribution and recognition and find some way of promoting justice for everyone. One way this could be done is through the promotion of socialism in the economic sphere and deconstruction in the cultural sphere. However, Fraser's preference is for a Left that supports only the identity politics that can be coherently combined with a politics of social equality. This has reference to West's project to co-join the politics of identity recognition and economic redistribution, given his belief that African Americans are oppressed on both these fronts. He wants to see the idea of class decentered to include social movements as well as the traditional economic definition, and is concerned not just with the exploitation of the "working class" but also the exploitation of women and African Americans. West does not want the identities of race or gender to be dissolved into the identity of a social class, but rather believes that identity politics can function as a galvanizing force for Left visions and arguments. This emphasis on identity politics does not mean that distributive justice is no longer necessary; rather, the two must be coupled if the Left is to survive and address the concerns with which people are struggling. Thus West wants to transform both the state of Left theory and the ongoing condition of the urban poor.

Radical democracy and the critique of liberalism

In his call for the extension of democracy, West can be located in the tradition of Ernesto Laclau and Chantal Mouffe in proposing a left-wing project of radical democracy that will be open to the identity politics of hitherto silenced voices. Contemporary radical democrats seek to rethink socialism within the context of a fragmented society and they suggest that the Marxist binary and antagonistic opposition between the proletariat and the bourgeoisie does little to aid our understanding of postmodern society. Instead, they argue that the working-class struggle against capitalist relations of production is simply one facet of a broader struggle for democracy. A redefinition of the struggle for socialism is posited whereby relations of ethnicity and gender are as important as class relations and where socialism is defined not just as the emancipation of a particular class, but also as an extension of democracy throughout society. The aim is to extend leftist demands for freedom and equality beyond the economic sphere of wages and working conditions to the political sphere of citizenship rights. Thus the radical democratization of society will emerge from a variety of autonomous struggles involving distinct democratic antagonisms.

The radical democrat's redefinition of socialism as a basis to the democratic project is accompanied by a redefinition of democratic practice. Crucial in this regard is an examination of the association between democracy and liberalism, with a particular focus on foundationalism and capitalism. First, the radical democrat is influenced by postmodernism's celebration of pluralism and rejection of metanarratives and so rejects the liberal foundationalist approach to democracy that is based on natural liberty and absolute rights. The empowerment of emergent voices of difference calls into question liberal notions of democracy that encompass the state as the fixed center of politics. Rather than viewing democracy simply as processes of government, the radical democrat broadens the notion of democracy to encompass the political culture as a whole and focus on the political potentialities of ordinary citizens. Second, radical critics of liberal democracy suggest that the radical potential of democracy has been obscured by the over-identification of democracy with capitalism. C. B. Macpherson, for instance, discerned a central tension in liberal democratic theory's attempt to "reconcile the claims of the free market economy with the claims of the whole mass of citizens to some kind of equality."[9] While he understood democracy as a rejection of the notion that the market should determine human value, within liberal democracy capitalism has emerged dominant. The strong association of liberalism with capitalism limits the scope of democratic accountability by ignoring the domination created by capitalism: capitalism is viewed not as market domination but as market freedom offering opportunity and choice as opposed to coercion or compulsion. Capitalism and democracy are not complementary but contrasting systems, in that the former is concerned with economic and property rights and the latter with personal rights and democratic accountability. Arguing that liberal democracy consolidates capitalism, Macpherson called for the realization of "post-liberal democracy" and a revolution in democratic consciousness to free democracy from the competitive nature of liberal capitalism. So, while radical democrats will defend liberal values such as individual rights and democratic procedures, this is supplemented by demands for social and economic equality and participatory democracy. In this sense the task of the Left is not to *renounce* liberal democratic ideology, but to *deepen* it. This process of expansion must occur within the economy, as the removal of economic inequality would be a step toward a more democratic society.

Because of the strong association of liberalism and capitalism, it is unsurprising that Marxism often portrays itself in complete contrast to liberalism. However, West suggests that a Left politics that can only imagine an antagonistic relation to liberalism is a bankrupt politics. In this regard he stresses that contemporary American liberalism is not as radically individualistic as many on the Left assume. For instance, John Rawls's "difference principle" evaluates political and economic systems in terms of their effect on the least advantaged. Moreover, the Declaration of Independence and the American Constitution were shaped by liberalism, and it was liberalism that led to the expansion of the welfare state in the postwar years. In other words, many ideas important to the Left find their roots in liberalism, and so any intellectually compelling social vision must take as its starting point the achievements of liberalism. Thus West suggests that the task of the Left is not to discard liberalism, but rather to revise, rework, and reconceptualize some of the central tenets of liberalism, such as political obligation and participatory citizenship; it must build on the best of what liberalism has to offer. This reworking requires recognition that liberalism, by the standards of the Left, is an unfinished project in the sense that it holds corporate power unaccountable, tolerates passive and depoliticized citizenship, rests on an impoverished conception of the human subject, and is insufficiently democratic and egalitarian. But recognizing these deficiencies, West sees liberalism not so much as the culprit but as having succumbed to powerful economic interests. Although liberalism may be considered the domain of white male elites, this tendency runs counter to the radical potential he detects at the heart of liberal ideology: an ideology which "can be mined in order to enlarge the scope of freedom. . . . My kind of left oppositional thought and practice builds on and goes beyond liberalism."[10] Leftists should also be aware that while liberalism is inadequate, its views on race, labor, and women appear radical in America when placed against the dominant cultural conservatism, and so may be the most radical option feasible within American society and thus potentially a vital ally for the Left. West believes that unified action with liberals (as with feminists and African Americans) will offer leftists *entry* into current political discourse, and once they are established in that discourse they can present their leftist perspective to wider society.

One perspective that West draws upon in his reworking of the liberal tradition is communitarianism. Communitarianism has become a fashionable term, and this poses inevitable problems in that it is used loosely to encompass thinkers whose views span the political spectrum. However, one can say that communitarian critics of liberalism such as Michael Sandel and Michael Walzer criticize liberalism's absence of a shared conception of the good. They view liberalism as irreparably individualistic and instead stress the need for a social and community basis to political life. In adopting the communitarian critique of individualism West does not apply this narrowly to liberal theory, but more generally to society as a whole, lamenting the breakdown of neighborhood bonds and the collapse of spiritual communities that have created rootless, dangling people. He views rampant individualism, the decline of civil society, and the prevalence of polarizing rhetoric as indicative of the multi-layered crisis in America. West believes that human beings have a basic need for community and relationships; indeed his main criticism of market culture is that it creates a narcissism that erodes the ability to participate in community and so contributes to the fragmentation of society. He bemoans the massive breakdown of nurturing systems for children in a market-driven society, and suggests that the result is denuded individuals who lack existential moorings and the cultural apparatuses to deal with the absurd. West claims that the remnants of community must be nurtured, yet stands apart from communitarians such as Alasdair MacIntyre who talk about community in a very conservative sense that regards it as a preserver of tradition. West wants to preserve the family and other elements of civil society for radical ends related to the liberation of the oppressed. He does not simply wish to restore previous forms of community, but rather is concerned with those who have been excluded from previous bonds of community – either because they cannot be heard or are excluded from the conversation. He thus wishes to construct new and inclusive forms of social life.

West's Marxism

Our consideration of West's conceptualization of Marxism will center on the paradoxical way in which he sees Marxism as "indispensable *and* inadequate, something to build on but also something to bring serious critique to bear on."[11] Because West rejects historical materialism, argues that modern capitalism is no longer subject to the crises and class conflicts that Marx predicted, and sees little privileged role for the working class, it would seem straightforward to conclude that, while unequivocally part of the leftist tradition, he is not a Marxist. Yet in many places he explicitly describes his thought as Marxist and stresses the valuable way in which Marxism tracks social misery, such as that found in contemporary management-labor tensions. West suggests that elements of the Marxist tradition, in particular what he refers to as the "vulgar Marxism" of Stalinism, have done a disservice to the whole tradition and he seeks to separate this strand from what he sees as the more progressive Marxism of Councilism which is committed to the norms of individuality and democracy and retains societal relevance.

West's thought points to an ongoing debate within Marxism concerning what constitutes Marxism. In attacking the dogmatism of much Marxism, West portrays himself as a "progressive" Marxist, and this suggests that there must be some orthodox image of Marxism that he stands in contrast to. However, the issue of "orthodoxy" is difficult to gage because what is orthodox by the standards of one tradition is often unorthodox to another. Indeed, while the perspectives of Lenin and Stalin are often referred to as Marxist orthodoxy, their dominance within the Marxist tradition has been superceded by adherence to the reinterpretation of Marxist theory offered by the Frankfurt School's critical theory, and by extra-Marxist sources such as poststructuralism. The question of orthodoxy is no clearer even when we look at Marx, because arguments can be constructed that his true heir is Lenin or Gramsci or the Frankfurt School, and so on. What West is really getting at when he rejects "dominant" or "orthodox" Marxism are perspectives tied to a dogmatic presentation of their principles, which thereby are unable to seriously consider the insights offered by feminism, race, and spirituality. What he attacks is not so much orthodoxy in the sense of a particular figure, but rather a closed state of mind. West's Marxism will always be unorthodox no matter who is held up as the icon of orthodoxy, as his perspective is inspired by something beyond his politics, namely his Christianity, and is open to the influence of other ideologies on his political thought.

The Left has continued to survive despite the repeated herald of its demise in the post-communist era, yet many see it as an anachronism that points to the past rather than a force that anticipates the future. Although Rorty suggests that West continues to speak of himself as a Marxist for purely sentimental and nostalgic reasons, West believes that Marxism is not exhausted as a political position and continues to be a valuable political vocabulary.[12] At the heart of West's work is an attempt to look at the way in which existential concerns are shaped by the processes of capital accumulation and the constraints the rule of capital places on the life chances, particularly of African Americans.[13] This means that Marxism is crucial to him. West believes that Marxism provides vital illumination concerning the operation of power in modern society and is indispensable to an understanding of monopolies, oligarchies, and plutocracies. He also admires Marxism's emphasis on the powers of human agency and the importance it ascribes to individuals seizing their own destiny collectively, and thus links Marxism to the Romantic movement of the early nineteenth century.[14] Moreover, Marxism's international spirit is very much in keeping with his stress on coalition building and global approach to politics (as opposed to narrow nationalism). While West is not a purist in the manner he utilizes Marxist theory, constantly seeking to remold it in ways relevant to present realities, the influence of Marx on his thought is indisputable. West's attempt to rework aspects of Marxist theory does not constitute a rejection of that theory, but rather an attempt to ascribe to it more power than it previously held. In short, he seeks not the demise but the revitalization of the Left. As we shall see, there are certain areas in which he finds Marxism wholly inadequate, and these center on a typical ignorance of race, religion, gender, culture, and existential concerns. West suggests that ideologies must adapt to keep pace with societal trends and thus seeks to extend Marxist discourse, so that it can account for cultural phenomena as well as economic relations in society. He also believes that, for reasons of political survival, progressive Marxism must be open to the possibilities presented by the emancipatory visions of the new social movements. The Left should engage with these movements in coalition building around the issues they espouse in order to advance leftist ends. However, this call for the Left to abandon dogmatic presentation of its principles in order to engage with other progressives has led some to conclude that West's Left credentials are questionable.

West's view of the merits of Marxism has certainly changed through time, and a cursory reading of his work seems to suggest that he has increasingly distanced himself from the Marxist tradition. Undoubtedly, his attitude to Marxism has been complicated by his philosophical critique of foundationalism. In *Prophesy Deliverance* West identified Marxism as the "best" theory for advancing the goal of human liberation and "the most powerful and penetrating social criticism," but his most recent work describes Marxism not as the master discourse, but as simply one theory or method among many, or indeed as a "paralyzing theory that clings to a belief in the existence of a system out there – 'capitalism,' for example."[15] In a 1998 interview with George Yancy, West states that not only is he *suspicious* of but "against general theories of oppression" and instead "places stress on historical specificity, on concrete circumstances and situations."[16] To be clear, he still feels that Marxism can be politically useful today, yet inevitably several figures on the Left are perturbed by this apparent shift in West's perspective, and this will be discussed in chapter 8. However, I would question just how cataclysmic this shift is. It is true that a change in emphasis can be detected, yet it is my contention that West's work has *always* been guided by his spirituality and open to progressive insights, no matter what their origin. Recent concerns about a shift in direction by West seem to overlook the fact that he has always tried to co-join Marxism with communitarianism and liberalism. More surprisingly, such critics also overlook the fact that West has always had an ambivalent relationship with the Marxist tradition, evident in his frequent remark that Marxism is "indispensable but inadequate." Thus it is worth noting another remark from his interview with Yancy:

> The Marxist intellectual tradition remains indispensable in order to keep track of certain forms of social misery, especially these days in terms of the oligopolies and monopolies that take the form of transnational corporations that have a disproportionate amount of wealth and power. . . . I don't see how we can understand the market forces around the world and the fundamental role of transnational corporations, the subordination of working people, the tremendous class conflicts going on around the world at the marketplace between management and labor without understanding some of the insights of the Marxist tradition.[17]

West attempts to broaden and rework Marxism, but he does so without eliminating the remnants of Marxism. He considers the specific contribution of Marxism to be its understanding and critique of capitalism, and values Marxism as a method of analysis rather than dogma, suggesting that Marx left room for cause and effect. In other words, economics alone does not cause history to march forward; humans have a role to play in this development if they are truly to make their own history.

The critique of capitalism

In *The Ethical Dimensions of Marxist Thought* West attempts to demonstrate that Marxism is primarily a critical social theory with strong normative and analytical dimensions. He suggests that in the "Theses on Feuerbach" Marx moved from being a philosopher to a social theorist and radical historicist. In so doing he demonstrated his disenchantment with the idea of philosophy as the quest for certainty and foundations, and instead stressed the historical and fallible nature of human knowledge. In the place of traditional philosophy, Marx put a theory of history and society that called for action to overcome certain conditions, aiming not to interpret the world but to change it. West suggests that it is the failure of certain later Marxists to understand Marx's shift to radical historicism that renders their work unhelpful today. In particular, he charges Friedrich Engels and Karl Kautsky with the fundamental misinterpretation of Marx's social theory in their suppression of his ethical values of individuality and democracy. They misread Marx's "metaphilosophical move" by attempting to ground ethics in scientific beliefs; for while Marx rejected philosophic aims in order to describe, explain, and change the world, they sought to fulfill philosophic aims. West suggests that scientific and epistemological-philosophical interpretations of Marxism do little to aid the urgent political struggle of the twenty-first century, and he attempts to redress this balance by asserting that Marxism, in the sense he believes Marx himself meant, is a social theory of histories, cultures, and societies, and is concerned with concrete struggles rather than epistemological debates.[18] West thus calls upon the Left to offer historical and theoretical rather than abstractly philosophic judgments, and one of his aims in publishing *The Ethical Dimensions*, fifteen years after he wrote it as his doctoral dissertation, was to counter the Left's paralyzing "epistemological obsession" and to try to reclaim the cause of morality for progressive thought. In this regard he stresses that although Marx was opposed to moralizing, he used a moral standpoint to critique capitalism. He also maintains that if leftists look to Marx, they will find concrete political struggle and social and historical analysis.

West suggests that the Marxist critique of capitalism is based on the normative values of democracy and individuality in community, and he echoes Harrington's emphasis on Marx's definition of communism as a struggle for democracy whereby workers will have control over their workplaces, thereby allowing their individuality to flourish. West contends that an open-ended interpretation of democracy constitutes the central normative value of the Marxist critique, concluding that the Left's ambivalence toward the concept of democracy does not stem from Marx. He maintains that Marx's critique of capitalism retains valuable insights as it offers a reasonably accurate reading of capitalist society, thus providing cultural critics with the analytical tools necessary to understand and critique capitalism with a view to fighting for a radically free and democratic society. The Marxist critique helps West to keep track of forces of degradation, oppression, and exploitation in society, and so plays a crucial role in informing his liberationist Christian perspective. He extends the Marxist critique to include the culture surrounding capitalism, arguing that market forces have shaped both the economy and our understanding of value and use. His point is that corporate activity is preoccupied with commodification which reinforces a market mentality and spiritual impoverishment. Market morality is concerned with hedonistic self-indulgence rather than the value of human life; it leads to nihilism and individualistic competition without concern for others, and destroys the social fabric by viewing people as objects who either aid or hinder one's quest to consume.[19] West also suggests that the "quick fix" dimension of market morality mitigates against substantive struggle by demeaning ideas of character and discipline.

Class politics

It will come as no surprise to find that West is not a purist in his emphasis on class politics, as he sees no role for the proletariat as a leading political agent in modern society, at least not in the way that Marx conceived. He suggests that there have always been divisions in the construct of the proletariat and so simultaneously casts doubt on how useful this concept has *ever* been and on whether there is any role it can play in modern society. West does not privilege class over race, and so rejects the notion that the proletariat lies at the center of social transformation while other groups are marginal. He views the idea that the working class could be the central agent of change today as a "noble though nostalgic vision" devoid of power.[20] Instead, he calls upon the Left to embrace the way society has changed from when Marx wrote and replace the politics of the proletariat with the politics of difference, suggesting that differences of race, gender, and sexual orientation have assumed the role of the proletariat in Marxist theory. Nevertheless, James Cone suggests that West has "almost singlehandedly helped us see the importance of economic and class issues within the black community."[21] So although West views race relations as the most important issue in the United States, he suggests that identities of race and gender are unintelligible without reference to class – racial explanations alone cannot account for the societal location of African Americans confronted by the dual oppression of race and class. Here West points to the black underclass who are locked into a particular level of the labor force through the interaction of racism and classism; the key needed for their release has been taken away in the sense that they have little or no means to acquire the skills necessary for release. He views class inequality as a major cause of the violence, rage, and nihilistic despair to be found in the inner cities, and so calls for a redistribution of wealth in society that would liberate and extend the possibility of meaning to those at the lower end of the class scale. For this reason, he insists that "class politics must be the prism through which black politics are elaborated" because class is a "fundamental determinant of black oppression."[22] West seeks to unmask the oligarchic and plutocratic nature of the upward distribution of wealth in America, and class theory takes him to the core of the manner in which wealth and power operate, providing explanation for the rich–poor disparity. The legacies of white supremacy and economic inequality go hand in hand, and so he is critical both of African-American theorists who play down class divisions and economic analyses and of Marxism's failure to explore racial oppression. Therefore, contrary to some misreadings of West (particularly concerning nihilism), nowhere does he suggest that class divisions are unimportant. However, the shift that *can* be detected in his work is from the call in *Prophesy Deliverance* for an overthrow of the class system, to the call in *The Future of American Progressivism* for greater class mobility. Throughout West's work an analysis of class and economic factors is crucial, but the response developed from that analysis has shifted.

The importance of race

West believes that Marxists and African Americans have a deep, yet often unacknowledged, need of each other. African-American thought offers socialism the positive attributes of "deep moralism, combative spirituality and aggressive pessimism," while Marxism's class politics offers an explanation for the position of blacks in society.[23] Yet West maintains that Marxism offers an inadequate critique of racism and is insensitive to non-class identities as it relegates discursive structures (the ideological superstructure) to an insignificant role *vis-à-vis* the economic base. While many Marxists ignore the complexity of superstructural phenomena, West attempts to accentuate the relative autonomy of the ideological superstructure from the economic base and thereby offer a social theory that accounts for both race and class domination. Here he draws on Gramsci's concept of hegemony – the formal ideas and informal habits and outlooks that support the existing order. While Marx posed ideology as the structural legitimation of the rule of the oppressor class, Gramsci's concept of hegemony deepens Marx's understanding of the legitimation process. Hegemonic culture is comprised of the traditions and current practices that "subtly and effectively encourage people to identify themselves with the habits, sensibilities, and worldviews supportive of the status quo and the class interests that dominate it."[24] The notion of hegemony allows for the dialectical interplay of the economic base and the superstructure, and so avoids mistaking the economic factor as the absolute determining influence on society's evolution.

Rethinking Marx in the American context requires an understanding of the complexity and irreducibility of racism; this means that racial oppression cannot just be seen as the simple result of economic oppression. West considers Marxist theories of African-American oppression to be "bland and glib," as they highlight the crucial role of racism in the capitalist economy yet ignore the integral role of racism in the cultural and psychological spheres. Such theories ignore the complexity of racism and also tacitly assume that racism only emerged with capitalism, when in fact it long predates capitalism.[25] West offers two explanations why American Marxists ignore race. First, Marxism developed in European societies where race was not a crucial issue, and so presupposed European models of history and experience that downplayed the significance of black people as historical agents. Thus for Marxism to be of benefit to African Americans it must become less Eurocentric. Second, Marxism emerged in the context of an industrial capitalism preoccupied with economic production, and the primacy of economic explanations within Marxist theory leads class reductionists to dismiss race or subsume it under class exploitation. West is adamant that a Marxism that is not cognizant of the extra-economic roots of racism is deficient, claiming there is a moral and political imperative for the Left to consider racism. He lays enormous personal stress on the moral obligation to confront racism and thereby build a more democratic society where all members are seen to possess equal value. He also suggests that the Left's neglect of issues raised by African Americans is one reason why the Left is currently weak. To regain visibility in public discourses he suggests the Left should cultivate a support base among excluded groupings. He believes that once the Left has gained entry into public discourse by centering its ideas on the issues with which people are concerned, it will be able to show people the linkage between race and larger matters of wealth distribution.[26]

Culture and religion

An emphasis on culture is central to West. He suggests that culture provides meaning to life and can offer ethical and political resources to resist domination; it is a crucial source of self-identity and self-preservation that binds people together, and so constitutes the first stage in organizing people to transform the status quo. Notwithstanding the work of the academic cultural Left, West considers "mainstream" Marxism to be paralyzed in the realm of culture, as it has tended to emphasize redistribution and ignore the cultural politics of recognition. While economic reductionist Marxism is eager to view the oppressed as political or economic agents, West discerns a stubborn refusal to view them as cultural agents. Consequently, he detects an inadequate conception of the capacity of the oppressed to change the world, which makes it difficult to envision, let alone create, a socialist society of democracy and freedom. He argues that economic reductionist readings of culture and religion as purely negative and dominatory are too narrow, rigid, and dogmatic, and considers this ideological narrowness to be "tantamount to political suicide."[27] It is true that religious values and culture *can* function repressively as instruments of oppression or pacification as Marxists allege, but equally those values can also serve as instruments of resistance to oppression. This latter liberatory potential is borne out in the role of the church in black liberation struggles. West's point is not simply that culture has been *ignored*, but that it has been *misinterpreted* when viewed as something vague that pertains to attitudes and values, when in fact it is also as much a structure as the economy or politics.[28] Thus Marxists need to *enlarge* their understanding of culture and religion. Industrial capitalist societies are divided unequally along ethnic, class, and gender lines, and culture is one of the principal sites where these divisions are established and contested – it is in the realm of culture that subordinate groups try to resist the imposition of meanings that bear the interests of dominant groups.

Crucial to West's understanding of culture as both a structure and an expression is Raymond Williams's "cultural materialism." Williams viewed culture not as transcendental and ethereal, but rather as "a whole way of life" that incorporates languages, practices, ideas, and attitudes, as well as institutions and structures of power. His theory of culture incorporates culture as the material productive process (which links culture to the way capitalism affects human relations and values) and culture as specific practices, such as the arts.[29] Thus he recognized both the importance of the content of culture and the mode of reproduction of ideas, questioning how capitalism impedes access to production and power. Following this, West observes that culture can function as an oppressive structure of domination, yet is also a powerful means to express the concerns of human existence. He also recognizes that while humans create culture they are also shaped by it.

West's emphasis on being organically linked with the struggling community requires an appreciation of that community's culture, and so he devotes attention to music as it is the realm where black humanity is most powerfully expressed, giving him insight into the lives of the oppressed.[30] He maintains that if African Americans are to be galvanized for political action, those leading the movement must be aware of the culture as well as the working environment of the oppressed. Marxism's strength lies in its ability to "keep track" of impediments in the economic sphere that preclude democratization, yet West argues it fails to appreciate the manner in which power operates outside the workplace and overlooks the fact that the market is part of culture. Racism and other forms of social domination are not purely attributable to modes of production but also to cultural traditions, and so he calls on leftists to address the culture of consumption and compulsive spending in America and the way in which big business and advertising have penetrated the realm of culture.[31] Turning to religion, West views it as a crucial aspect of the culture of the oppressed and calls on Marxists to take it seriously as a positive and liberating force. Like culture, religion can be a source of dignity, survival, and vitality that provides meaning in people's lives and fosters genuine structural change in society. He believes that religion can form an alternative to capitalist culture by providing the "existential moorings and emotional assurance" that capitalism neglects.[32] Christianity embraces dread, despair, leaps of faith, and questions concerning the meaning and absurdity of life. It can thus negate Marxism's inadequate grasp of the tragic and enable Marxism to address all areas of modern life. Moreover, because prophetic Christianity seeks to empower people to struggle for freedom and justice it can be of assistance to the Left by providing a much-needed utopian dimension to Left theory and practice.

Capitalist markets

Market values have exerted profound influence on the distribution of wealth in society and on community values and relationships, and West views capitalist market culture as one facet of the crisis in American society. However, he is not entirely critical of markets and can be viewed as a market socialist who cannot envisage America functioning without markets. He follows Alec Nove's desire for a socialism and equity that will not lead to the collapse of the economy, recognizing that lack of access to markets, technology, and capital will ultimately be bad for democracy. In a 1993 interview in the *Boston Globe* West stated, "Markets do play a very important role in our economy. I don't want to downplay that. I don't want in any way to be cast as one who trashes markets."[33] He does qualify this "non-trashing" approach in another interview where he suggests that although markets are inescapable, questions must be raised concerning the way they are regulated; centralization, hierarchy, and markets are inescapable realities in modern society, but these economic structures have to be liberated from sexism, racism, and classism.[34] Thus, while markets have a place, this must be balanced with unrelenting critique of liberal capitalism. Despite this qualification, the portrayal of markets as being in any way positive is anathema to many Marxists and shows West's distance from "traditional" Marxism.

To understand West's views on markets we must note the distinction he draws between market *economy* and market *culture*. His argument is that while markets in and of themselves are inescapable and necessary in modern societies, the culture of consumption and addiction that accompanies the unregulated market is a highly destructive force; for instance, he holds the market values of hedonism and narcissism responsible for the "gangster" mentality and violence seen on the streets of America. Because market culture is driven by hedonism, narcissism, and egoism, it contributes to the fracturing of civil society by allowing no space for the family or other civic institutions to develop moral content. The market is a "preoccupation with the now" dominated by values of consumerism which produces "addiction to stimulation" and consumption that undermines human ability to develop rich relationships.[35] Market mentality views profits as more important than human life and leads to cultural decay in close relationships and in society as a whole. West also suggests that one way capitalism perpetuates itself is that market forces create despair and nihilism, which breed cynicism toward social change and inability to consider alternatives to capitalism. In this sense consumer culture promotes a passive citizenry, spiritual impoverishment, and moral shallowness.

West centers his critique of capitalist markets on its values of consumption and stimulation, which he sees as eroding the individual's ability to participate in community. In so doing, he calls on Marxists to adapt to changing circumstances and accept markets as a necessary part of economic life while constantly questioning the intent and values of the market. This suggestion has unsurprisingly provoked attacks on West from sections of the Left who see his attack on market culture and market values as wholly inadequate. His support for market socialism raises questions concerning the strength of his desire for wholesale social change and demonstrates that he does not seek the revolutionary overthrow of the capitalist system, but rather the democratic transformation of it. However, we must note that West was unrelenting in his critique of the way President Clinton unquestioningly took plutocracy for granted when addressing inequality. West does attack "the system," but that attack is couched in moral exhortations uncharacteristic of sections of the Left. Although leftist analysis remains crucial to his assessment of the capitalist market, he replaces dogmatic presentation of leftist principles with a stance of pragmatic realism. He suggests that the Left should accept that markets are inescapable, and from *that* premise should work to increase the accountability of markets. It is for this reason that West is able to acknowledge and accept the role of markets, while condemning the culture of consumption and calling for a redistribution of wealth to benefit and liberate the downtrodden in society. His perspective remains that of the underside.

Conclusion: the direction of the Left

The American Left has been weak for some time: the Republicans dominated the 1980s and the Democrats under Clinton were a centrist rather than leftist party. Further pessimism has been bred within the Left by the collapse of communism and the pervasiveness of capitalism. However, West insists that the Left must resist the temptation of pessimism, cynicism, or negativism, and find some way out of the engulfing disillusionment to convince people that the Left still has something to offer. He presents three specific challenges – existential, intellectual, and organizational – necessary for the rebuilding of the Left.[36] First, on the existential and ethical level, questions must be raised concerning *why* one should continue to work and hope for social change, and what sustains hope in the face of the hopelessness bred by the strength of capitalism. Despite demoralization, leftists must energize themselves to continue to believe in the possibility of social change. Intellectually, the Left must preserve explanations and descriptions of misery, as well as ideals such as justice, equality, freedom, and democracy. Leftists must preserve a sense of history that will enable them to build upon past experiences and recall the memories of non-market values such as love, concern, and community. In a society dominated by the market, West believes that such memories are subversive. Finally, in terms of the organizational challenge, there must be an examination of leadership and mobilization, and the Left must propose effective strategies and tactics. West stresses the importance of grassroots politics, as well as organized groupings such as the DSA, that highlight connection in a time of fragmentation and polarization. He urges the Left to articulate issues such as unemployment and health care in order to gain the attention of the public and so expose them to left-progressive viewpoints. West suggests that the result of the self-examination induced by these three questions is that the Left should be open to the possibility of alliance with non-leftist progressives. Thus, in order to survive, the Left must abandon dogmatism and adopt a more "sophisticated" approach.

West recognizes the inadequacies of a traditional Marxist position. He sees no merit in Marxism as a general theory or master narrative that turns its hand to everything. Quite simply, he finds that attitude paralyzing. Some will inevitably read that as a claim that Marxism is now obsolete for West, but that is not West's intent. He does not reject Marxism; rather, he wants to revitalize a modest Marxism as a local theory that can serve his struggle for liberation. Marxism persists in fragments for West and remains important as a *method* of social research, and a theory and praxis of emancipation. This Marxism does not exist in isolation and West supplements it with a variety of other paradigms, as demanded by specific situations. It is important to grasp that this is not a new argument of West's. Throughout his work it is the extent to which Marxist theory proves useful in bringing about practical policies, such as the redistribution of wealth and the erosion of racism and patriarchy, that determines its usefulness in the eyes of West. Because of this, he is always willing to shift from a Marxist position in order to achieve practical goals. Thus it is most helpful to view West's politics as a form of American radicalism that incorporates insights from Marxism into a more general radical democratic perspective preoccupied with democracy and liberation. Such a definition highlights his fundamental concerns, but does so in a manner that encompasses the way his leftism, while crucial, is determined by his prophetic Christianity and draws extensively on "non-leftist" sources such as communitarianism and pragmatism.

6

The Multicontextual Public Intellectual

West's work encompasses an enormous diversity of themes that at first glance may appear unrelated to each other. However, it is my contention that there are two factors that bind his myriad of concerns together in a coherent fashion. First, we have seen that liberation theology gives a foundation to his quest for black liberation and emphasis on the culture of the oppressed, his preoccupation with democracy, his attack on nihilism, and his attempt to foster dialogue and coalition building. The other unifying force is what he terms his "vocation" as a public intellectual that compels him to be multicontextual and draw on a diversity of influences. The focus of this chapter will be threefold. First, we will consider in general terms what it means to be "an intellectual." Consideration of the historical development of an intellectual's role in society will help us to contextualize West and to establish what difference, if any, there is between an intellectual and a "public" intellectual. Second, we will consider the recent phenomenon of the black public intellectual, a category in which West is widely viewed as one of the leading exponents. Finally, we shall specifically consider the tensions and dilemmas that the role of public intellectual poses for West. We will assess how successful West has been in this role and the implications it may have for his thought as a whole.

Historical development of the intellectual's role

"Intellectual" is an open social category whose members seek to explain the fundamental notions of society through engagement in creative mental activity. In its purer form, the intellectual stands outside the power structures of society and offers opinion in the name of high ethical or intellectual principles, and so is more concerned with the quest for "truth" than with official truths of states. Most theorists hope that their thought will have some bearing on the world, and may even improve it, but this process requires *listeners*, because speaking or writing in and of itself can have no impact. Therefore all intellectuals must relate to some form of public, either with the desire to educate the public on a matter they deem important or to express their own socio-political agenda. This requires intellectuals to have some connection either with those who exercise a degree of social power, such as political parties or policy elites, or with social movements who seek to challenge established centers of power.

While the idea of "the intellectual" can be traced back to the time of Plato, the notion of the intellectual is essentially a child of the Enlightenment's emphasis on progress and human reason. Intellectuals played a key role at the time of the 1848 revolutions, and it was at this time that the social category of the intellectual began to develop collective self-consciousness. This culminated in the Dreyfus Affair of 1896 that solidified intellectuals as a distinct group with a moral mission to perform in society. Dreyfus, a captain in the French Army, was falsely convicted of espionage and sentenced to life in prison-exile. The affair polarized France and came to a head when a popular novelist, Émile Zola, published an open letter on the front page of a Parisian newspaper accusing members of the French Army of forging evidence and covering up the facts of the case. The following week a petition signed by literary figures and professors supported his letter, and this heralded a new era when teachers and scientists began to take public sides in a conscious attempt to influence public opinion. The affair saw a thin line of demarcation between the role of professional critic and the intellectual, and so pointed to the emergence of the "public intellectual" whose views were articulated through new means of expression, such as journalism and public gathering places like bookstores and salons.

Nineteenth-century American interpretations of the intellectual defined the prime role of the intellectual as educator. An aristocratic conception of the "genteel intellectual" was imported to the American colonies from the Old World, whereby elites were distinguished on the basis of superior cultivation and higher learning and were based in universities from where they attempted to set the cultural standards for society at large. However, figures such as Emerson dissented from the aristocratic intellectual tradition they were born into. Along with Thoreau, Emerson attempted to turn transcendentalism into a program of self-help and moral education. Another reaction against the "genteel" idea of the intellectual was the pragmatic progressivism inspired by James and Dewey. This was essentially a form of middle-class activism and a vehicle for moving out of the universities and drawing-rooms of aristocratic society into urban immigrant ghettos. For instance, Jane Addams started Hull House in a Chicago immigrant neighborhood in 1889 and sought to instill in the educated a sense of social responsibility. She attempted to synthesize the Christian virtue of "good works" with utilitarian ideas of the expanded system of higher education and thereby use the intellect to reform society through direct action. Like Addams, Dorothy Day's Catholic Worker movement attempted to mediate social and cultural divisions, and so bridge the divide between the academy, the professions, and the wider community through her newspaper and hospitality houses. Cultural radicalism was also crucial in defining the role of intellectuals in the early twentieth century. The artists and writers centered in Greenwich Village utilized small magazines and salons based on European models such as the Bloomsbury Group to complete the break from the early aristocratic tradition through an emphasis on feminism, Freudianism, sexual liberation, and modernism in art and literature.

In the years after World War II American intellectual life gathered around two poles: the professional world of the academy where intellectuals were specialized according to discipline, and the freer realm of the urban social critic which drew upon cultural radicalism and new social movements. While critical theorists such as C. Wright Mills moved between both poles, the influence of the Cold War forced intellectuals to choose one side, with the result that the academic pole became dominant. The Cold War had a profound impact on intellectual development in the United States. Military expenditure not only drove economic growth but provided research grants and fellowships, cultivating new fields of study in higher education, with the result that academics had to conform in order to acquire money from federal research funds. The political pressures of American foreign policy largely determined research agendas, and so although there was much support for scientific research and area studies of Latin America, China, and Japan that would aid foreign policy development, some research areas were eliminated and area specialists were not hired. Moreover, the McCarthy witch-hunts insured that there was a decline in leftist discourse within universities.

It is in this context that it is most helpful to think of the public intellectual's role. Of course, all intellectuals require some association with a public for their work to have impact, and as such it seems superfluous to refer to certain intellectuals as "public" intellectuals. However, if we consider the polarization that the Cold War induced in American intellectual life, the term "public intellectual" acquires certain meaning through its attempt to bridge the gap between academics and social critics. While in the pure form of intellectual activity there is no need for such a prefix as intellectuals freely engage with publics, this period saw many American intellectuals fail in this regard. Thus the New Left's attempt to re-define the vocation of the intellectual in their desire to transcend the boundaries of the purely "academic" was extremely important. The SDS's *Port Huron Statement* of June 1962 stressed that academically based knowledge and the development of theory were essential for effective politics; some way was needed to synthesize the roles of the activist and the intellectual, increase the social relevance of the university, and find ways for those based in universities to link with social movements. However, the New Left failed to achieve this synthesis. In the early years the intellectual was seen as privileged and distant from action, and emphasis was instead attached to the organizers who left the comfort of the academy to devote themselves completely to social change. Then, in the late 1960s, when organizational forms of the New Left collapsed, many opted for life in the academy over professional organizing. From their base in the academy they attempted to change the status quo in their academic disciplines and institutions.

The debate concerning the role of intellectuals is illustrated in recent works emphasizing the political limits of the academy. In *The Last Intellectuals* Russell Jacoby laments the demise of public intellectuals and suggests that Left intellectuals have secured a niche in the academy and consequently are less engaged in the process of social transformation, choosing to direct their energy exclusively toward theoretical discourse. Although these leftists may enjoy a degree of legitimacy in the academy, the price has been conformity to the institutional logic of the academy. In this line of argument, acceptance of disciplinary specialization and peer review make the hope for a public as a sustaining framework for politically engaged intellectual work seem implausible. Jacoby suggests that not only does the academy create bored intellectuals, but more significantly it deprives the public of the radical services of intellectuals who no longer articulate a sense of public engagement or political emancipation. Following Jacoby, Robert Boynton suggests that, in contrast to previous generations, most current American intellectuals are "private figures, their difficult books written for colleagues only, their critical judgments constrained by the boundaries of well-defined disciplines. Think of an intellectual today, and chances are he is a college professor whose 'public' barely extends beyond the campus walls."[1] Against Jacoby it could be argued that accommodations to the academy have been only partial as many academics are still committed to producing change through their work. For instance, Dick Flacks stresses that feminism is concerned with political identity; an activist core of locally based peace, environment, social justice and human rights groups includes a high proportion of intellectuals; and intellectuals from feminist and black communities have a wide following outside academia. He suggests that while current intellectuals may appear to be politically disaffiliated, this is simply because there is no longer an intellectual collective identity.[2] Another objection to Jacoby is presented by Allan Bloom in *The Closing of the American Mind*. Like Jacoby he is concerned with leftist intellectuals of the 1960s generation, but he suggests that a false politics has entered the academy that impoverishes the sense of truth the academy should provide. While Jacoby believes leftist intellectuals are lacking in the realm of political engagement, Bloom sees this group as too political, thus wrecking the academy and America and Western civilization as a whole. Therefore both writers want to establish a limiting boundary between the academy and politics, but for markedly different reasons.

What does it mean for an intellectual to address "the public"? "The public" is a vague and ambiguous term; taken at face value it implies public in the sense of the whole population, while in practice its actual meaning embraces a more limited conception. For instance, Edward Said and Noam Chomsky are labeled "public intellectuals" despite the fact that it is questionable whether their work can be described as "accessible" to the entire population. Although their works generate an appeal beyond the confines of the academy, the degree of meaning and relevance to "ordinary" members of society is limited. Another question we must consider when defining "the public" is how feasible is it to think of the public as a single monolithic construct in a postmodern age? Instead, it is more helpful to think of many publics who interact and overlap with each other, namely the public of the academy, the public of the church, the public of the workplace, and so on. All intellectuals seek to engage with at least one of these different publics, and so to refer to West as "a public intellectual" does not tell us a great deal about what distinguishes him from other intellectuals. Thus we need to scrutinize what publics are being addressed. In my opinion, West should be thought of as a *multicontextual* public intellectual who reaches beyond the public of the academy to the publics of TV talk-shows, grassroots political organizations, and prisons. It is not in any sense unusual for an intellectual to engage with these publics, but there is something novel in the attempt of the current group of prominent black intellectuals to consciously address these diverse groups simultaneously as part of a larger quest for black emancipation.

The new black public intellectuals

Much attention has been drawn to the new generation of black public intellectuals that emerged in the early 1990s, of which West is undoubtedly one of the most prominent. This group, which also includes bell hooks, Manning Marable, Michael Eric Dyson, and Henry Louis Gates Jr, can be characterized as diversity-stressing cultural pluralists, often deeply critical of nationalism, based in the most prestigious of American universities. They have access not only to scholarly journals, but also to major newspapers and television chat-shows, while their books are prominent in the bookstores of shopping malls. Michael Bérubé suggests that "they have consolidated the gains of the Civil Rights and Black Power movements" in that "they have the ability and the resources to represent themselves in public on their own terms," thereby undermining the pathology that comes from constantly seeking white approval in the way required of their predecessors.[3] They attempt to engage critically with popular culture in order to benefit the community from which they have emerged, and are not simply concerned with race-based identity politics but more generally with the importance of American citizenship for race relations. Thus they are concerned with what it means to be an African American and the bearing that meaning has on citizenship in America. The impetus for this new momentum among black intellectuals lies in Gates's creation of an academic "dream team" at Harvard and the boost this provided to Black Studies. Other factors that led to the group's emergence and prominence are the "Afro-Americanization" of popular culture and an explosive period of race relations, encompassing the O. J. Simpson trial, the Clarence Thomas–Anita Hill hearings, and the 1992 Los Angeles riots. Black public intellectuals have attracted attention by their willingness to confront contentious issues.

This intellectual trend is not without precedent in American life, with two pertinent examples being the Harlem Renaissance of the 1920s and the "New York intellectuals" of the 1930s–50s. The Harlem Renaissance produced a significant flowering of black intellectual thought and culture, evident in the work of writers and artists such as Alain Locke and Jean Toomer. The New York intellectuals were a mostly male group of Jewish writers, such as Irving Howe, Lionel Trilling, and Edmund Wilson, who grappled throughout their work with the issue of being both Jewish and an intellectual in America. However, the parallels are limited. For instance, the current renaissance of black intellectual thought is not confined to one city and so has much wider regenerative implications than the Harlem Renaissance had. Regarding the New Yorkers, Bérubé observes that not only did some of them develop into neo-conservatives, but also they were "often the worst kind of armchair quarterbacks and fence sitters, 'activists' whose only activism consisted of essays in *Dissent*."[4] Thus they chose not to take stands on crucial social issues such as the war in Vietnam, school desegregation, or the women's movement. As well as achieving much more attention than their predecessors, the new black intellectuals are willing to take stands on social issues and have an explicit concern with popular culture. A sense of constituency is crucial to them as their professional status depends on their engagement with African-American culture, not repudiation of it. Therefore a fundamental challenge for black intellectuals concerns whether they represent or rather betray "their" socio-cultural constituency.

There is more to "black public intellectuals" than the name suggests. If the sole criterion for attaining membership of this group is the ability to speak and write clearly and substantively on a range of public issues for a broad audience, then many black scholars can be seen as part of the phenomenon; yet William Strickland, Gloria Wade-Gayles, and Na'am Akbar are not regarded as such. Apart from the fact that the most official designees of the title "black public intellectual" teach at elite eastern universities, they also speak in important ways to a *white* public and in effect their work functions as a translation, interpretation, and explanation of black culture to white people. This goes some way toward explaining why black public intellectuals are simultaneously lauded and sharply condemned, and why talk of the ascendancy of black intellectuals has been followed by a tirade of damning indictments. Some critics suggest that these intellectuals focus too narrowly on racial issues and are too open to the seduction of fame and fortune that will ultimately corrupt them. One particularly vocal critic is Adolph Reed, who in a controversial essay in the *Village Voice* accused West and Gates of falling prey to "the Booker T. complex," whereby they act as "authentic" spokespersons of the black community for whites when they actually lack viable constituencies or genuine accountability within the black community.[5] While Reed contends that the basic audience of black intellectuals should be blacks, other commentators such as Bérubé suggest that these intellectuals tell *all* Americans important things about America and help whites to understand black experiences of racism. Of course the difficulty with this role is the temptation to present some artificial black "common agenda" when in fact there are a variety of black experiences and agendas. Therefore the issue of who can be considered a "black public intellectual" is important, because unless there is space for the emergence of larger numbers of diverse black intellectuals, the stars who do ascend will find it difficult to avoid being drawn into the role of spokesperson for unheard African Americans located outside Ivy League institutions.

Manning Marable suggests that the new black intelligentsia is one of few examples of left of center influence in America's current political climate of decline of both the organized labor movement and the liberal wing of the Democratic Party, together with the disarray of the civil rights movement.[6] He suggests that the group is characterized by a commitment to theoretical and cultural engagement in an attempt to analyze race, gender, and class in the post-civil rights era of attacks on affirmative action and multicultural education. Of course, not all of the new black intellectuals are politically progressive (although most are), and so it may be more helpful to speak of figures like West as "oppositional" intellectuals, rather than simply "public" intellectuals. But although leftist black intellectuals are prominent, they lack influence in the realm of practical politics, as opposed to the cultural political concerns of gangsta rap and the movies of Spike Lee. Here they rely on a broad understanding of "the political," yet as Bérubé notes, "not every kind of 'political' work has political effects."[7] He believes that to be politically effective intellectuals must address public policy, and is critical of the way leftist intellectuals choose to ignore this area and focus instead on improving democracy through cultural politics – an option that he views as "easier" than practical politics as it is more satisfying and open to intellectual virtuosity. African-American intellectuals working for black liberation must wage war on all fronts and hence devote some attention to provoking change through policies and senate subcommittees, rather than simply focusing on cultural politics. They must, in short, become fully integrated into the machinery of social policy.

One difficulty for these intellectuals concerns how they balance the lure of media and commercial success with an oppositional stance, as they may become so much a part of the "system" that they will lose their ability to be properly oppositional. The danger is that those who become accustomed to the media spotlight, high salaries, and large book advances become less confrontational, talk increasingly of inclusion in the white academy, and become increasingly adept at reducing ideas to neatly packaged sound-bites for TV producers. Undoubtedly, part of their media prominence is related to changing modes of expression and there is nothing to suggest that precursors of the new black intellectuals would not have used television had that means of expression been available to them; indeed, television is a logical progression in approach for those wishing to speak to the world outside the academy. What is significant is the question of whether adopting the televisual approach has forced the new intellectuals to adapt their message. What is the price of this new-found significance in the eyes of Oprah viewers? Furthermore, regardless of whether their ability to provide media sound-bites undermines their substantive theoretical work, their commercial success *strengthens* their place in the academy, as it clearly adds to the prestige of the department if they can hire a few "celebrities," as the Afro-American Studies Department at Harvard testifies. Thus the problem is that these intellectuals can be doubly commodified by both the media and the academy, losing both their radical oppositional edge and their organic links to the community from which they have emerged. This question of how an intellectual can balance media fame with serious scholarship takes us to the heart of West's work.

Substance and accessibility in West's work

Gates refers to West as the "preeminent African-American intellectual of our generation," and diverse ranges of newspapers and magazines have applauded his astute intellect and ferocious moral vision. West has developed into a fully fledged intellectual celebrity, with frequent appearances on television and extensive profile articles in high-circulating publications such as *Newsweek* and the *Washington Post*. He is in high demand as a speaker on the lecture circuit, doing a staggering 150 speaking engagements a year in addition to his commitments at Harvard. In June 1993 *Time* reported that West and Lerner received a $100,000 advance for *Jews and Blacks*, "an almost unheard-of-sum for a scholarly work."[8] His move to Harvard from directorship of the Afro-American Studies program at Princeton made the headlines, with *The Journal of Blacks in Higher Education* describing Gates's feat in luring West to join his "dream team" as "probably the most important acquisition of superstar talent since the New York Yankees acquired Roger Maris on December 11, 1959." By way of context, in 1990 Black Studies at Harvard was on the verge of receivership with only one tenured faculty member and widespread student disillusionment, and so Yauw Miller concludes that the acquisition of West "effectively completed the transformation of the department from an academic backwater to a pulse center for black thought."[9]

West strives to balance his media prominence with "work on the ground," and there is a close correlation between his understanding of his role as an intellectual in society and his sense of political engagement in a variety of progressive campaigns. He believes that intellectual debate must be linked to political practice so that ideas are transformed into action; although theorizing is not to be discarded, it must not take precedence over action. West borrows Gramsci's phraseology to refer to himself as an "organic" intellectual who is actively engaged in concrete political struggles, and strives to fuse the life of the mind within the academy with forces outside the academy working for the expansion of democracy. Yet, despite the acclaim West has received, Leon Wieseltier dismissed his work as "almost completely worthless" and "noisy, pedantic and humorless," while Ellen Willis claimed, "Far too much of West's oeuvre conveys muddled views in jargon-riddled prose, a Zelig-like amalgam of mix and match personae, and worst, perhaps, the picture of a man who has come to believe his publicity."[10] Therefore, the central questions we must address concern whether his work does lack substance. Has it been toned down in order to secure media prominence? How accessible is his work to "ordinary" people? Is he really a celebrity rather than an intellectual? Has he been commodified? Before addressing these questions we must outline West's views on the responsibility of intellectuals and how this relates to his multicontextualism. We will then be in a position to judge his accessibility and intellectual substance.

The responsibility of intellectuals

West's intellectual work must be situated in the midst of his diagnosis of the times as nihilistic. He places a social responsibility on intellectuals to connect with the day-to-day realities of the black communities and urges them to be "truth-tellers" about the state of America and make constructive criticisms about societal defects. For instance, the truth must be told about the distribution of wealth in America, where "10 percent of the population own 86 percent of the wealth."[11] The intellectual should then move on to assess what such distribution says about a society that calls itself a democracy, and this should provoke a progressive intellectual to produce analyses that induce transformative action. Thus West attempts to use intellectual activity to struggle for those who have been oppressed and dehumanized by turning easy answers into critical questions addressed to those in power, with the aim of putting social misery on the agenda of those with power.[12] His intellectual work responds to suffering and crisis by offering a vision of hope underscored by a sense of the urgency of transformation. This demands a lived rhetoric that is exemplified with integrity in word and deed. He also calls on Left intellectuals to engage in moral and spiritual discourse, arguing that the language of love and support can no longer be the monopoly of the Right as these are fundamental human notions and crucial responses to crisis.

Intellectuals must also respond to the challenge of re-legitimizing the public sphere. West stresses that the fundamental role of the public intellectual "is to create and sustain high-quality public discourse addressing urgent public problems which enlightens and energizes fellow citizens, prompting them to take public action."[13] This task is compounded by what he observes as the waning of public spheres in America. This process began during the Reagan-Bush years when a high premium was placed on the private spheres of family, school, and home, using them to attack the realm of the public in the name of the people. Consequently, politics has shifted into a sphere where there is some level of public discussion, namely the academy. Thus the challenge is to reconstruct publics in an age where the private is cast as sacred. West wishes to recover critical politics in American public life and believes that the general public sphere needs to be reconstituted and broadened, while the current exclusiveness of the academy as the arena for public debate must be dismantled. Intellectual endeavor must be broadened if public debate about issues such as race and the nature of American society is to be revitalized.

Multicontextualism

The focus of West's ideas lies in transforming work to liberate the oppressed. As the oppression of "the wretched of the earth" is multifaceted, West's response must be eclectic, multicontextual, and draw upon a diverse range of intellectual tools. He thus entertains "a variety of social analyses and cultural critiques which yield not one grand synthetic social theory but rather a number of local ones which remain international in scope and historical in content."[14] West views himself as an "intellectual freedom fighter" who utilizes all the intellectual weaponry at his disposal in order to speak at different levels to a diverse range of groups. There are two main facets to this multicontextualism. First, in terms of the content of his message, he rejects the specialization of academic disciplines and seeks to rupture the established codes that separate traditions, so that his work has an appeal to scholars in fields other than African-American Studies and to public spheres beyond the academy. He chooses to speak on a broad range of issues ranging from philosophy to art and music. These interests do not develop simply by chance, but rather emanate from his desire to explore and express his message of radical democracy and racial healing at as broad a level as possible. Although critics argue that his work lacks depth because he spreads himself too thinly, admirers suggest that he proves it is possible to speak with depth and insight on a wide spectrum of issues, with bell hooks enthusing that "there are few intellectuals in the United States able to speak in such an informed way about so many subjects, whose influence reaches far beyond the academy."[15]

The second dimension of his multicontextualism is his utilization of a range of media to speak to different kinds of publics. He recognizes that there is no monolithic public sphere but a number of specific publics, each with their own concerns. West attempts to speak specifically to each of these publics in order to energize each public for political action to change their circumstances. Different languages are required in different communities, and so he is willing to change the means of presentation depending on who his audience is. Thus *The American Evasion* was directed toward academic philosophers whereas he had a considerably broader audience in mind in *Race Matters*, as is evident in terms of both style and content.[16] Because West strives to be multicontextual, he recognizes the importance of maintaining his place within the academy by keeping pace with the current trends of academic thought. Equally, however, intellectuals must resist the temptation to remain cloistered within the academy and preoccupied with the furtherance of one's university career rather than speaking to publics on the broad issues of the day. For instance, concern with the inscription of phallocentricity in Dickens's portrayal of Little Nell is all very well, but West sees such academic questions as operating blissfully detached from the everyday concerns of the population. So although West's utilization of television appearances and participation in public forums have opened up his ideas to certain publics, this has been alongside the more traditional academic accolades he has received from the public of the academy. His aim is to be located in the academy but not confined to it, and to present intellectual concepts in ways to which many publics can relate. When we consider the enormous influence exerted by the information and entertainment industries, it is natural that West should use such media to address the specific publics that comprise the larger public sphere, which explains his foray into the world of hip-hop with his CD *Sketches of my Culture*. West made the CD for the same reason that he speaks in prisons, schools, and churches – in order to make connections and take his work beyond the confines of Harvard or Princeton. He looks for different modes of communication to engage people with, and as such the CD is an innovative teaching strategy and an unconventional attempt to make his intellectual pursuits relevant to publics outside the academy; in particular, it is an attempt to communicate more directly with young people.

West finds fascination in the fact that generally if someone is associated with the White House, Louis Farrakhan will be reluctant to speak to them, or if there is an association with leftists such as the DSA, the mainstream becomes wary, yet he has been able to engage with all these groups.[17] While in one sense this appears to be positive, it raises the question of whether the reason all these groups listen to him is because he changes his message like a chameleon to suit each group of listeners. Undoubtedly, multicontextualism contributes to West's visibility, but does he develop this multicontextuality at the expense of consistency and coherence? If so, is this too high a price to pay? It is my contention that his multicontextualism helps to explain his work and actually contributes towards *making* it coherent. This is because West seeks to use the life of the mind as a force to induce social change. That requires him to respond to a variety of crises by speaking in a multiplicity of contexts to specific groups, but always with the basic intent of furthering the project of black emancipation.

Organic intellectual?

West believes that intellectuals should be engaged in society in a critical manner and so he strives to address both the academy and the general population in ways coherent and intelligible to each grouping. For this reason he prefers the broader label "intellectual" to "academic" as it fits better with his ideas of relevance, praxis, and engagement. He invokes Gramsci's distinction between traditional and organic intellectuals to point to the fundamental distinction between academics and intellectuals: "an academic usually engages in rather important yet still narrow scholarly work, whereas an intellectual is engaged in the public issues that affect large numbers of people in a critical manner."[18] He likens academics to Gramsci's traditional intellectual; they "revel in the world of ideas while nesting in the comfortable places far removed from the realities of common life." Organic intellectuals, on the other hand, are linked to prophetic movements and "take the life of the mind seriously enough to relate ideas to the everyday life of ordinary folk." They are therefore willing to go further in their academic pursuits by attempting to make their work accessible to those located outside the academy. West concludes that "organic intellectuals are activistic and engaged; traditional intellectuals are academic and detached."[19]

West equates his self-characterization as an intellectual freedom fighter, who fuses intellectual engagement, political transformation, and existential struggle, with being an organic intellectual. He views himself as a "critical organic catalyst" and points to his commonality of interest with the social group on whose behalf he acts. However, his presentation of Gramsci is not entirely accurate. Gramsci believed that organic intellectuals spring from a social class and are politically related to it inasmuch as they fulfill some strategic function and are related to the political structures of that class, such as trade unions. But for West the primary characteristic of an organic intellectual is that they link the life of the mind with a sense of political engagement. West wishes to be organic in the sense of being rooted in black organizations such as the church and encouraging other African Americans to organize politically. This is evident in an interview with Peter Osborne where he admits, "I want to say 'be organized' rather than 'be organic'." What West means by "being organic" is therefore "a much more fluid and constructed notion of participating in the organizations of people."[20]

While on the basis of West's own interpretation of Gramsci he can be seen as an organic intellectual, when we consider his political relation to his own social class he is not as organic as he claims to be. Indeed, an argument could be constructed that Public Enemy are more organic intellectually than West is, in that they are rooted in their class and ethnic structure, seek to explicitly articulate some sense of community to that community, and provide a space where people can engage in collective practice. In contrast, West seems less concerned with the particular social class from which he emerged than with some notion of "the black community" that produced him, and it is on this basis that he claims to fulfill Gramsci's criterion of an organic intellectual. Central to his work is the quest for black liberation, and related to this is his emphasis on black culture as sustaining the community in the face of oppression. He also seeks to develop a sense of moral community and encourage a sense of active political engagement whereby the oppressed will strive to create their own liberation. However, his emphasis on the black community as a whole rather than a particular social class raises its own problems. For instance, it is strange that while he emphasizes class elsewhere in his thought, he plays it down here. Also, although he stresses that African Americans should not be thought of as a monolithic whole, he appears to counter this when writing about his role as an organic intellectual, referring to the black community as if it constitutes a *class* (or acts as a substitute for what Gramsci meant by class) when rather there are many black *communities*. Although the various African-American communities share many things in common, such as an emphasis on culture as a sustaining force and the historical legacy of racism, the values of the black middle class of which West is a part are quite distinct from the concerns of those blacks living on the poverty line. Thus West, as a member of the black middle class, cannot claim to be organically linked to the black underclass unless he conflates class into community and treats blackness as if it constitutes a class in Gramscian terms. This is precisely what West does, despite the fact that he urges against such an approach in the rest of his thought.

Adolph Reed suggests that West presents himself as "authentically black" yet lacks viable constituencies or accountability among African Americans. He likens him to Booker T. Washington as a "freelance race relations consultant and Moral Voice for white elites" whose status is dependent on designation by these white elites rather than by any black electorate or social movement.[21] West's standing as an organic intellectual is further compromised by the way in which Joy James views West and Gates as contemporary manifestations of Du Bois's "Talented Tenth" – a black elite committed to leading black non-elites toward political, social, and economic equality. James suggests that what brings greater status to black intellectuals, such as lucrative publishing deals, simultaneously pushes them away from the black masses.[22] Thus, although West rejects the conception of the black intellectual as the spokesperson for the black community, that is the role in which he functions and deep ambivalence can be discerned in his conception of the intellectual's vocation. On the one hand he calls for "collective intellectual work that contributes to communal resistance and struggle" and which will stand in contrast to "the solitary hero, embattled exile and isolated genius – the intellectual as star, celebrity, commodity."[23] As such, he promotes grassroots political activism and calls for unrelenting critique of elites. Yet on the other hand he suggests that "most of the important and illuminating discourses in the country take place in white bourgeois academic institutions and . . . the more significant intellectuals teach in such places."[24] In this regard he downplays non-academic intellectuals who are involved in their communities but who are not celebrities and hence not as "visible" as West. Thus James concludes that while "West's rhetoric criticizes the Talented Tenth" he revitalizes elites through "his valorization of academe as the most important intellectual site."[25] Location in prestigious white universities and the privilege of advanced degrees and university affiliations segregates intellectuals such as West from practical struggles in the black community. In contrast, James upholds Charlene Mitchell as a model of a non-elite, non-academic, and organic intellectual. Mitchell is a leader of the democratic-socialist Committees of Correspondence, who educates people through newspaper articles, speeches, and organizational position papers, yet is an activist intellectual without degrees or a university appointment.

Marginality and commodification

In his early work West adopted self-imposed marginality and an insurgency mode, asserting that the priority of black intellectuals should be to create "institutional networks that promote high-quality critical habits primarily for the purpose of black insurgency." He emphasized that intellectual work committed to fostering social change should not be built on the middle ground but on the margins, outside the world of "aimless chit-chat," where one could speak for and to the community to which they are organically linked.[26] According to West, black intellectuals face "a grim predicament. Caught between an insolent American society and an insouciant black community, the Afro-American who takes seriously the life of the mind inhabits an isolated and insulated world."[27] The black intellectual is thus isolated and estranged: on the one hand facing hostility from black communities while, on the other, denied full entry into the academic white world. As Lewis Gordon observes, "In both cases there is a form of legitimation crisis – because the black academic's credentials for 'belonging,' so to speak, are held hostage, by both communities, to suspicion and incredulity."[28]

West is now a superstar courted by television networks and major newspapers, and as such can no longer be viewed as marginal in the academy; yet it remains an open question as to whether he is alienated from the black community. West is acutely aware of the danger of "commodification" by the media and academy. He believes there can be no escape from commodification, and so the challenge is to hold commodifying forces at bay.[29] However, it is very difficult to combine oppositional politics with celebrity status and media success, as James Cone observes: "one of the best ways to destroy someone is to expose and promote him. It's very hard to be critical of a system that makes a hero out of you."[30] Similarly, David Goldberg notes that the language commanded by public representation is not value free but rather drags one toward the center of the political spectrum, because if a book is going to sell it needs to sound centrist. The critical voice becomes corporatized, "agents take over, fees become exorbitant, contractual conditions mediate critical engagement. . . . The critical voice begins to quaver beneath the weight."[31] A major challenge for West concerns how he balances the forces of commodification, whereby the media makes him a superstar and the academy attempts to lure him with the cult of professional expertise, with the attempt to remain "organically" linked to a black community. West maintains that "since some of the aims of professionalism in the academy are to tame the comic [and] domesticate the subversive . . . I resist professional incorporation even as a highly visible voice in the academy."[32] Yet he admits that there can be no absolute escape from commodification. As there is no escape it is possible to conclude that West's academic achievements coupled with the process of becoming a media celebrity have removed and alienated him from the black community, because, as a social location, Harvard is far from the ghetto. However, West claims that although his views may be *marginal* in the black community, he does not feel *estranged*.[33] The tension between organic connections and commodification may be irreconcilable in a media-dominated age, but West does mobilize his media exposure to focus on and invoke changes in the infrastructure that directly affect African Americans. Thus the challenge is to draw something positive from the inevitable march of stardom-commodification. Fame must be channeled in ways that will benefit and work toward the liberation of the oppressed. This is one reason why he plans to shift 25–30 percent of his lectures to high schools over the next few years: young people see him on television and so are eager to hear him speak in their own school.[34] Their willingness to listen is an important first step to his desire to see them mobilized politically to effect change.

Accessibility and impact

Accessibility and intelligibility are crucial if the term "public intellectual" is to mean anything beyond an inherited label that certain intellectuals, most notably cultural critics, have received. West attempts to balance scholarship and theoretical discourse with more popular rhetoric so that his work will have some degree of relevance for "ordinary" members of society. The question of the impact West exerts outside academia is impossible to gage, but clearly impact is linked to accessibility in that people can act politically on his message only if they comprehend what that message is. In the realm of the media he uses to impart his ideas, West is undoubtedly more accessible than many other intellectuals. Moreover, West seeks to appeal to a range of publics and portrays himself as being just like ordinary people in that he too listens to music daily "for sanity" and has experienced police harassment because of his skin color.

However, there are limits to this apparently high level of accessibility. Although West strives to present ideas in an accessible yet non-simplistic manner to various publics, his intelligibility is not aided by a frequent use of jargon and obfuscatory language. Indeed, James Cone began his Aims of Religion speech at the University of Chicago in April 1998 by joking that West has the ability to make things sound as complicated as possible. This complexity is evident, for instance, in West's discussion of whether Charlie Parker's music is modernist or postmodernist. There is a tension at play here stemming from his attempt to combine theoretical discourse and the concerns of the academy (the modernist–postmodernist debate) with more popular rhetoric and cultural concerns, such as music. So, while West can be seen as accessible in terms of the *medium* he utilizes to present his ideas, much of his *message* comprises complex theoretical language; this mitigates against the accessibility of the message, as not everyone is willing to try to understand intellectual jargon.

There is a temptation to over-emphasize the level to which even the most "public" of intellectuals can be accessible to the public. For instance, the number of "ordinary" people who have heard West speak or have read an article he has written in a magazine and remembered his name is probably limited, despite his high celebrity profile. While he is undoubtedly more publicly prominent than many intellectuals, he remains marginal within the complete picture of American society and in comparison to celebrities from the world of music and film. The public world outside the academy in which he immerses himself is one of meetings at the White House or rallies associated with groupings such as the DSA or the NAACP. However, it does not end there. A common aim of the diverse groups he associates with is to end the misery and suffering of ordinary people, and West accompanies sitting in the cloistered committee rooms of such organizations with preaching in black ghetto churches and teaching in prisons. Thus while there are clear limits to the degree to which even politically engaged intellectual work can impact upon political change, it can at least attempt to do so. But a prerequisite for this is accessibility, and this is not as strong in West's work as one might imagine, partly because he is entangled in the bind that when he uses a certain type of "accessible" language elements in the academy complain that he is being "unscholarly," while at other times different elements dismiss scholarly academic jargon as elitist and inaccessible.

Intellectual substance

There is a danger that West's role as a critical intellectual may be compromised by his status as a media star who is required to speak in sound-bites and that he may substitute superficial celebrity punditry for theoretically rigorous criticism. Thus the most significant charge leveled against West by his critics is that he has sold out to the media and as a result his work is a form of diminished scholarship. Of course, some of this criticism stems from jealousy rather than an attempt to offer constructive criticism, and pertinent examples of what West refers to as the "recent wave of venom" directed against him are the polemical trashings of his work by Leon Wieseltier and Adolph Reed; he views these as a backlash against both the tremendous visibility he has received in the media and the academic success at Princeton and Harvard.[35] However, setting aside the fact that their motivation might stem from jealousy, such critics raise an important challenge that takes us to a central tension in West's work, namely how successfully he combines theoretical discourse with popular rhetoric. In his attempt to combine work in the academy with the accessibility of television, West leaves himself open to criticism on two fronts. On the one hand his intellectual activity is too theoretical, jargon-ridden, and lacking in organic links to a marginal community, while on the other hand it is simultaneously unscholarly, spotlight chasing, and lacking in substance. Clearly, West has striven in recent years to increase the accessibility of his work to "average" citizens, but has this been done at the expense of substantive intellectual work? Harvard President Lawrence Summers clearly feels that it has.

During the Christmas 2001 holiday period details of an October meeting between Summers and West became public and exploded into a national controversy that vied for headline space with al-Qaeda and Enron. During their meeting Summers complained that West does not do enough pure academic work, as opposed to popular work, and urged West to write a major academic book. He apparently called West's CD an "embarrassment" to his professorship, questioned his role as political adviser to Bill Bradley and Al Sharpton, quizzed West about whether he had canceled classes to campaign with Bradley in 2000, and urged West to help tackle Harvard's grade inflation dilemma in his introductory course on black studies, one of the most popular courses on campus. Summers ended the meeting by saying, "I look forward to seeing you every two to three months to make sure you're doing scholarly work that is in some way commensurate with your position."[36] Such "monitoring" would be a patronizing approach to an assistant professor, let alone to one of just seventeen University Professors in the Harvard faculty – Harvard's highest distinction. West was incensed that Summers should challenge his credentials and integrity at their first formal meeting and claimed that in his 26-year teaching career he had never felt as attacked and insulted as he did during the meeting with Summers. The incident escalated into a race war when Jesse Jackson and Al Sharpton entered the fray, with Jackson depicting the academic conflict as a case of racial discrimination. Jackson flew into Boston on New Year's Day to seek "clarity" on Harvard's diversity policy and called for Harvard to convene a conference on racial justice, while Sharpton threatened to sue Harvard for interfering in his potential presidential bid. Meanwhile, speculation mounted in the press about the potential defection of prominent black faculty members, including West, Gates, and Anthony Appiah to Princeton. Eventually, on April 12, West announced he was accepting a job at Princeton. His final salvo at Summers was to brand him "the Ariel Sharon of American higher education" in interviews with National Public Radio and the *New York Times*.[37] For West and his colleagues the issue is not that he was rebuked by Summers, but that he was rebuked unfairly. As such, West maintains that Summers is entitled to talk about the work he is doing, but he wonders how Summers can make an evaluation without reading his books or listening to the CD. West claims that criticism is important (even when it is painful), but "the one thing I do not tolerate is disrespect, being dishonored, and being devalued."[38] He makes a similar point in the context of Wieseltier's attack, when he says he must be accountable to all the criticisms made of his work, but finds this difficult when "you see that people sometimes have no intention whatsoever of saying something that might be empowering to you so that you can learn if you listen. Rather they're just engaging in trashing that would somehow disempower you."[39] When West says he wants to be treated with respect he is not demanding agreement or affirmation; rather the point is that disagreement should be mediated with civility.

The confrontation with Summers raises important questions. Should a university president question the scholarly work and political views of a tenured professor? Should Summers say it is "unbecoming" of a Harvard professor to record a hip-hop album, and would a chamber music CD be equally unbecoming? Was he right to push West to spend more time on scholarly works and less on books that reach the masses, or is this myopic and elitist? We must remember that one reason Harvard hired West was *because* he was a public intellectual and a highly visible star who could consolidate their Afro-American Studies program. They wanted someone who does high scholarship yet also speaks to the broad audience of society, and so it seems disingenuous to attack him now for doing just that. Moreover, it is easy to be critical of public intellectuals such as West and in the process of dismissing their work overlook the substantive ideas that led to their prominence in the first place. West is only in his forties, yet has held tenured positions at the elite establishments of Princeton, Yale, and Harvard, and this is something he would have been incapable of if he lacked sufficient intellectual depth. These positions have contributed to him becoming a celebrity in the world of academia, possessing a monumental reputation, and there is no doubt that West is a distinguished scholar who has demonstrated his familiarity with Marx, Foucault, and Du Bois in his more substantive works. However, that is not the issue here and nor is the fact that he is a very powerful speaker with the ability to move his audience. The question is how much depth lies beneath his style and performance and whether his televisual image undermines his undoubted intellectual acumen. Is he, as Wieseltier contends, a pretentious egomaniac and a superfical thinker?

West's best-known work is *Race Matters*, in which he consciously attempted to reach a broader audience. Peter Schuck contends that the essays in this volume "do not pretend to be scholarship but are instead a mode of tendentious discourse conducted at a high level of generality."[40] While it may not be West's most profound work, the essays contained therein must be viewed as representative of his work in the 1992–3 period. For instance, the chapter on black-Jewish relations was the basis for many of his lectures on the subject, while the introduction was originally published in the *New York Times*. Therefore to view *Race Matters* as a specific toning down in order to reach a broader audience is misleading, and the content of the book must stand on its own merits. On closer examination we can see that while his language may be diluted and the reference to towering intellectual figures such as Marx and Hegel may be sparse in relation to his earlier works, his message remains constant in terms of its basis in the quest for black liberation. Thus *Race Matters* is less *philosophical* in tone, but not less intellectual; it is simply a different form of intellectual activity. Although less concerned with philosophy, *Race Matters* tackles important public issues such as affirmative action, the failure of black leaders, and black–Jewish relations. The fact that these issues are often controversial, combined with the manner in which West constantly seeks to challenge assumptions, means that the reader will be provoked into thought. In this sense, the book performs an important intellectual service in that it seeks to extend and expand public conversation about the crisis of race in America.

Much of West's work takes the form of essays, short journal articles, or published versions of dialogues, speeches, and interviews. Of his many books only *Prophesy Deliverance*, *The American Evasion of Philosophy*, and *The Ethical Dimensions of Marxist Thought* could be classed as "traditional" full-length books, and while *Keeping Faith* could be added to this list in terms of its intellectual depth, it is in fact yet another collection of essays and articles previously published elsewhere. The complaint of some critics is not so much that West is too willing to make money out of regurgitation of old material, but that a short article lacks the sustained analytical substance found in a book. However, West views essays and transcribed dialogues as an essential part of his intellectual vocation, as it is through dialogues and articles in "popular" publications that he seeks to make his ideas accessible and heighten public awareness of his views on democracy. Unless people understand how important democracy is they will not be in a position to work for its advancement, and while the average person is unlikely to pick up a 250-page book on democracy, they may garner some crucial points regarding democratization from an opinion column in a newspaper. However, this argument overlooks the fact that there are limits to the accessibility of opinion columns, in that not everyone wants to read the *New York Times* on a regular basis. To complicate things further, when we think of more "accessible" publications such as *Rolling Stone* or *Harper's*, there is a stigma of "unscholarly" attached. The academy is still locked in the elitist premise that legitimate scholarship is that read by those within one's respective field rather than by the masses. Thus a transformation of attitudes is needed that would enable an article in a popular magazine to be considered on its own merits without the pejorative condemnation of it being intrinsically unscholarly. Indeed we could argue that there is more intrinsic worth to be found in an article in an extra-scholarly and widely read magazine than a 200-page monograph on the same subject.

Another response to the elitist charge that aspects of West's work are unscholarly is that he utilizes scholarly conceptual tools to analyze American society even when writing for "popular" publications. Concepts such as democracy, individualism, dignity, and double-consciousness are an integral part of his work, and it is rather ironic that his attempts to popularize these concepts have led to charges of sell-out and lack of scholarly commitment. Such criticisms imply that an attempt to make one's ideas accessible to as many different publics as possible is an easy option pursued only by those lacking in the realm of cogent scholarship. Yet those prepared to adopt the challenge of making their work widely accessible and comprehensible could actually be seen as *more* committed intellectually as they take time to re-explain and reconceptualize their ideas. Academic Left phrases such as "hegemony is leaky" must be made intelligible as political positions, and such a process requires time and energy.

Conclusion

It is figures such as West who reject Jacoby's claim that the academy has destroyed public intellectuals. Bill Moyers observes that West has been seen in "some very unusual places" for an intellectual: "the storefronts and streets of Harlem, the shantytowns of South Africa, one of the worst high schools in one of the worst districts in Brooklyn," places which are "so far from Princeton."[41] However, West finds nothing "unusual" about an intellectual expressing their ideas to people located outside the academy, and he seeks to create new space for intellectual work outside the academy where citizens can debate public issues. As such, he offers a model of the intellectual as a democratic agent, stimulating informed discussion about social issues. West preaches in churches and teaches in prisons alongside his work in the academy because he feels a deep sense of urgency concerning the need for social change. He insists that intellectual work must serve some political ends and believes he has an intellectual, political, and moral responsibility to contribute to social change by energizing people politically so that they can build their own liberation. Mere critique is insufficient and so political organization is the means to put rhetoric into transformative action. A prerequisite for that process is that people have some understanding of why change is needed and of concepts such as democracy and justice, and the way America falls short of the claims it makes about itself. Hence he engages in a multicontextual attempt to make his thought more accessible to a range of publics. In many ways this is a noble agenda requiring deep intellectual commitment, but his attempt to balance the demands of the oppressed community that produced him with the academy and media prominence creates deep tensions. For instance, institutionalization in the academy and commodification by the media both weaken the organic intellectual impulse. A deeper tension lies in his attempt to combine theoretical discourse with popular rhetoric and here West is entangled in a bind not of his own making. There will always be voices in the academy who dismiss West's attempts to popularize his ideas as "unscholarly," just as there will be other voices who complain that his work is insufficiently accessible to the communities he claims to be organically linked to.

7

The Politics of "Conversion": West's "Love Ethic"

West considers American public life to be in a state of crisis and deterioration. This is manifest in racial balkanization that affords African Americans second-class citizenship, the "gangsterization" of everyday life, a predatory market culture, and the erosion of civil networks that nurture citizens. West recognizes that the specific crisis in black America and the more general crisis in American democracy tend to reinforce each other – the growth of a culture of anger polarizes citizens and prompts the problematization of African Americans, while the inequality of this marginalization in turn reflects back on the quality of American democracy. In Chapters 7 and 8 West's intervention in these crises will be considered. Of fundamental importance is the intellectual armory provided by prophetic Christianity, as it is the source from which he derives the language of conversion. He suggests that Christianity offers a loose conception of a civic code based on values of love and respect from which a tentative idea of a common good can be constructed. We will begin by considering precedents for the use of spiritual language in American public life, most notably the civil faith heritage that makes his spiritual-ethic language plausible. Moving on, we shall see that, given the bifocal nature of crisis, West recognizes the need for "conversion" on a dual level. On the one hand he is concerned with the specific liberation of African Americans from invisibility and marginality through self-love and an accentuation of blackness. Simultaneously, to surmount polarization and balkanization he wishes to fashion the fragments of identities such as "blackness" into some form of whole based on what holds people together as human beings. As such, he seeks to simultaneously assert black visibility and *transcend* race. The dual forms of liberation he proposes do not occur in isolation from each other, as the personal liberation of African Americans from the oppression of problematization is dependent on white people learning to respect black humanity, and that requires them also to respect the humanity of other white people with whom they differ ideologically. Relationships both within and between communities must be strengthened, and the dynamics of this healing center on love and respect for both oneself and others.

The love ethic: sources and precedents

A metaphor of salvation runs throughout much of West's work and there is a strong biblical overtone to what he identifies as "the most fundamental question facing this country," namely, "what does it profit a nation to conquer the whole world and lose its soul?"[1] West's response to the withering of his nation's soul is explicitly articulated toward the end of the essay "Nihilism in Black America," where he calls for a "politics of conversion" grounded in a "love ethic."[2] This love ethic shapes and guides his political aspirations. West considers nihilism to be the greatest threat confronting black America, suggesting that it is a "disease of the soul" that requires a spiritual response of love that affirms both love of self and love of others. Crucially, West does not envisage a sentimental display of love, but rather love as generating a sense of agency among the oppressed through an affirmation of their humanity. Additionally, he believes that love prompts other values such as civility, respect, integrity, and accountability that if practically implemented can collectively contribute to the restoration of America's fragmented sense of community. In a 1996 interview with Audrey Edwards, West called for a "spiritual awakening" in America.[3] In contrast to the manner in which many Christians use such terminology, West is not calling for spiritual revival in the sense of widespread conversion to Christianity. Rather, his understanding of "spiritual awakening" is associated with the values of humility, self-criticism, and the rejuvenation of public life as evident in both civil religion and the Social Gospel.

There is a highly ambiguous relationship between religion and politics in America that stems from the fact that the American Constitution prohibits a religious establishment but protects the free exercise of religion. One might expect separation of church and state to lessen the impact of religion on American life, but the reality is that religion has played a crucial historical role in the self-definition of the American nation. For instance, Tocqueville saw religion as the foremost of America's political institutions as it restrained people from naked self-interest and thus allowed republican institutions to survive. Partial clarification of the ambiguity is found when we realize that the instigators of church–state separation were not atheists but religious dissenters who wanted protection for the free exercise of (their) religion. It is in this context that one can discern a strong tradition of civil religion in American life.

In the contemporary American context, "civil religion" is a term formulated by Robert Bellah in his 1967 essay "Civil Religion in America." The term was also used by Rousseau, who saw civil religion as a transcendent ideology focused on the nation state that would provide meaning for citizens by locating them both in their society and in history. While Rousseau interpreted this civil religion in a strict sense as a set of religious dogmas to which every citizen must subscribe, Bellah used the term to denote a set of widely held beliefs about the history and destiny of America. So, in the contemporary sense, civil religion is an overarching and rather vague sense of spirituality that centers on well-established rituals, symbols, values, and allegiances, and which pays homage to America's belief in religious pluralism. Evidence of civil religion in America is found in the biblical imagery and references to God's hand of providence that have pervaded national speeches and documents. Specifically, one can point to the blending of themes of God and country in the national motto "In God we trust," the inclusion of "under God" in the Pledge of Allegiance, the inclusion of patriotic songs in church hymnals, the display of the American flag in church buildings, and the trappings of religious ceremony at presidential inaugurations. Civil religion has had a profound impact on American history, evident in the Abolitionist movement, the relationship between the Social Gospel and the early Socialist Party, and in the Civil Rights movement, as well as in the more negative dimension of expansionist war and oppression of minorities; it thus functions as a legitimizing force for the actions of political leaders. In such a national context it should not be at all surprising that West elects to use a metaphor of spirituality to describe aspects of public life.

Phillip Hammond suggests that American civil religion is premised on the idea of civility and mutual reciprocity.[4] A central tenet of American civil religion is the display of tolerance toward religious expressions that differ from one's own, and this is quite distinct from specific claims to special righteousness or Messianic mission. This creates confusion when one considers the Christian Right. It is in the heritage of civil religion that they locate a mandate for their call on America to repent, and civil religion forms the basis for their patriotic language that equates religious belief with national purpose. However, in contrast to the inclusive rhetoric of heroes of American civil religion, such as Abraham Lincoln and Martin Luther King, the narrow ideological fundamentalism of the Christian Right intensifies the self-interest of specific groups. Their articulation of a particularistic expression of religion tends to be far from tolerant toward opponents and as such does not equate with the necessarily vague and pluralistic nature of civil religion. Much of the ambiguity surrounding the reception of religious language in the public realm stems from the specific *nature* of that language, and so, while the particularistic language of the Christian Right is greeted with fear and suspicion in certain quarters, there is widespread acceptance (at least retrospectively) of King's words of moral inspiration that were steeped in Christian symbolism.

The problem with conceiving West as part of the civil faith tradition is that, like the Christian Right, he too calls upon America to "repent" and his conception of repentance is strongly informed by a specific Christian perspective. In West's case this stems from his interpretation of the Bible as a social critique based on an alternative vision of a society governed by the kingdom values of love and justice where the oppressed will be emancipated. His interpretation of Christianity is at odds with the Christian Right because he recognizes that personal salvation alone is inadequate – he sees an additional need for a strong social awareness that struggles against structural injustices. West openly acknowledges that some interpretations of Christianity are "better" than others because of the degree to which they conform to his interpretation of the Bible, and so, as we saw in chapter 4, West suggests that the Christian Right are *mistaken* in their interpretation of the Bible. West has no trouble saying that his moral position is better than others, and this counters the vague nature of civil religion. Given their fundamental theological differences, it is unsurprising that West and the Right use words such as "repentance" and "conversion" in different ways. Of the two, West's usage is undoubtedly closer to the spirit of civil religion. The Christian Right point to social crises of abortion and homosexuality, calling on Americans to repent from ways of personal immorality. In contrast, West's sense of repentance is based on the more universal and inclusive values of love and community. These values have a broad appeal; indeed few people would claim to be opposed to "love," as such. Thus West's rhetoric is more likely to find a receptive audience through its elasticity, and indeed the allure of civil religion lies in its articulation of highly ambiguous values and symbols, such as love. Yet the problem remains that when people look beyond the rhetoric to the ideas that underpin West's message of love, they may be alienated by the specific theological and political stance he presents. Like those on the Right, there are limits to the degree to which he can be conceived as a civil religionist, given his articulation of a distinct theological agenda, but the important point is that he takes advantage of the strong tradition of civil religion in America to articulate his transformative vision in spiritual-ethical terms.

West suggests that the reconstitution of the public sphere required for surmounting the crisis in democracy needs the language of moral value. Thus another precursor to his call to conversion is Rauschenbusch's *Christianizing the Social Order*. As we saw in chapter 4, Rauschenbusch perceived the potential of Christianity as a basis for a global democratizing process and had a vision of society as a cooperative commonwealth. Rauschenbusch called for the social order to be brought into line with Christian ethical principles and asserted the moral values of Christianity in the public realm. Similarly, West believes that Christianity has a prophetic vocation in the public sphere, through which he wishes to challenge the dominant ethos of society. He stresses that the public conversation of morality cannot be conceded to conservatives, such as the Republican's language of "family values" which is essentially a morality premised on patriarchy and heterosexism; their reactionary agenda cements social and class divisions and does nothing to restore the moral value of community. West rejects the pietism and self-righteousness so often associated with the Right's moralism, adopting a broader understanding of morality that condemns those whose sole emphasis on personal morality (and how that personal morality is played out in a social context) results in a downplaying of matters of social morality, such as the disintegration of community, racism, and the way market culture values profits and consumption more than human life. West maintains that it is possible to salvage a legitimate role for religion in public life while contesting the politics of the religious Right. His work offers progressive politics of economic justice and social equality grounded in moral and religious values, and through an emphasis on the political relevance of prophetic Christianity's focus on "the wretched of the earth" he attempts to show general "secular" audiences how religious conviction can provide a moral framework for social change. He does not seek the adoption of Christianity as a state religion, but rather desires widespread informal acceptance of the Christian values of love, concern, and community – values that have the potential to transform a polarized America into an egalitarian democratic society where the value of all is accented. He maintains that the formation of a new social ecology and a reconstitution of the public sphere is dependent upon the injection of moral substance into politics. Crucial to this process is the (re-)introduction of a deep morality into the politics of the Left – the Left must recapture the moral language that has become the domain of the Right.

West rarely refers explicitly to specific biblical passages to justify his arguments, yet by choosing to adopt the language of civil religion and the Social Gospel he invites us to make explicit the biblical sources upon which he undeniably draws. A central message of the Bible is that one should love God and love others, and West is committed to the "fundamental claim" of the Christian Gospel: "To follow Jesus is to love your way through the darkness of the world."[5] Thus the love ethic is at the center of his interpretation of Christianity and also constitutes the basis of his socio-political agenda of liberation. West believes that all individuals are made in the image of God and so it follows that they are entitled to the respectful treatment of love, which recognizes the value, dignity, and true potential of every person. He thus highlights democracy and individuality within community not just as two crucial norms that arise from a prophetic Christian worldview, but also as principles grounded in love of self and of others. For West, the values of love and respect are reflected in the formation of a community whose strength is to be judged by how the weakest members within it fare. His love ethic is far from sentimental as it is tied to a specific liberationist agenda that seeks justice for the oppressed, and thus stands in contrast to the vague application of "love" in modern society. Thus, when West thinks of love, he thinks of "that which keeps one keeping on. Motion, movement, resilience, resistance."[6]

The precedent for his grounding of love in struggle and justice can be located in the Bible. For instance, Jesus did not say love your enemies if you feel like it or it is expedient or practical to do so; rather, there was no concession in his radical command to love others relentlessly. Moreover, "love" and "justice" are generally referred to in conjunction in the Bible. This is because it is love that points toward the type of society that justice requires. Without justice, love can be naïve and sentimental, while justice without love can be harsh and unfeeling; but when love and justice are combined one can advance beyond works of love in the sense of charity and attempt to remove structural injustice in the name of love. Robert McAfee Brown suggests that the main principles of biblical justice include (i) a preferential option for the poor evident in the frequent biblical admonitions to care for widows and orphans – the most deprived people in Israelite society; (ii) social ethics where the concern is not so much with evil individuals who wish to increase profits so that children will starve, but rather with the entire structure in which those individuals operate; (iii) realization of the need for self-criticism to insure that justice is embodied in one's own life; and (iv) the claim that to know God is to do justice. Hence Brown argues that Micah 6:8 ("What does the Lord require of you but to do justly, to love tenderly, and to walk humbly with God") is not three separate assertions but one assertion made in three ways. One walks humbly or engages with God by loving others and doing justice.[7] Thus love, dignity, and community constitute the defining characteristics of the biblical concept of justice.

West attempts to bring the weight of the biblical tradition of love and justice to bear on American society and articulates a vision of America where the dignity of all is accented through love. He believes that this love ethic has important political implications because it informs one's attitudes, concerns, and motivations and thus, if taken seriously, the Christian love ethic can transform society by addressing both the crisis of racial oppression and the crisis of eroding systems of care with the incivility that this breeds. This is because love can change the lives of individuals who for so long have been told that they are worthless, and can also prompt a change in democratic practice, together with the social structures and injustices that affect human beings. Some might object that West over-emphasizes the political power of love when he portrays it as a social value and political force that can be applied to strangers, because love is really an emotion that we develop in connection to specific persons. West's talk of love fails to acknowledge moral proximity and the idea that we feel greater emotional regard for those closer to our immediate lives. Can we really love in the abstract, or must there be an explicit connection to a specific person in a specific location? While I might "respect" people living in Afghanistan on the basis of our common humanity, can I really say that I "love" those people who are not personally known to me? But when West talks of loving others he is talking about respecting others and showing concern and compassion for them. That is precisely the same way in which the Bible speaks of loving your neighbor, but it is a usage of the term "love" that we have lost today. Some progressives consider talk of "love" as naïve or as an abstraction that detracts from struggles for justice, and claim that as both a concept and a strategy talk of "love" lacks the clarity that a response to exploitation demands. Yet there is nothing sentimental in West's emphasis on the transformative power of love to move people to work for justice and liberation. It is worth remembering that Martin Luther King saw love as the only force that could empower people to take life-threatening risks in pursuit of the eradication of injustice. King's emphasis on love is reflected in his vision of a "beloved community," and was something deeper than sentimentality or an emotional display; rather, he believed that justice is the embodiment of love and that power is love implementing the demands of justice.

Self-love: overcoming invisibility

In a 1991 *Dissent* essay, "Nihilism in Black America" which is reprinted in *Race Matters*, West highlighted the pan-generational crisis of economic and moral despair evident in the black community, and identified nihilism, rather than oppression or exploitation, as the major threat to black survival. These arguments continue to be the most controversial and misunderstood aspect of his work. West does not use the term "nihilism" in the Nietzschean philosophical fashion as the affirmation of atheism, but rather to explain the existential and psychological mood of the black ghettos whereby nihilism is exemplified in the brutality of street life with its violence and crime. As in past generations, economic deprivation and racial ostracism persist, yet these forces have been joined by a diminished sense of self-worth, an absence of self-love and love of others, family breakdown, a decline of community bonds, and depression about the future. These feelings of meaninglessness and despair leave existential marks on all African Americans, culminating in "a numbing detachment from others and a self-destructive disposition toward the world" evident in the "walking nihilism of pervasive drug addiction, pervasive alcoholism, pervasive homicide, and an exponential rise in suicide."[8] This has profound political implications: those whose lives lack meaning are unable to engage in the necessary work to overcome oppression because their sense of possibility has been debilitated.

West views nihilism as an outworking of the inevitable self-hatred that stems from centuries of white domination. It is a bigger threat today than in earlier generations, partly because the "televisual style" politics of leaders such as Jesse Jackson is an inadequate response to nihilism. At a deeper level, West points to the strength of a market culture that values pleasure-seeking over love and care. African-American culture has been pervaded by the market moralities of pleasure, profit, and consumption to the point where individualism and consumerism reign supreme. Consequently, the cultural buffers that sustained people and countered despair in past generations, namely church, family, and civic institutions, have been undermined by the predominance of market values. People have become "culturally naked" as the seductive images of "comfort, convenience, machismo, femininity, violence and sexual stimulation that bombard consumers . . . edge out non-market values – love, care, service to others."[9]

West suggests that nihilism is "a disease of the soul"; it is "not overcome by arguments or analyses" but rather "tamed by love and care."[10] Although George Yancy is critical of West's "anti-intellectual" use of the term "nihilism" whereby "thinking has been reduced to feeling," most critics are troubled by an apparent shift in West's focus from structures and class politics to psychology with conservative overtones.[11] In short, they feel that his existential focus on love has detracted from consideration of structural political issues. David Goldberg contends that the love ethic mutes West's earlier "more radical focus on political economy and the continuing legacy of racist discourse."[12] Henry Giroux asserts that West "fails to connect the specificity of black nihilism to the alienation that results from systemic inequality, calculated injustice, and moral indifference that operate as a daily regime of brutality and oppression."[13] Even critics who share West's concern with social morality feel that nihilism is no real explanation for what ails black America, as nihilism is not a cause but a consequence of suffering. Thus Michael Dyson is "deeply sympathetic" to West's call for "a politics of conversion, where a love ethic is central," yet maintains that the spiritual despair and collapse of hope in black America is "the pernicious result of something more basic than black nihilism: white racism," and he worries that West's emphasis on nihilism puts the onus on suffering African Americans to overcome nihilism.[14]

Building on this argument, Stephen Steinberg condemns West's portrayal of nihilism in ghetto culture as deeply pathological in that it blames the victims for their nihilism. Steinberg argues that West considers social breakdown independent from the forces that produce it and "divorces nihilism from political economy, thus implying that moral redemption is to be achieved through some mysterious turning of one's soul."[15] He sees West's logic as trying to change the person who is nihilistic rather than the system, and insists that this simply validates conservative arguments. Steinberg is not alone in detecting neo-conservative overtones in West's love ethic, as Molefi Kete Asante claims West's emphasis on personal values downplays the need for a strictly class analysis of African-American troubles and inadvertently aligns West with the black conservatives from which he distances himself.[16] Similarly, Kofi Buenor Hadjor asserts, "Whatever their subjective intentions may be, those who help to convert social problems into moral ones will always end up pointing the finger at the individual."[17] These commentators share concern that West's emphasis on the spiritual and psychological conditions of blacks depicts nihilism as stemming from the tragic nature of the human condition, rather than from capitalist domination or racism, and also detracts attention from pressing structural issues. Hence Goldberg insists, "Response to racism requires, minimally, not that my neighbors love me but that they treat me fairly," while Dyson claims, "Love alone, even a complex, socially rooted understanding of love, cannot provide the material basis for the permanent high self-regard that will need to be in place for black folk to stop snuffing one another out."[18] He considers love to be a luxury that can only come into play when people have the resources in terms of employment, education, and housing to improve their condition.

How accurate are these criticisms? Does West, intentionally or not, locate the problem with the victim and suggest that victims are to blame for their own victimization? Does he articulate a conservative theory when he suggests that social critique begins with individual change? Some of West's critics seem to have been so taken aback by his suggestion that love is a cure for nihilism that they did not manage to read the remainder of *Race Matters*, for it is difficult to see how anyone familiar with his work could accuse him of overlooking the structures of racism and capitalism that produce nihilism. Those who chide him for an emphasis on individual pathology rather than social analysis overlook the fact that he ties despair to broader inequality in America. His argument is that racist stereotypes and corporate market institutions *shape* nihilism, and so nihilism is "the tragic response of a people bereft of resources in confronting the workings of U.S. capitalist society."[19] It is true that some of his arguments overlap with those made by conservative social commentators, but this does not mean that West articulates an inherently conservative theory. Instead, "Nihilism in Black America" continues his critique of both liberal structuralist and conservative behaviorist approaches on the grounds that both are reluctant to attack capitalism and racism, and concludes that the love ethic *entails* structural change. West suggests that critics such as Steinberg "equate a philosophic notion of 'nihilism' with a socio-logical concept of 'passivity' or an existential response with a pathological reaction." He bristles that this is "a category mistake that produces a misreading of my work and flies in the face of my two decades of writings that highlight structural and institutional analyses of white supremacy."[20] Elsewhere he concedes, "Maybe the language of nihilism suggested a downplaying of structural reali-ties, hence a leftist knee-jerk designation of a blaming-the-victim perspective," but insists that "even an uncharitable yet close reading would see my focus on existential agency within a capital-ist, white supremacist civilization, not a self-blaming victimization with no historical contexts."[21] In short, West's critics miss the point that love comes accompanied by justice.

West's political theology seeks liberation for those oppressed by namelessness, problematization, and double-consciousness. A crucial part of this liberatory process is a turning away from the internalized self-contempt inherent in the socialization process of white supremacist society that views blacks (explicitly or implicitly) as second-class citizens. Because African Americans have been told repeatedly that they are somehow less than human, their minds, bodies, and souls have been colonized by self-hatred. Decoloniza-tion comes only through the "conversion" that affirms one's humanity, and so for West the fundamental premise of liberation is humanity and love. He views self-love, self-respect, and self-regard as potent weapons and preconditions for human agency, and strives to generate levels of self-confidence among African Americans who for so long have been told by society that they are worthless or problematic. He recognizes that "you can't generate agency and insurgency when people feel themselves lacking worth," and stresses that without a love ethic people who have been "hated for so long" will be unable to conceive of themselves as "agents in the world who can make a difference in it."[22] Only when African Americans unshackle themselves from society's demeaning picture will they be confident enough to shape the conditions of their own destiny. Black self-love is thus subversive in a white supremacist society. There is no recognition when one is viewed through stereotypical images, and this renders one simultaneously invisible and hyper-visible. Therefore the struggle for justice is a quest for recognition, visibility, and self-definition, and to secure liberation and equal citizenship the differences that have been rendered invisible must be recognized and accented.

Given the historical basis of white supremacy in the difference of skin pigmentation, it might seem odd to point to *difference* as a means to overcome this domination. Indeed the response of some to racism is that difference should be rejected in the pursuit of a color-blind society. However, difference can have two distinct intentions: to dominate or to empower and liberate. So although racism recognizes differences in a dominatory fashion, West's conception of difference is based on a self-defined celebration of blackness and is therefore liberatory. As African-American liberation entails overcoming both invisibility and hyper-visibility, West argues that liberation cannot be premised on ignorance of differences of color. Attempts to be "color-blind" deepen rather than alleviate the problem, as color-blindness is not race neutrality but rather the *omission* of race, the denial of continued racial subordination, and a guise through which whiteness remains invisible. West therefore concludes that equality can only be built from the premise of race-consciousness. While West values the moral reasoning that may lead one to ignore differences of skin pigmentation and see only humanity and the content of one's character, in this instance such reasoning seems to assume that race is an appendage to a person's humanity and therefore peripheral to their social existence. Given his insistence that blackness cannot simply be eliminated, he is suspicious of those who claim not to see black but just a person when they look at an African American. Blackness cannot simply be forgotten as it is integral to the life experiences and collective memory of African Americans, and so to downplay the difference of blackness is to downplay part of one's self. Thus it is difference-induced domination rather than difference *per se* which must be minimized.

Love of others: race transcendence

West stresses that it is impossible to be race-neutral, yet racial awareness must not be translated into the creation of a dual world of white and black. As such, his call to love blackness is distinct from the self-love and difference advocated by Afrocentrists. He rejects uncritical group-centered politics that is reliant on racial reasoning because self-love is only one part of his love ethic; also vital to the equation is respect for others. The differences that comprise a person's identity must be accented, but so too must common concerns that cut across those differences, and one's unique identity as an African American should not be asserted at the expense of the identity of others. West adopts a moral perspective that respects rather than demonizes the differences of others, and calls for an ethical approach to politics that will advance inter-group coalitions as a means to reach some form of unity amidst diversity. West's love ethic encourages people to turn from self-centeredness to interconnection. This approach attempts to draw upon the best of nationalist and integrationist responses to the need for racial justice and tries to construct a common vision of black liberation from the diverse perspectives that comprise "the black community."

West views America as an increasingly atomized society that emphasizes possessive individualism and he stresses that the privatism of egocentrism must be challenged if polarization is to be overcome and community rebuilt. His conception of community is premised on non-market values and so is fundamentally at odds with society's dominant narratives, such as the message that accumulation of wealth leads to happiness. Instead, West suggests that accumulation leads only to emptiness because consumption is valued more than human life. However, the dominance of market values problematizes the extent to which people will voluntarily adhere to non-market values such as love and concern. Nevertheless, West believes that when people are faced with the stark choice of learning to stand together or of disintegration, they will choose the former and realize that community or commonality is in the best interests of all members of society. With his metaphor of the sinking boat, West hints that society might become so harsh that fear will compel people to work across racial differences. Yet he does not give any indication as to why we should believe this. What about stubborn racists who will never accept black humanity? Will they choose commonality with those they hate in order to save America from destruction? West's response would be that one should never give up hope, no matter how grim the evidence may look. He stresses that unless people come together and develop a sense of commonality, any remaining sense of what it means to be an American will evaporate. As he sees the future of America at stake here, one cannot simply give up and wallow in pessimism about the attitude of stubborn racists, but rather should strive to turn the evidence around. The first step would be to work for a moderation in the attitudes of racists. As with much of West's thought, he portrays a grim and apocalyptic scenario and then makes a huge leap of faith to believe it can be surmounted.

The love ethic is an outworking of West's liberatory vision, and so he links the idea of conversion with an articulation of leftist politics and with spiritual wrestling against the "darkness." There are three facets to his notion of social liberation. First, people must individually reform their attitudes. They must question their personal addiction to market values of stimulation and titillation and the way in which this addiction has displaced humane interaction with others. From that premise people can advance to the second stage, where non-market values of equality and community can be articulated through interpersonal toleration and the creation of bonds of trust that will enable one to treat others with respect despite the presence of strong ideological differences. Third, West discerns a need for something more than respect: an attempt to understand the arguments of others. This requires the reconstitution of the public sphere as an area where disparate groups can dialogue and discover tentative areas of common ground to supercede cultural fragmentation. West maintains that it is possible to locate a sense of common good discursively; this good is people living in a community based upon ethical principles and characterized by civility rather than contempt towards opponents. He favors a process of civil communication where individuals can retain their unique identity, needs, and concerns, while recognizing what holds them together as Americans by finding common ground in values such as love. However, he also notes that the common good is not a homogenizing force; rather, because it is reached discursively and through interaction with others, it shifts in accordance with the concerns of the population.

Crucial to this conception of social liberation is the construction of alliances. There are a number of reasons why coalition building is so important to West's perspective. First, coalitions provide a way to reconcile distinct identities by finding common ground in shared values or shared ends. Second, there is the pragmatic reason that coalitions are important for the project of the Left. West realizes that by itself the American Left is not strong enough to transform society and surmount polarization. Because concrete action on specific issues is more important than dogmatic adherence to orthodox leftist principles, West wishes to broaden the political concerns of leftists and break their crippling insularity. He discerns strong, yet highly disorganized, progressive forces operating at the grassroots level – in the culture industry, student activism, Habitat for Humanity – and sees it as the Left's task to channel these groupings into an organized expression that will attack the defects of society rather than remain on the defensive. If the Left develops an organization around disparate movements it may be able to push it in a leftist direction, and so he strives to create new discursive spaces in the public conversation in which Left perspectives can be aired. For instance, the rejuvenation of public life would provide a basis for discussion of issues such as inadequate health care, distribution of wealth, and substandard housing.[23]

One specific form of coalition advocated by West is between African Americans and white liberals and feminists. Inevitably his advocacy of interracial coalitions as a political strategy has been attacked by Afrocentrists, such as Sister Souljah, who are concerned that West downplays the importance of race. West certainly advocates moving beyond a narrow vision of race, because although race is central in the life experiences of African Americans, it is not an exclusive force as gender and class also have an impact. Consequently, the anti-racist struggle must be linked to other forms of political resistance around class and gender struggles. West is a cultural or racial pluralist who acknowledges differences and yet refuses to view any culture or race as superior to others; thus he is critical of Black Nationalists who cling to a romantic vision of race based on homogeneity and separatism. West offers a critique of "the pitfalls of racial reasoning" as heard in arguments about racial "authenticity" and in appeals for African Americans to close ranks behind any black perceived to be under attack. Here he points to the controversy surrounding the nomination of Clarence Thomas to the Supreme Court, when racial reasoning and appeals to racial authenticity led to collusion with sexism and to a closing of ranks behind Thomas, even though many of his political commitments were antithetical to the interests of many African Americans. These narrow notions of racial solidarity leave no room for critical thinking; yet, without space for dissent, racial solidarity can become a form of domination. That is not to say that race no longer matters, as quite clearly it does; rather, the argument is that the consequences of racism are not a reason to "close ranks" and become narrowly parochial. While the rationale of black authenticity presumes a fixed essentialist conception of blackness, West reminds us that blackness is historically constructed, not given. Thus his appeal for racial transcendence entails deconstruction of the notion of an essential blackness by stressing the diversity within African-American communities. He rejects both racial stereotypes and racial essentialism as illusory absolutes that are static, one-dimensional, and ignore complexity and multiplicity. In rejecting essentialist notions of blackness, West points to the diversion of interests along class and gender lines which make any conception of unified black interests an anachronism. Although a loose sense of cultural heritage and experiences bind African Americans together regardless of gender, age, or class, it is not possible to speak of "*the* black community" as a monolithic whole, as clearly the interests of middle-class blacks differ from those of the urban poor. "Race" is a hybridity, and so blackness must be deconstructed in order to view the identities that make up that construct. Thus there can be no one authentic way to "think black," and instead the differences and competing identities among African Americans must be recognized. Of course this perspective poses its own problems – for instance, given the differences between African Americans can there be any form of agreement concerning the meaning and purpose of liberation?

Like his arguments concerning nihilism, West's desire to build race-transcending coalitions is easily misunderstood. This is because many, such as Howard Winant, assume that to "transcend" race means to *eliminate* race. Moreover, as Dyson observes, talk of transcending race often means transcending or "getting beyond blackness," as blackness has been "so completely identified with negative attributes – limited, narrow, particular – that we can rarely imagine it representing a universal ideal."[24] Just how can West simultaneously speak of accenting and eliminating blackness? Quite simply, he does not. West has no desire to eliminate race and nor does he advocate color-blindness or race neutrality. So, while Winant asserts that "the 'solution' to the race 'problem' is not transcendence but recognition, not denial of difference but respect for it," West seeks recognition *and* transcendence, or love of self and love of others.[25] His quest for the transcendence of race is not associated with color blindness, suppressing race, or erasing difference, as any attempt to deny or evade the presence of race simply reinforces the power of race. Instead, it is transcendence of the limitations of current racial discourses and of a narrow focus on race that excludes categories such as gender and class. West does not say "let's forget about differences"; rather he wants different people to develop coalitions and participate in each other's struggles for social justice. His vision of interracial coalitionary politics wants people from different social groups to come together with their different ideas about social norms and work out a political consensus about what norms should prevail. Thus the goal is to build consensus without rejecting claims of racial legitimacy. He wants to find common ground across group lines that will be able to respect difference, with the aim of enabling different groups to at least tolerate each other as they pursue common *and* different ends. As such, his call for race transcendence argues for programs that will eliminate all forms of social misery no matter what their shade. For instance, coming together to fight for affordable housing for poor people is part of the process of creating the bonds of trust and commitment that are necessary to eliminate racism.

Unity and diversity

West's vision of humanity is dependent on a conception of a common good that brings together the fragments of American society without undermining the differences between these fragments. He attempts to reconcile the apparently binary opposition of unity and diversity through a celebration of diversity that also focuses on what people hold in common. Crucially, he understands consensus and community as dynamic and open to change and regroupings, and so, although he recognizes the importance of building communities of similar interests, he does not view these interests as static nor necessarily common. When he refers to "community" or "coalitions" he does not seek homogeneity or dogmatic assimilation to the ways of others, but rather recognition of diversity that dialogically mediates interests. West's construction of a collective form of identification based on identity as "citizens" stands in addition to one's other identities. As such, he does not speak of single community membership as a closed totality, but rather recognizes that there are many communities to which a person relates and belongs. His recognition of a complex dynamic of multiple identities means that no single one of his various identities as Christian, African American, or radical democrat can claim to fully represent his interests; none has any claim to superiority, and so there is no definitive articulation of what his identity is. West's vision of community life acknowledges membership of smaller communities and strives to build a community of communities by blending differences in the name of consensus that will prevent societal self-destruction. However, he must strike a delicate balance, as reconciling love of self with love of others is an endeavor fraught with difficulty. In the first instance, equality and difference are often paired dichotomously, prompting the conclusion that equality is antithetical to difference. Second, the excesses of either form of love mitigate against expression of the other. In other words, the quest for commonality to surmount polarization can produce an impulse of assimilation and race neutrality, while emphasis on self-love can evolve into Afrocentrism premised on the exclusion of non-blacks and thereby increase polarizing trends.

West's attempt to balance African-American recognition with a quest for a common good is nothing novel as a prime concern of democratic theory has long been identity and commonality. Some theorists suggest it is possible to set aside differences through dialogue and thereby establish consensus, while others suggest that the attempt to reconcile difference with equality as citizens is an impossible dream as people will not voluntarily set aside difference to unite with those from whom they differ fundamentally. In *The Disuniting of America*, Arthur Schlesinger suggests that America is coming apart because too many groups are emphasizing their cultural diversity above their common identity as Americans. Following from this perspective, Robert Bellah argues in *Habits of the Heart* that private interest should be subordinated to the common good. Like Bellah and Schlesinger, West is concerned with the fracturing of America and urges the development of a common good premised on an ethic of regard and concern for others. However, he diverges from them in asserting that the interests of personal identity should not be sacrificed. West sees no value in a common culture of Anglo-American regionality that masquerades as universal and portrays other cultural traditions as parochial. Instead, he strives for a sense of commonality that promotes the values of democracy and equality while maintaining a strong awareness of difference. We must embrace both unity and diversity as both exemplify the love ethic: diversity stresses particular identity and is built on love of self, while unity is an outworking of love and respect for others. People must find things in common, yet difference must not be absorbed into the universal.

A dominant ideological response to the question of how we balance difference and equality is "multiculturalism." Multiculturalists such as Will Kymlicka claim that minority cultures are not sufficiently protected by insuring the individual rights of their members and so must also be protected with special group rights or privileges. They view American culture as a complex intermingling of diverse perspectives and demand that society give space and voice to "minority" perspectives in order to counter prejudice and preserve distinct ethnic, religious, and racial identities. Multiculturalism is essentially a movement of the Left that emerged from the new social movements of the 1960s, and it is evident, for instance, in multilingual policies and in campaigns to change college curricula on the grounds that knowledge as currently taught serves white male interests and thus contributes to domination. Critics of multiculturalism, such as Schlesinger, contend that diversity breeds divisiveness and that such fragmentation undermines civic harmony. He derides the new "cult of ethnicity" that he sees as based on denial of the idea of a common American culture. Given West's attempt to balance commonalty and diversity it is worth considering where he stands in such debates. In one obvious sense he is a multiculturalist: he respects cultural diversity and the positive portrayal of difference and supports programs such as affirmative action. Additionally, his contextualism and historicism rejects the monolithic, homogenetic, and universal and favors diversity, multiplicity, and specificity. Ultimately, however, he finds multiculturalist attempts to balance diversity with a common identity as Americans problematic. He acknowledges that there is some truth in Schlesinger's arguments; while the politics of identity must be affirmed, the flux of identities – from Louisiana Cajuns to Oregon skinheads – poses a threat to common values. As such, multiculturalism leads to a proliferation of small publics, yet fails to address the crisis of balkanization and disdain for public life: "the notion of a public life that you enter without necessarily being obsessed with your own, smaller public we hold at a distance."[26] West recognizes that democracy cannot survive as a culture of fragments without a cementing center and thus he highlights the importance of a sense of "Americanness" which distinct identities share; although the legacies of white, Latino, and black are different (settlers, immigrants, or slaves), all three can view themselves as American New Worlders.[27]

West also discerns deeper weaknesses in multiculturalist arguments unidentified by conservative critics, such as the compounding of the dichotomy between difference and equality. West stresses that each person has a multiplicity of identities – for instance he is a Christian, a radical democrat, an African American, a professor at Princeton, and is from California. At certain times and in certain contexts one identity will become salient within the larger identity of his overall thought. However, multiculturalists highlight *group* membership as the cornerstone of identity and thus tend to construct "difference" as a form of group homogeneity untroubled by internal distinction. Such group homogeneity places a premium on how one responds to threatening external "enemies" and in the process cements fragmentation. Another flaw West detects with multiculturalist arguments is that they are built on notions of white supremacism. He suggests that "multiculturalism" is a term created by Eurocentrics to explain the non-white population. It is thus an extremely limiting term as whites too often assume that multiculturalism has nothing to do with them, as it refers only to "ethnic minorities." Although "multiculturalism" is regarded as a recently invented means of dealing with the problem of race in America, America always has been multicultural. The existence of multiple cultures and races in America is not new; but what is new is the deliberate focus on race. West observes that because Americans are so deeply shaped by a discourse of "positively valued whiteness and negatively valued blackness" the assumption is that multiculturalism only goes on when blacks and whites interact.[28] Thus the multiculturalist emphasis on race overshadows the multicultural diversity among white Americans. Indeed, "If all the black, brown, red, and yellow people in America were to disappear tomorrow, leaving no trace of their histories, the country would still be multicultural. But there would not be a heated debate about multiculturalism."[29] West is also critical of the reluctance of multiculturalists to grapple seriously with the scars of racial constructs. He calls for the inauguration of a full and frank discussion of racism and suggests that the absence of this in multiculturalist discussions betrays a sense of complacency concerning the degree to which white supremacy has been dismantled. Rather than easy talk of political correctness there must be serious conversation about suffering that seeks to empathize with the other. This is "not simply a question of various peoples coming together and feeling happy about being different." Rather, talk of identity and diversity must be linked to moral vision and social analysis because without some rooting in a democratic ideal that questions hierarchies and degradation, diversity can become "idolatrous, ahistorical and cathartic."[30]

West's attempt to fashion diversity into an integrated whole is dependent upon transcending prevalent expressions of multiculturalism in order to create a democracy that is at the heart committed to change. He thus links questions of diversity and identity to the future survival of democracy. His discussion of multiculturalism is grounded in the history of all Americans' struggles with the question of what it means to be human and how one can understand evil and pain. West stresses the need for dialogue and civil communication as a means to realize a common good which can restore communal bonds of trust. Here the call is not for unanimity, but for citizens to recognize the good in others and locate things in common with each other in the midst of their disagreements. For instance, as Jean Elshtain suggests, common ground can be found in a desire for safer streets.[31] It is through public deliberation and interaction with others that one recognizes what aspects of one's specific identity are shared with other citizens. As such, it is only through a discussion of race that one can hope to eradicate inequality and injustice. However, existing power relations (based on race or gender) and historic mistrust and suspicion pose obstacles to the dialogical adjudication of conflicting views, and so West recognizes that "dialogue in and of itself is not ultimately going to create the bridges; but dialogue is a crucial element in creating a bridge."[32] Through robust dialogue one gains greater understanding of the issues at stake, culminating in the point where pride in one's own identity can be accompanied by recognition of the value and uniqueness of other people's identities.

Although West stresses dialogue, he rejects Bruce Ackerman's liberal perspective that requires dialogical process to conform to a neutrality constraint.[33] West does not want coalition parties to embrace impartiality. In part, this is because as a pragmatist he sees no true and universal moral principles, but he also rejects such impartiality as a form of false unity that wants judgments to be detached and neutral. Unlike Ackerman, who wants to *reduce* plurality, West wants to *accent* plurality while searching for a shared stock of ideas that are acceptable to all in the culture, no matter what their moral or political views are. West wishes to preserve difference yet also establish some unity or commonality *within* that diversity. He thus seeks a form of universality that is rooted in particularity, and rejects a faceless, empty universalism that wipes clean all the particulars. The point is that if we are "to hold on to an ideal of universalism, then it's got to go through particularity"; we must discern "overlapping universalisms within our particularities" and attempt to "articulate universality in a way that is not a mere smokescreen for someone else's particularity."[34] West thus

opposes both racial assimilation and the elimination of racial differences, as both approaches devalue those forced to accept the
dominant culture or identity by hiding particularities. Instead, we
must affirm our differences and we *need* the particularities of our
different backgrounds and traditions in order to understand our-
selves. This is because our traditions enable us to make truth claims,
without which we are simply faceless atoms, controlled by the dominant discourses. Differences should not merely be tolerated but
defended. They must also be challenged in conversation, and here
West stresses that we all have "cultural baggage" and "a certain set
of assumptions" that we bring to a conversation, but those presup-
positions must be "open to scrutiny. When we leave public conversation, we ought to be different from when we entered."[35] Thus
what makes this public dialogue a democratic conversation and not
a cacophony of incommensurable voices is that the claims of our
traditions should be inflected by democratic norms.

West recognizes that the ideal of a homogeneous society is
mythical, for although diverse identities can experience commonality there will also be friction, as each person belongs to a variety of
communities whose interests are not always compatible. Therefore,
for a society to be "democratic" and respect all of its citizens, no one
section can claim to represent the totality. As such, West questions
the merit of perfect harmony in social relations and concurs with
Chantal Mouffe that radical democratic efforts to recover and
reformulate the notions of "common good," "civic culture," and
"political community" must be made "compatible with the recognition of conflict, division and antagonism."[36] Recognition of a
plurality of social agents means that antagonism and struggle are
inescapable. In a fragmented and plural society there can be no
"rational" consensus that negates antagonism, as such a claim is
based on delusions of neutrality. Indeed Mouffe argues, "To present
the institutions of liberal democracy as the outcome of a pure
deliberative rationality is to reify them and make them impossible to
transform."[37] It follows that West does not seek racial *harmony* but
racial justice. He is aware that "harmony" can easily be accompanied
by unquestioned racial hierarchy or may function as a coercive consensus based on some form of exclusion. Thus his coalition building is a coming together which recognizes that there are substantial
differences and that one has to *construct* a coalition. As such, we
should not confuse unity with unanimity, as West is not seeking
harmonious agreement on every issue. His democratic theory takes
difference seriously enough not to seek the universalization of

difference that false unity would entail. In his recognition that conflict and resistance are inescapable he likens radical democracy to
jazz music:

> The interplay of individuality and unity is not one of uniformity and
> unanimity imposed from above but rather of conflict among diverse
> groupings that reach a dynamic consensus subject to questioning and
> criticism. As with a soloist in a jazz quartet . . . individuality is pro-
> moted in order to sustain and increase the *creative* tension with the
> group – a tension that yields higher levels of performance to achieve
> the aim of the collective project.[38]

He concludes that respect for cultural diversity will enable people
to cultivate a sense of belonging to the larger community. This sense
of belonging is vital if polarization is to be surmounted and community restored. West is respectful of difference and believes we
should work for temporary agreements; we should figure out how
different and even clashing interpretations can overlap or converge
to generate some kind of consensus. We must engage across chasms,
aware that a gravitation toward happy consensus paralyzes debate.
The aim is to cultivate a culture of dialogue and conversation with
one another across political and ideological lines, not necessarily
seeking an outcome of happy reconciliation but recognizing that the
engagement itself, and the commitment of those struggling with
you, is as important as the outcome.

Conclusion

In this chapter we have seen that West believes America's crisis of
spirit must be confronted by a value-based response. He believes
that a moral vision must undergird any movement for social
transformation and so his political vision of communitarianism
and emancipatory leftist politics is dependent on spiritual and
religious values – specifically, the language of civil religion and
of Rauschenbusch's "Christianizing" mission. In this regard he
believes it is possible to balance the universality of love for others
with the particularity of love for self. West's quest for love and
meaning may be desirable at the abstract or theoretical level, but
how is this to be achieved politically? For his work to realize its
desired political consequences of securing liberation through a re-
invigoration of democracy, he must offer a clear agenda of how his

love ethic can be implemented in society. The next chapter will consider the tensions in his love ethic, such as the difficulty in combining the vague rhetoric of civil religion with invocation of a specific liberationist agenda and quest for justice, and also the controversy surrounding some of the guidelines that he has offered for expanding democracy.

8

Achieving Democracy: Applying the Love Ethic

West's critical social theory is both "explanatory-diagnostic" and "anticipatory-utopian"[1]; it offers an analytic diagnosis of present crises and normatively explicates those crises in the name of a better future, thereby opening the door to liberatory transformation. His picture of redemption is based on both despair concerning the reality of crisis, and hope and belief in the possibility of a better and more democratic future. Despite prolonged disappointment, West remains inspired to create change. He recognizes that there will be limits to change as it is impossible to rid the world of all evil, but relates this tragic dimension to melioristic hope and a commitment to political praxis. The contradiction between realism and idealism forces us to question the practical value of his love ethic as a response to crisis. This is because, although his love ethic can be considered a laudable and theoretically desirable ideal, the degree to which its implementation is possible seems questionable given the stark picture he paints of crisis in American democracy. Yet the question of the love ethic's practical value is crucial, given West's approach that claims to reject theoretical obsession and focus instead on praxis.

Niebuhrian realism suggests that while *individuals* can strive to be moral and live by criteria of compassion and love, it is impossible to expect all society to live by these standards. Compassion may work on an individual level, but in our fallen world any compassionate society would be swallowed by other societies without such compassionate leanings. So, although West's love ethic may be desirable, its practical implementation remains naïve to realists.

However, the Christian utopian belief in hope and a better future is often misunderstood. West maintains that while evil cannot be eliminated, it can be pushed back, and likewise Rubem Alves suggests that Christian utopianism does not point to the possibility of a perfect society but to the non-necessity of the present order of imperfection. Alves also argues that "reality" must be understood as a human construction, and as such it can be demolished and rebuilt by humans. Thus to use "reality" as a criterion for ethical judgment is a form of idolatry which fails to recognize that all social systems are under the historical judgment of God. History from a biblical perspective is not self-enclosed but open to surprise, and so we can think of the presently unreal as potentially real.[2] The basis for West's "audacious hope" is a refusal to be a prisoner of the past and of previous social-system constructs. Although pessimism posits limits to change and to the levels of justice that can be attained, that should not preclude one from entering the process of struggle; some advances can always be made, and this is better than no change at all. Indeed Gary Dorrien claims, "the church that does not struggle for 'things not seen' betrays the hope of the poor and oppressed." He views a liberationist theological perspective such as West's as crucial to the continuance of social Christianity because "it brings to Christianity the perspectives of those who have no choice but to struggle for a just social order."[3]

Acceptance of the need to envisage and work for change fails to diminish the weight lent to realist arguments by the virtual absence of historical evidence of societies attempting to live on the basis of pure compassion. Desirable as a love ethic may be, there seems to be little evidence that its implementation is a realizable ideal. Thus West's leap of faith and audacious hope for transformation may appear incredulous and incognizant of the difficulties of transformation, despite the apocalyptic pictures he so often paints. The love ethic might even seem foolish. But echoing 1 Corinthians 1:20 and 27, West says "Surely in a moment of such pervasive fatalism and pessimism and cynicism we will be cast as foolish. But what a compliment to be called foolish by the world . . . I serve a God who told me that the foolish will be cast as wise, once the world is turned upside down."[4] It is hard to see how the politics of conversion would work in practice, as the love ethic has never really been tried before on a broad scale. However, there is a very powerful example of this sort of ethic in global politics that counters realist arguments, namely the post-Apartheid years in South Africa. Prior to the transition of power there was widespread fear that (a) the whites would not hand over power and the black people would rebel against the regime, or (b) that once in power blacks would seek revenge for Apartheid. In both scenarios there was fear of widespread violence. However, the transition of power from white to black was accomplished with relative calm (albeit in a context of widespread fear of social disorder if change was not forthcoming), and crucially the new bearers of power did not respond with the revenge anticipated by some in light of the experience of human history. As Brown notes, "words like 'reconciliation,' 'forgiveness,' and 'compassion' were on black lips and exemplified in black lives. . . . The lesson of South Africa is that *we are never entitled to close the door marked hope*."[5] These values of reconciliation and compassion sit at the center of West's love ethic, and so we must conclude that his politics of conversion is not as implausible as it might initially appear. With that in mind, this chapter aims to probe how West's love ethic might be applied and considers his practical suggestions concerning how democracy might be expanded in America.

We will focus on arguments outlined in three of his most recent books, *Jews and Blacks*, *The War Against Parents*, and *The Future of American Progressivism*. These works are essentially applications of his basic approach in which he presents political programs aimed at reviving democracy and enabling the best possible flourishing of human life. For instance, his work on black-Jewish relations and on the construction of a parents' movement speak to his quest for social liberation, and are grounded in his desire to build progressive alliances that cut across ideological lines in order to counter the prevailing power of global capital. In assessing the extent to which his love ethic can contribute to transformed democratic practice, it will be suggested that deep tensions inhibit the degree to which his work can effectively promote positive change. Although I reject the arguments of West's critics concerning the inadequacy of love as a response to nihilism, serious problems exist in tying the vague and universal language of love with a specific liberationist agenda. The difficulty is that for West's appeal to love to have any real meaning it must be supplemented by specific proposals for change; yet once such an agenda is articulated it undercuts the inclusive nature of love and the levels of potential political support begin to crumble. In fact, the concerns raised by many on the Left about West's arguments in *The War Against Parents* hint at this very problem.

Black-Jewish alliance

Of all West's work on coalitions, it is his work on black-Jewish alliance that is the most fully developed. As such, it provides a number of principles that can be used to inform general alliance building efforts and also points to some dilemmas inherent to such a politics. The pretext for this work was the growing paranoia among Jews and African Americans toward each other that West detected in the early 1990s. In the context of collapsing progressive forces in America, he viewed this paranoia as particularly damaging given his conception of both Jews and African Americans as political progressives. This prompted West to engage in dialogues and a subsequent book, *Jews and Blacks*, with Michael Lerner, the editor of the Jewish magazine *Tikkun*. West's attempt to construct a black-Jewish alliance is partly a political attempt to buttress progressive forces in America, but more importantly it is "a moral endeavor that exemplifies ways in which [two pariah groupings] can coalesce in the name of precious democratic ideals – ideals that serve as the sole countervailing force to hatred, fear, and greed."[6] Believing that cooperation between the two groups can play an important role in rejuvenating the radical democratic tradition in America, he asserts that black–Jewish dialogue must be built on a fundamental respect for the "other" and regulated by the ideals of democracy, decency, freedom, and justice. West contends that the principles developed through this dialogue hold true for society as a whole, providing a basis from which to surmount polarization. These principles include awareness that dialogue requires vision, active listening, and open questioning, with a democratic spirit of flexibility that is willing to "bend without breaking." The compromise that this entails is "not about the violation of principles [but] the application of principles to circumstances," and as such places a premium on integrity.[7] West asserts that if dialogue is to achieve anything, the grounds upon which one enters dialogue – such as one's principles, strategies, and objectives – must be made clear from the outset to partners in dialogue and there must also be belief that the other person is movable and recognition that one can learn from others.

Coalition building is often a vicious circle: incivility rises when consensus breaks down and leads to oversimplification, increased anger, frustration, and entrenchment. As such, the degree to which alliance building can surmount polarization must be limited, and

West does admit that the O. J. Simpson verdict and Million Man March left his efforts for black-Jewish healing "in shambles."[8] Black Nationalists have been skeptical of West's dialogue with Lerner and feel that in the process of black-Jewish exchange "black interests" will be lost. Groups such as the African United Front tend to understand West's condemnation of black anti-Semitism as an assault on the blacks and accuse him of attacking blacks while ignoring white racists and anti-black Jews. West has attempted to reassure such fears by stressing that his dialogue with Jews is connected to the goal of ending black suffering – blacks cannot conquer intolerance and racial scapegoating alone and so a progressive multiracial coalition is required; he has also developed a fuller dialogue with Black Nationalists by endorsing the magazine *Race Traitor* and supporting Al Sharpton. In August 2001 West was named chair of Sharpton's 2004 presidential exploratory committee. But West's most notable and contentious engagement with Black Nationalism is his friendship with Louis Farrakhan, leader of the Nation of Islam. The problem is that, given Farrakhan's derogatory remarks about Jewish people, West's dialogue with him is viewed by many as undermining his dialogue with Jewish groups. From West's perspective, Farrakhan must be spoken to and not condemned outrightly as "a fascist" because he represents a large constituency whose voice must be heard if substantive dialogue is to occur.[9] Thus, in *Jews and Blacks*, responding to Lerner's characterization of Farrakhan as a "racist dog," West asserted, "I wouldn't call the brother a racist dog but a xenophobic spokesperson when it comes to dealing with Jewish humanity."[10] Undoubtedly, West's attitude to Farrakhan has moderated as a result of his dialogue with Black Nationalism. In a 1984 article West condemned Farrakhan's portrayal of Judaism as "a gutter religion" as a "despicable characterization," yet in *Jews and Blacks* there was some equivocation: "What he meant was that Judaism has been used to justify various forms of domination. He was wrong in the monolithic use of it, but we know that every religion has been used to justify domination."[11] Elsewhere, West stresses that a distinction must be drawn between Farrakhan's radical anti-Semitism and Nazism, for although "Farrakhan says terrible things about the Jews, he does not advocate that people physically attack Jews. He is different from the neo-Nazi skinheads who advocate the actual physical injury of Jewish human beings."[12] Some might consider this an exercise in outrageous semantics on the part of West. There is no disputing West's rejection of anti-Semitism, but such explanatory attempts seem to point to justification for Farrakhan's remarks rather than condemnation, and suggest to some a certain moral weakness on the part of West. Not only is his rationalization of Farrakhan's positive remarks about Hitler morally offensive to Jews, but it also gives West's critics further ammunition, with Adolph Reed observing, "West has been twisting himself like a pretzel, overtaxing his prodigious capacity for double-talk" in his support of Farrakhan.[13]

Obviously West objects to some of Farrakhan's statements, yet he refuses to denounce Farrakhan personally. This is because West draws a distinction between moral criticism and the demonization of Farrakhan. He suggests that Farrakhan has a deep love for black people but a limited vision of how to achieve black freedom. Thus West engages in moral criticism through condemnation of Farrakhan's anti-Semitic rhetoric, believing that the basis of mature dialogue is the ability to engage critically with those of a different perspective to oneself. Dialogue does not entail agreement but wrestling with the views of others, and indeed, on this basis, we could argue that it is *Lerner's* "racist dog" language that lacks in civil discourse and that will prevent the open and civil public discourse that West suggests is needed. West maintains that he has approached dialogue with Farrakhan from a position of integrity grounded in consistent principles and he has made it clear to Farrakhan from the outset that he unequivocally opposes anti-Semitism. West suggests that dialogue is predicated upon some faith that the other person is movable and here he points to a moderation in Farrakhan's attitudes toward Jews and women: there are now some women in leadership positions in the Nation of Islam and he is more willing to engage in critiques of corporate power. He also contends that, following their conversations, Farrakhan has realized it is anti-Semitic to talk about "the Jews" and that rather the stress must be on one's political and moral perspective. In 1998 West said "I must give him credit because throughout the past three years the press hasn't caught him making an anti-Semitic remark once. He's referred to Jews many times, but he always talks about particular Jews – what conservative Jews are doing and so on" instead of talking about "*the* Jews doing this, *the* Jews doing that."[14] West maintains that his dialogical experience with Farrakhan proves that transformative possibility is always lurking.

Nevertheless, the issue for West's work as a whole is whether dialogue with Farrakhan is worth the expense of alienating other groups with whom he wishes to build alliances. For instance, there was much controversy surrounding the NAACP-sponsored National African American Leadership Summit held in Baltimore in June 1994, at which West was present. Jewish leaders condemned the NAACP for extending an invitation to Farrakhan and some condemned West for attending a meeting at which Farrakhan was present.[15] A group of protestors, including Michael Lerner, gathered outside the conference; during the protest, in a move unpopular with black extremists, West approached the protestors and embraced Lerner before returning inside. West defended his presence at the summit on the grounds that the summit's focus was on black suffering and pain, with the aim of generating strategies to "address the state of siege ravaging much of black America." Farrakhan's presence was essential as his is "one noteworthy voice . . . trying to understand and overcome pervasive black social misery."[16] West believes that he has a moral obligation to work with Farrakhan if the areas on which they agree can be used to build better communities and heal some of the deep divisions among African Americans. Yet in the process West has angered those wounded by Farrakhan's words, thereby jeopardizing black–Jewish healing. It also puts West in a seemingly oxymoric position as a racial healer who is also a friend of racial extremists, and begs the question of whether either side can take him seriously. However, despite these very real difficulties to building black–Jewish healing, this is the practice of the love ethic and the enactment of West's democratic ideals. Farrakhan's ideas are not so dangerous that he cannot be engaged in civilized discourse about the problems confronting African Americans, and West gets further challenging Farrakhan close up (around a dinner table, for instance) than condemning him from a distance with no connections. Moreover, West and Lerner's continuation with serious dialogue despite their intense disagreement over Farrakhan in itself provides hope as it illustrates a model of dialogue that can cope with difference rather than happy consensus. West tries to be a voice of moderation in debates and as such can accept the humanity of a person without accepting the legitimacy of their political program. The process of engaging in dialogue with a person does not entail that you must agree with them, and so an obvious, but as yet unexplored, dialogue partner for West is white racists. West claims to acknowledge the humanity of everyone, and as racists must comprise part of this "everyone," he should be speaking to them too. In short, to be consistent, West needs to talk to the Ku Klux Klan and include them in the net of his love ethic.

A parents' movement

In *The War Against Parents*, co-authored with Sylvia Ann Hewlett, West calls for the formation of a 62 million strong parents' move-ment (along the lines of the American Association of Retired Persons) to demand more support for child-rearing. The impetus for the book was their engagement in the Domestic Strategy Group prior to the 1992 presidential election – an advisory group com-prised of liberals and conservatives whose mandate was to explore the causes of America's social malaise evident in the fracturing of families and communities. In 1995 this was followed by their cre-ation of the Task Force on Parent Empowerment that aims to create the intellectual foundations for a parents' movement and insure that parents' voices are heard in the public square. West suggests that the family has acted as a crucial countervailing force to forms of domination such as capitalism and white supremacy, and so views the family as a radical rather than conservative force in society. He considers parenting the ultimate non-market activity and maintains it can offer a new political morality to replace liberal individualism. A central claim of *The War Against Parents* is that America's well-being depends on the care, nurture, and love of others that is exemplified in parenting – democratic life relies on people who are capable of commitment and responsibility. Because parents are economic providers, as well as emotional and moral providers, West sees the undervaluing of parenting in contemporary America as lying at the root of the "social capital" crisis. Parenting weaves a web of love and so "when parenting breaks down, the mechanism that transmits self-love is shattered, and this seriously compromises society's ability to pass from one generation to the next the values of compassion and commitment to others, which are the essential raw material of community-building and citizenship." Thus the erosion of parenting has "a huge impact beyond the home: com-munity life shrivels up and so does our democracy."[17]

Despite the prevalence of "family values" rhetoric in American politics, Hewlett and West contend that of all Western industrial nations America has the poorest record of family support. Not only do 30 percent of working women have no right to time off for preg-nancy or childbirth, but the government "does a better job under-writing the breeding of horses than the raising of children." This is because "If you own a horse, you can deduct from your tax bill the cost of food, stabling, training, vet and stud services, transportation to and from horse shows, attendance at horse shows, and a host of other expenses."[18] In contrast, parents faced with the growing financial burdens of housing costs, medical costs, and college tuition costs receive little help from government. This is very different to the 1950s when West suggests that the federal government buttressed family life. For instance, his parents benefited from the provisions of the GI Bill, which offered a 2 percent mortgage, free college education, and health insurance. West thus detects part of the source of the "war" against parents in corporate downsizing, declining wages, and government cutbacks. He emphasizes the economic factors that put families under stress, such as the sagging wages that force a person to work two jobs, noting that high levels of "wealth and income inequality result in parents being more overworked and underpaid than 30 or 40 years ago."[19] Parents are overworked and underpaid and hence undervalued, thus making it difficult for them to provide the regular nurturing that children need, and so West claims that, "any serious talk about family values" must address the need for "a decent and liveable wage for working parents."[20] Fifty years ago government policies strengthened family life by providing economic security for families, but today government is irresponsive to the tax burdens and the financial weights of mortgage and rent confronted by parents, and the erosion of government-funded programs for housing, urban development, and education have left many families vulnerable to poverty and dislocation. Today's parents are more beleaguered than ever, partly because government provides fewer supports to help parents come through for their children.

It is not just government policies and economic factors such as corporate greed that wage war against parents, but also the media's portrayal of parents in an unfavorable light. For instance, TV shows such as "Married With Children" portray parents as jokes. More dubiously, West and Hewlett also point the finger at feminism, which they suggest has elevated the rights of women above the rights of children and degraded fathering. They suggest that feminism is concerned with individual freedom and self-realization at the expense of community cohesion, and as such it has been no friend of families. The most damaging of the "excesses" of feminism has been "a set of attitudes that center on the expendability of men," and they are critical of celebrities such as Madonna and Rosie O'Donnell who in raising children without a father "have made single motherhood a chic thing to do – the ultimate liberated act of a strong woman."[21] Against this, West and Hewlett are adamant that children need two parents. We should note that West does not make an anti-feminist argument that *mothers* should be at home to look after children; rather the argument is that children need both their parents. West has one son born from his first marriage and is acutely aware of the difficulties facing non-custodial fathers and stresses that marginalized fathers need to be returned to responsibility and involvement.

In a 2001 article based on experiences of people they met during a promotional tour, West and Hewlett claim that their book actually underestimated the virulence of the attack on parents and the depths of despair bred by the emotional intensity of that war.[22] By way of response to this war, Hewlett and West advocate a Marshall Plan to rebuild families and a Parent's Bill of Rights inspired by the GI Bill of the post-World War II years. They call for greater economic security for parents, and their top priorities are flexibility for parents in the workplace (flexitime), which would afford more time with children, and livable wages. Specific features of their Bill include tax codes that are supportive of marriage, paid parental leave for both parents, family-friendly workplaces, mortgage subsidies for families with children, an extended school day and year to minimize children's unsupervised time, child-targeted funding for health and education, mandatory ten-day paternity leave, priority seating on buses and priority parking in shopping malls for parents with small children, paid days off for family responsibilities, and the reversal of welfare cuts. One particular aspect of the Bill that has raised the ire of a number of commentators is legal protection of the two-parent heterosexual family. West and Hewlett are "firmly convinced that most children benefit from the sustained loving attention of two parents" and contend that "the best way of ensuring an increase in the number of two-parent families is to bolster the institution of marriage."[23] They want to see a general cultural recommitment to marriage, and as such strongly reject narcissistic divorces and advocate a three-year waiting period for divorce. They are adamant that children need two parents and contend that their *biological* mother and father should raise them as, unlike "substitute parents," they have "unique genetic investments in their children."[24] Inevitably such arguments shock many people to the degree that they are unable to think about the deeper point being made, namely that concern with the family is a civic issue as democratic life needs the commitment found in family life. But ultimately there are major problems with the agenda of West and Hewlett, not least the astonishing implication of their biological argument, which is that a child would be better placed with abusive biological parents than with loving foster parents. Also, while some commentators are concerned that their agenda is heterosexist, Iris Young suggests that it is antifeminist and looks for remedies in a "nostalgic idea of family."[25] Certainly, West and Hewlett offer a generous reading of organizations such as Promise Keepers and the Nation of Islam, which are considered patriarchal by many, and although they call for an egalitarian model of the family to replace the traditional patriarchal model, they are critical of non-traditional family structures and appear not to support the legal right of gays and lesbians to marry and raise children. There is also a danger that they stigmatize single mothers. These are not the only problems. West and Hewlett recognize that the electoral power of parents is declining: in 1956, 55 percent of eligible voters were parents, but by 1996 this had fallen to 35 percent. They attempt to surmount this obstacle to their movement building through the dubious policy proposal of giving parents the right to cast votes for their children aged under 18, thereby tripling the size of the parent voting bloc.[26] Aside from the fact that this is thoroughly undemocratic, it is also hugely problematic. For instance, are parents under the age of 18 to be given votes to cast for their children despite being unable to vote themselves?

West and Hewlett's agenda seeks to intertwine economic concerns with values and so cuts across the traditional lines of conservative and liberal. Despite the misgivings of those on the Left, they hope that their Bill will unite parents behind an agenda that spans the lines of race, class, and gender. They claim that "if parents can mobilize behind our Bill of Rights" this will "transform our democracy, for we are not talking about narrow interest-group politics here. We are all stakeholders in this critical endeavor."[27] In other words, parent power can be a powerful healing force in American society. They point optimistically to survey data evidence that their policies have overwhelming levels of parental support (ranging from 70–95 percent) as hope for the creation of a parents' movement.[28] Their policy proposals also form the basis to the May 1998 report of the Institute for American Values, "A Call to Civil Society: Why Democracy needs Moral Truths."[29] Jean Elshtain chaired the group and members included West and other professors, politicians, and community organizers from across the political spectrum who wish to see restoration of the institutions of civil society. While centered on the idea of strengthening the married couple as the basic unit of child-rearing, they also advocate the return of a "family hour" of prime-time television with reduced violence and sexual content, incentives to give more charitable donations to anti-poverty groups, and an end to state lotteries. In their desire to reverse the deterioration of social morality and incivility they place the emphasis on voluntary civic action as the basis for the development of a public moral philosophy. Although this sounds like a conservative agenda, the fact that the Report's signatories come from across the political spectrum suggests it may be possible to forge a broad consensus around the desire to bolster the family and restore civil society.

The Future of American Progressivism

A recurring theme in *The War Against Parents* is that greed is a fundamental cause of inequality and social misery. In identifying greed rather than private ownership of the means of production as his target, West calls for a more equitable distribution of wealth as a means to reinvent the American Dream. West builds on this analysis in *The Future of American Progressivism*, where he presents a reform package of policies aimed at democratizing the market economy in America. Among other things, this package calls for broad-based taxation of consumption in the form of a value added tax, whereby savings are exempt from taxation (61–4); implementation of a social inheritance program that gives everyone a fund to use at major moments in their lives, such as going to college or starting a business (62); child-targeted food, medical, and dental support (67); a preferential system in education and hiring for the socially disadvantaged, but not one based exclusively on race (73–4); greater social support for education and training (76, 81); a democratizing of access to productive resources through establishment of venture capital funds (78); the creation of non-governmental citizen's action councils to deal with neighborhood issues (83); and public financing of political campaigns to enable conviction rather than private money to determine who runs for office (87–8). These are sweeping proposals that aim to deepen and re-energize American democracy by undermining the greed of corporate capitalism. Crucially, the goal of many of these policies is to *narrow* the gap between rich and poor by lifting up the rearguard. We should note that these arguments are not entirely novel, as in *Race Matters* West attacked consumer-driven selfishness that has discredited the common good, and also called for a mix of government, business, and labor in large-scale public intervention.[30]

It is not difficult to imagine why some on the Left are appalled at West's policy proposals. His priority in *The Future of American Progressivism* is not to transform capitalist property relations but rather is more incremental, focusing on reforming the law and tax code and on creating joint ventures between private capital and public institutions. So *is* West less radical than he once was? Has his radical voice been muted by the lure of celebrity? With this question in mind, it is worth reflecting on the issue of class politics: does class still matter to West, or has he evaded it? Clearly, class is an important theme in *The Future of American Progressivism*. West has long been concerned with inequality of wealth and continues to discuss the role that class plays in determining life conditions. However, a shift is apparent in that his recent emphasis is on corporate greed, rather than class *per se*. More troublesome for leftists is West's attempt to narrow class divisions rather than do away with them. Whereas in *Prophesy Deliverance* West placed an emphasis on worker control over the process of production, his emphasis in *The Future of American Progressivism* is on loosening the stability of America's class system in order to create greater social mobility.[31] West wants to redistribute wealth rather than reorganize the mode of production of wealth, and so, while he once advocated the abolition of private ownership of institutions, he now wants to increase ability to climb the class ladder. His democratic experimentalism wants to see greater freedom of initiative and there is a strong message of self-reliance in his emphasis on increased social mobility. For instance, one role of schools is to "equip the child with the means to think and to stand on his or her own feet," while the social endowment principle is a "tool of self-reliance, not an alternative to self-reliance."[32]

West's perspective has matured and he has become more of a mainstream figure who accepts capitalism as the framework within which to advance the struggle for democracy. It seems that he is now more concerned with improving conditions of life and work under American capitalism than with moving beyond capitalist property relations. In other words, he is now less concerned with building an international movement against capitalism than with saving *America* from racial division and moral dissolution. West is concerned with political possibility and therefore suggests that the Marxist idea of trying to change the entire system is beyond reach and thus paralyzing; instead he focuses on specific ways to improve America. Yet, while *The Future of American Progressivism* has an incrementalist and ameliorative orientation, it should be noted that

West still seeks radical transformation in America and his policy initiatives are directed toward American progressives. Although he favors communitarian democracy and a mixed economy as an alternative to unbridled capitalism, he continues to challenge the foundations of capitalist society, and in particular its racism and greed. He suggests that American democracy is teetering on the verge of disintegration; so for government, economy, and society to be organized more democratically there needs to be a change in consciousness and culture to sustain new arrangements. The specific proposals of taxation on consumption, private pension reform, and child protection laws are offered alongside his ideal of radical democracy in which people would be empowered to live lives of freedom and dignity. In that sense, his emphasis may have shifted but the goal and the ideal remain. This ideal informs his long-term activism, while the specific policies are to be applied in present circumstances. West has a broad vision of change, but it relies on local efforts, and so the policies outlined in *The Future of American Progressivism* are meant to be concrete steps to ameliorate the present.

Love and liberation

"Democracy" is a central reference point of American political discourse and a widely invoked ideal in political rhetoric. The United States was one of the countries where liberal democratic ideas were first articulated, and it prides its leadership role in worldwide democratization processes. Although American democracy has proven itself to be responsive to "the people" through constitutional amendments and a proliferation of elections, increased levels of citizen dissatisfaction with government performance, apathy about the political process, and declining levels of political participation suggest that any over-confidence in American democracy is misplaced. Rather than viewing "democracy" simply as processes of government, the radical democrat broadens the term to encompass the political culture as a whole, and as such West suggests that American democracy is in a state of crisis that runs much deeper than citizen cynicism and apathy. He contends that, from its inception, American democracy has been predicated upon white supremacy and that there has always been a sharp divergence between democratic rhetoric and the practice of American democracy. Yet, although West condemns the dehumanization within current democratic practice, he points toward the future possibility of a democracy that actualizes aspirations for justice, freedom, and happiness. His call for a radical reconstruction of American democracy is not based on a revolutionary overthrow of liberal democracy, but rather on radicalization of the democratic tradition whereby the political principles of democratic practice are transformed to conform to the ideals of American democracy. He seeks to deepen American democracy and holds that African Americans' unique perspectives on the workings of democracy can contribute to this task.

West places the democratic imperative at the center of progressive politics and he seeks to reconcile the tension between what America is and what it aspires to be. Thus he condemns the class injustice, racial hatred, and rationalized selfishness prevalent in America, searching for ways to re-energize American democracy and thereby find liberation from these forces of oppression. His vision of radical democracy is open to new political languages and hitherto silenced voices, and attempts to unify a variety of struggles in order to transform society. He maintains that diverse groups, despite their differences, can find common cause in shared commitment to the extension of democracy. West is attentive to difference, but recognizes that there must be provision within identity politics for the solidarity of community as it is in community that one's vocabularies are developed and one finds empowerment. As such, it is within a context of solidarity that the self-determination of marginalized groups can exert real political significance. Not only is community identification a crucial aspect of self-identification, but the politics of liberation must be based on something more than disconnected discourses fighting internally and externally, as the over-exaltation of difference deprives the marginalized of any meaningful language. So while people have different needs and require liberation from specific circumstances, West seeks to unify these fragments into a liberatory coalition. He believes that values such as love have a sufficiently broad appeal to encourage a shift away from privatism toward concern with a common good.

West's understanding of love is closely tied to concepts of justice, liberation, and struggle, and these concepts enable him to transcend the vagueness of much "love" talk to use love to impact change. Given the omnipresence of "love" in contemporary society, he recognizes that if his appeal to love is to have any real meaning it must be supplemented by more specific proposals for change. However, his grounding of the elastic conception of love in the specificity of the struggle for liberation and social justice is fundamentally at odds with the spirit of civil religion. His expression of social Christianity's love ethic is unrelenting in terms of the *demands* it makes of citizens, calling them to ways of sacrifice by resisting the lure of market values, such as wealth accumulation, and thinking first of the needs of others. Yet Stephen Carter suggests that American culture increasingly prefers religion as something vague and without political significance. While most Americans retain some level of religious affiliation, this is often viewed as a hobby that offers inspiration and encouragement but which can easily be forgotten should it prove too demanding.[33] Thus the dilemma for West is that once concepts such as "struggle" and "commitment" are entered into the equation of spirituality it ceases to reflect society's dominant ethos of convenience and thus becomes less than inclusive. This in turn questions the degree to which people will be willing to struggle for the implementation of the love ethic in society. West recognizes that it is not always easy to love other people but that one must persevere with such challenges for the mutual benefit of all; but it is questionable whether people will continue to find the love ethic attractive when confronted by someone whom it is difficult to display this love toward.

The problem is that because West attempts to be faithful to both the civil faith heritage and a liberationist perspective, he is not completely true to either. On the one hand, his liberationist theological perspective and emphasis on struggle compromises his civil religious rhetoric, while, on the other, he does not ground his quest for liberation in as strong a programatic agenda as he might were he not trying to be inclusive in a civil faith sense. Although West's strong vision of love in action may provoke some people into action to secure the liberationist ideal, a vision alone is insufficient as those people still require channels and direction for that action if it is to be at all effective. West suggests that once people grasp the seriousness of the crisis engulfing America they will realize that there is little option but to adopt a love ethic and thereby restore a sense of community and secure a degree of liberation. However, West's own emphasis on the depth of polarization in America and the dominance of market values problematizes the extent to which change can occur. By his own account the hope for surmounting society's mean-spiritedness is dim, yet until recently his work has offered little in terms of a concrete agenda regarding how to surmount the crisis. In essence, most of what he offers by way of an agenda for change is the call to love each other. When I asked him in 1998 to outline some practical ways to build coalitions, he pointed to (a) the necessity of quality leadership and in particular someone who is charismatic enough to bring people together, and (b) willingness to be visionary and flexible.[34] While these are undoubtedly crucial to the process of alliance building, in and of themselves they are an insufficient basis for change; if alliance building is to be more than a utopian leap of faith, we need to know more about *how* we get to the point of dialogue. Although his call to love is not a sentimental conception of love, but rooted in struggle and commitment, lack of a strong programatic agenda must prompt the questioning of his liberatory vision itself – because how useful is a vision if it offers no directions concerning its realization? He fails to address the vicious circle that incivility rises when consensus breaks down, prompting oversimplification of issues, increased anger, and yet more incivility; it will take more than a call to love and an awareness of the need for strong and visionary leadership to break that cycle. As such, the very misunderstanding that he wishes to surmount makes it hard to build the trust needed for coalitions. Moreover, what hope is there that, once constructed, alliances can be sustained? The logic of coalitions is built on perceived self-interest and so a coalition can easily break down if it is not in one's interest to remain in it. West's response is that we need courageous leaders who will educate people to focus on long-term interests and not just short-term ones. But how can this education occur in a racist society? We must conclude that West needs to be more precise about the terms and conditions required for unity in the face of diversity in America.

One might conclude that West is strongest when descriptive rather than prescriptive, and that he is a provocateur whose strength lies in wrenching hearts and troubling the nation's conscience rather than strategizing. In this regard he says he is "more interested in Socratic probing of the public than pronouncing blueprints for the public."[35] As such, it could be argued that West has done his job in terms of offering an inspiring vision and that others could undertake the task of creating a programatic agenda. However, this is no real excuse, given that West constantly stresses his own role in grassroots political organizations that are committed to building change. He also repeatedly condemns the Left's current state of exhaustion and its vocabulary of decline rather than anticipation; like Rorty in *Achieving our Country*, West encourages the Left to propose political projects rather than be spectatorial and retrospective. But although he calls on Americans to build coalitions and urges the Left to devise specific strategies and programs, he offers insufficient practical strategic guidelines concerning how coalitions can be built, thus failing to do that which he urges others to do. This failure has deep implications for his politics. Without a concrete agenda of how democracy can be invigorated and how his liberatory vision can be fulfilled his work might be viewed as largely irrelevant to the task of social change, despite his avowed commitment to the goal of inspiring change in society. Part of the difficulty here is that West's love ethic does not easily translate into political policy because America has never really enacted such a normative framework. Thus, we would be mistaken to dismiss West's love ethic as irrelevant to the task of social change, because something may radically take place if this love ethic was truly enacted. As such, it is reasonable to demand that West tell us more about *how* to enact this love ethic, particularly given the dearth of precedents for it in American life that make it hard to visualize how the politics of conversion might work in practice.

We must conclude that either West's analysis of the crisis is too bleak or that his response to that crisis is inadequate in terms of strategy. If his analysis is seen as too apocalyptic, it could be argued that lack of a programatic agenda is not such a major shortcoming after all and that his love ethic as it now stands is an adequate guide to the task of surmounting polarization. However, if we accept his apocalyptic characterization of American democracy it follows that we should demand a sharper programatic agenda from him. It is the latter conclusion that is more compelling. West's analysis of crisis, his hope and desire for transformation, and the manner in which he intervenes in traditions such as Marxism and Christianity, reshaping them in pursuit of the liberatory goal, are powerful. The vision of a love ethic is compelling and inspiring, yet West is thin on solid guidelines as to how one can reach that ethic's goals. Therefore, for his work to have the political impact that can inspire realization of his redemptive vision he must amplify and augment his arguments. West is clearly less concerned with hypothetical coalitions than with building actual consensus in real situations. But avoidance of the issues of *how* alliances are to be built and *how* change can occur in a racist society begs the question of whether it is all just utopian dreaming.

We have seen in this chapter that in recent works West has started to articulate a programatic basis for his struggle to revive American democracy. Although this remains sketchy on detail (for instance, he still has not told us in concrete terms how to build a coalition), it is at least a step in the right direction, and we must welcome

West's attempt to follow through on his commitment to social and economic equality. But with this programatic agenda we do see further problems pertaining to the delicate balance between love and liberation and between the universal and the specific. For instance, as we saw above, many progressives are bothered by the fact that West has criticized feminism and are troubled that he seems to have moved from a concern with global capitalism to a narrow focus on what ails America. Both of these concerns are the inevitable results of moving from broad and vague theoretical notions of love and justice to specific policy proposals – people *will* be alienated. Thus it is unsurprising that West's recent works, particularly those co-authored with Hewlett and Unger, have proved so controversial in progressive circles. These works move beyond abstract arguments and try to apply and work through the practical implications of West's perspective. But when ambiguous catch-all ideas are made specific, the inevitable result is some degree of alienation, as, to put it crudely, it is impossible to please all people all of the time. Equally, it should be noted that if West issued a call today for a violent assault on global capitalism, it is "moderates" such as Bill Bradley who would be alienated. Therefore, it appears that the vision of a love ethic starts to crumble when it is applied and once the concrete political ideas underpinning the rhetoric of love are galvanized. In an age of polarization it is easy to regard West's inclusivity and coalition building as a good thing, and large numbers can agree with West in the abstract that we should love; but once it comes to a concrete agenda the contradictions open, posing serious problems for West's objective of expanding democracy. It is hard to see a way out of the circularity that West's political agenda needs to pursue concrete policies, and yet such concrete policies can undermine the inclusivity by alienating some potential supporters.

Conclusion

West is a perceptive critic who seeks to redefine "America" and struggle against the grain in order to expand democracy in America. Although he is more interested in probing the public than giving blueprints, some degree of application is necessary and in works such as *The War Against Parents* and *The Future of American Progressivism* we see prophetic pragmatism in practice. Specific policy proposals relating to parenting, social relations, and taxation are offered alongside his ideal of radical democracy in which people would be empowered to live lives of freedom and dignity. West's vision of radical democracy entails the restructuring of social, political, and cultural institutions, and the development of community bonds of mutual trust and respect. We have seen that in addition to challenging social structures that produce maldistribution of wealth and class inequalities, West highlights the role of moral and spiritual values in the social reconstruction of American life.

Throughout this book I have defended West against the charge that he has "sold out" by highlighting the fact that his work is consistent when he is read as a liberation theologian whose spirituality determines his politics. Here I am not making a judgment on whether certain commentators are correct to say that *Prophesy Deliverance* is a more appropriate response to present troubles than *The War Against Parents*. My point is that these commentators are mistaken to present West as having radically shifted the substance of his views from those he held in 1982 to those articulated in more recent works. However, these criticisms have to be heeded because they do point to a difficulty in West's work, although not one typically identified. This difficulty is that despite West's emphasis on contextualization and moving beyond the abstract, his own arguments start to crumble once he begins to apply them. At the level of the abstract principle of "love" it seems that there could be widespread support for building broad coalitions; but once practical policies are presented of what goals these coalitions should pursue, things begin to unravel. This is because divergent groups or individuals may share a concern with "justice," but can mean radically different things by that term. Thus West ends up in the bind that on the one hand he *needs* to present a programatic agenda if his work is going to have the desired effect of producing change, while on the other hand *articulating* such an agenda erodes his support base.

Conclusion: Creative Tensions

West's liberationist praxis is informed by a profoundly ethical impetus to restructure capitalist society along more egalitarian and democratic lines. He takes up a number of intellectual tools to analyze the functioning and impact of life-denying forces such as racism and economic injustice, and proclaims himself "a blues man in the world of ideas" because he seeks to creatively interweave various intellectual strands in order to help us live in "barbaric" times.[1] First, his moral vision and the normative values of democracy, love, and justice emanate from prophetic Christianity, and his Christianity prompts his attempt to restore deep ethics to the practice of politics (as opposed to the shallow moral rhetoric of the culture wars). Second, his critical perspective is situated within the tradition of the Left. He links his analysis of democracy to economic injustice, and so the Marxist critique of capitalism is crucial to this analysis. A third tool is the jazz-like qualities of pragmatism that emphasize the innovation and experimentalism so crucial to the project of reinventing American democracy. Fourth, he realizes that to effect change his critical discourse must have public accessibility and through his intellectual work he seeks to encourage people to organize politically. In an age of political apathy, the participatory element of democracy must be nurtured, and for democracy to work effectively people must become politically active and recognize that they are historical agents responsible for their own actions and the quality of their interaction with others. Part of his democratic project is thus the re-legitimization of the public sphere and the attempt to reconstruct publics in an age where the private is cast as sacred. He wants to restore to public life a serious moral discourse characterized by quality, integrity, and civility.

Alongside West's hybridity as professor, political activist, media celebrity, and preacher, is his ability to fuse traditions. He self-consciously attempts to integrate seemingly unrelated perspectives and ideas, admitting that his work constitutes a "perennial struggle between my African and American identities, my democratic socialist convictions, and my Christian sense of the profound tragedy and possible triumph in human life and history."[2] This struggle means that his work is not an "over-arching synthesis" but "an articulated assemblage of analytical outlooks."[3] Given that West blends so many seemingly diverse ideologies, his thought can be viewed at the very least as undisciplined eclecticism and even as incoherent, inconsistent, and incomprehensible. His work abounds with tensions, such as how his anti-foundationalist perspective fits with his invocation of the "foundationalism" of Marx. Moreover, he is obsessed with building alliances. The multicontextual nature of West's thought means that he addresses a diverse range of audiences, and so it is natural that he should desire some coming together between those audiences. In *The American Evasion of Philosophy* his desire is to unify people of goodwill to build an Emersonian culture of creative democracy, while more recently in *The War Against Parents* he seeks to unify citizens to be better parents. But inevitably this concern with alliance building and forging a middle path creates the opportunity for even more tensions, and the previous chapter considered the very practical tensions that have arisen from the fact that alongside his attempts to build black-Jewish racial healing he has endorsed a racial extremist like Louis Farrakhan.

It has been my contention that, when understood in the light of his prophetic Christianity, his politics is not as inconsistent as it might first appear. The road on which West is journeying is one of justice, democracy, and community, and has been determined by his liberationist Christianity. Throughout the multiplicity of political theories West embraces, his destination and commitment to the values of democracy and freedom remain unyielding. However, West realizes that he needs more than one vehicle to reach his destination. So, while he sometimes uses the vehicle of Marxism or ecologism, a change in terrain requires a vehicular change. Additionally, if one vehicle runs out of gas, he is more than happy to hitch a lift with another that happens to be going his way along the progressive road, be it liberalism, market socialism, feminism, or trade unionism. Crucially, however, and keeping with the metaphor, while the vehicle may change the destination remains the same. This provides some level of coherence to the diversity of political ideologies upon which he draws.

Locating this coherence does not mean we can simply forget about the tensions that exist, as some of the tensions have implications for West's project of liberation and radical democracy. For instance, West acknowledges that Marxism and Christianity clash in the realm of possibility. While Marxists believe that human betterment is possible, Christians suggest that fallen human nature curtails the possibility of betterment so that while evils such as racism can be alleviated, they cannot be eliminated. His balancing of the Marxist and Christian traditions leads him paradoxically to be skeptical about the possibility for change, yet not unhopeful. He believes that some change is possible and must be striven toward, but that change will be incomplete given the plurality of voices with different demands. A similar tension is found in his adoption of both pragmatism and Christianity. As a Christian, West emphasizes humanity's fall and points to ultimate salvation provided by God. This implies that history is already written. Yet he also affirms the pragmatic view of history as open-ended and transformable. Thus he appears to argue that while humans must take responsibility for their own actions and possess the power to transform their lives, ultimately their fate lies in the hands of God.[4] An awareness of misery and evil tempers his leanings towards progress and hope, and so his work oscillates between the possibility of human progress and the human impossibility of paradise. Thus, while his work encompasses despair about the present state of democracy that subjugates African Americans, he retains hope in the imaginative potential of democracy to secure black liberation.

West's liberatory enterprise is inherently problematic given the conflicting ideas within it. Most significant is the dialectic of hope and despair at the center of his thought, and his appropriation of both Rauschenbusch's idealism that points to a Christian-inspired vision of a better world and a Niebuhrian pessimism that points to the Christian emphasis on human nature as fallen. From Niebuhr he develops a pessimistic awareness of fallen human nature that is evident in his characterization of the crisis in democracy, while from Rauschenbusch he develops an optimistic liberatory vision that can be seen in his response to crisis through a moralizing love ethic. This pessimism–idealism tension at the center of West's thought is not entirely of his own making as the dialectical interplay of "imperfect products and transformative practice, of prevailing realities and negation, of human depravity and human dignity, of what is and the not-yet" is central to the Christian Gospel;[5] it is also a deep existential problem that is at the very heart of human existence. Hence the problem is not with West's theoretic failure to reconcile hope and despair, for the problem is one that any of us face – it is the problem of making sense of human existence.

Recognition of the realism–idealism relation offers an explanation of why West can be evasive in terms of specific agendas and neglectful of the degree to which the polarization he laments blocks the realization of his vision. He seeks to connect the dark reality of oppression with the hope and vision contained in emancipatory politics. While his tragic conception has deepened through time, he has to maintain hope because otherwise it would be futile to continue the struggle for liberation. He contends that this tension between realism and idealism is "creative"; not only is it an inescapable part of his radical democratic project, but this tension produces his notion of "audacious hope" and perseverance. In the same way that conflict cannot be removed within a radical democracy, so too would the removal of conflict in the form of theoretical tensions in his work be a form of false consensus. West's project requires both leftist politics and Christianity (and both the idealist and realist inclinations of the latter). Thus to remove the tensions within his thought would not only necessitate the silencing of one of his identities, but would also force him to abandon the inherent conflict within the attempt to force American democracy to live up to its own ideal. Despite the tensions, his work retains a large degree of value in terms of its strong and compelling vision of the way in which moral values can undergird the movement for social transformation, together with his attempt to provide an ethical basis to democracy.

Notes

Introduction

1 Kakutani, "Rage and Reason," p. B2.
2 West interview with Yancy, *African-American Philosophers* (1998), p. 47; "Audacious Democrats" (1997), p. 262.
3 West, *The War Against Parents*, p. 4.
4 Cited in Russell, *Black Genius and the American Experience*, p. 214.
5 West, *Jews and Blacks*, pp. 16–19; *The War Against Parents*, pp. 12–13.
6 *Race Matters* cover material.
7 West, "Beyond Multiculturalism and Eurocentrism," in *Prophetic Thought*, pp. 3–6.
8 West, "The Tragicomic and the Political in Christian Faith" (2002), p. 6.

Chapter 1   Reading West

1 Rauschenbusch, *A Theology for the Social Gospel*, p. 165.
2 West, "The Religious Foundations of the Thought of Martin Luther King, Jr." (1990), p. 129.
3 McGovern, *Liberation Theology and its Critics*, p. 148.
4 West, interview with author (1997).
5 West, *The Ethical Dimensions of Marxist Thought*, p. xxix.
6 West, interview with author (1997).
7 West, interview with author (1998).
8 Brown, *Reclaiming the Bible*, p. 10.
9 Kraemer, *The Theology of the Laity*, p. 184.
10 West, interview with author (1997).

11   Ibid.
12   West, "Whither Liberation Theology?" (1984), p. 57.

Chapter 2   Race and American Democracy

1   West, *Breaking Bread*, p. 33; *Keeping Faith*, p. x.
2   West, *The War Against Parents*, pp. 14–15.
3   West, Lesley College Speech (1996).
4   Ransby, "The Black Poor," p. 6.
5   West, "The Crisis in Black America," in *Prophetic Reflections*, p. 203.
6   West, "Nihilism in Black America" (1991), p. 224.
7   Goldberg, *Racial Subjects*, pp. 161–2.
8   Ransby, "The Black Poor," p. 6.
9   West, "A World of Ideas," in *Prophetic Reflections*, p. 108.
10   West, "Learning to Talk of Race" (1992), p. 24.
11   West, "Class Day Address" at Kennedy School of Government (1995); "The Moral Obligations of Living in a Democratic Society" (1999), p. 9.
12   West, *Jews and Blacks*, p. 164.
13   Ibid., pp. 252–5.
14   West, "Black Theology and Human Identity" (1999), p. 13.
15   West, "Black Politics, Black Leadership" interview (1993), p. 774.
16   West, interview with Brod (2002).
17   West, 1996 speech quoted in Russell, *Black Genius and the American Experience*, pp. 207–8.
18   West, *The Future of the Race*, p. 78; "Moral Obligations," p. 7.
19   West, interview with Hadnot (1998), p. 1J.
20   West, "Black Music and Youth," in *Prophetic Reflections*, p. 25.
21   West, "The Postmodern Crisis of Black Intellectuals" (1991), p. 695.
22   West, *Cornel West Reader*, p. xvii.
23   West, "On Afro-American Popular Music," in *Prophetic Fragments*, p. 186.
24   West, Barnes and Noble forum (1998).
25   West, "Charlie Parker" interview (1991), p. 63.
26   West, interview with Yancy, *African-American Philosophers* (1998), p. 36.
27   West, *Reader*, p. xvi.
28   Ibid., pp. xvi–xvii.
29   West, *Keeping Faith*, p. xv.
30   West, "Subversive Anger, Subversive Joy" interview (1991), p. 543.
31   West, "Beyond Eurocentrism and Multiculturalism" (1992–3), pp. S150–1.
32   West, *The Future of American Progressivism*, p. 93.
33   West, "The Tragicomic and the Political in Christian Faith" (2002), p. 9.
34   West, Sterling Brown symposium (1998), pp. 1073–4.
35   West, "A Grand Tradition of Struggle" (2000), p. 44.
36   West, "Charlie Parker" interview, p. 60.

37 West, *Keeping Faith*, pp. xii–xiii.
38 West, *Reader*, p. xvii.
39 West, *Breaking Bread*, p. 34.
40 West, "The Future of Pragmatic Thought," in *Prophetic Thought*, pp. 31–2.
41 West, *Breaking Bread*, p. 34.

Chapter 3   Jazz Philosophy: Westian Pragmatism

1 West, interview with Yancy, *African-American Philosophers* (1998), p. 33.
2 Ibid., p. 38.
3 West, "West of Righteous" interview (1994), p. 111.
4 Ibid.
5 West, *Prophesy Deliverance*, p. 24.
6 West, "Philosophy, Politics, and Power" (1983), p. 51.
7 West, *The American Evasion of Philosophy*, p. 44.
8 Ibid., p. 114.
9 Rorty, *Contingency, Irony, and Solidarity*, p. 7.
10 West, *American Evasion*, p. 5.
11 Ibid., p. 209.
12 West, "Theory, Pragmatisms, Politics" (1991), p. 22.
13 West, "Reply to Westbrook, Brodsky and Simpson" (1993), p. 46.
14 West, "Fredric Jameson's Marxist Hermeneutics" (1982–3), p. 196.
15 West, *American Evasion*, p. 5.
16 Ibid., p. 207.
17 Rorty, "Intellectuals in Politics," p. 489.
18 West, *American Evasion*, p. 206.
19 West, "The Politics of American Neo-Pragmatism" (1985), p. 267.
20 West, *American Evasion*, p. 228.
21 West, interview with author (1998).
22 West, *American Evasion*, p. 6.
23 Gooding-Williams, "Evading Narrative Myth," p. 523.
24 West, *American Evasion*, p. 223; *Prophesy Deliverance*, pp. 48–50.
25 West, *Prophesy Deliverance*, p. 15.
26 West, "Pragmatism and the Sense of the Tragic," in *Keeping Faith*, p. 111.
27 West, interview with author (1997).
28 West, St John's College speech (2001).
29 West, *American Evasion*, p. 233.

Chapter 4   "Prophetic" Christianity

1 West, "The Religious Foundations of the Thought of Martin Luther King, Jr." (1990), p. 116.

2 Clearly there are also strong differences between the two traditions besides the differing social contexts in which they emerged. For instance, liberation theologians tend to stress the need for revolution whereas Social Gospelers espouse socialist gradualism and make a more explicit attempt to "Christianize" the social order. For a comparison of the two traditions see Sanks, "Liberation Theology and the Social Gospel."

3 West, "Subversive Joy and Revolutionary Patience," in *Prophetic Fragments*, pp. 161–5.

4 West, "Religious Foundations," p. 117.

5 Ibid., p. 118.

6 West, *Jews and Blacks*, pp. 100–1.

7 Dyson, "Martin Luther King, Jr.," pp. 95–6.

8 Sturm, "Martin Luther King, Jr., as Democratic Socialist."

9 King, *Stride Toward Freedom*, pp. 91–2, 97–9.

10 Cone, *A Black Theology of Liberation*, p. xiv.

11 Ibid., p. 63.

12 Ibid., pp. 119–24.

13 Harris, "Practising Liberation in the Black Church," pp. 599–600.

14 Wilmore, "Black Theology at the Turn of the Century," in Hopkins (ed.), *Black Faith and Public Talk*, pp. 236–7.

15 West, "The Historicist Turn in the Philosophy of Religion" (1985), pp. 44–5.

16 Remarks made in address at the "Black Theology as Public Discourse" conference, April 1998. See also *Jews and Blacks*, pp. 21–2.

17 Wallis, *The Call to Conversion*, pp. 5, 8.

18 West, "Critical Theory and Christian Faith," in *Prophetic Fragments*, pp. 122–3.

19 West, *Prophetic Fragments*, p. x.

20 Ibid., p. ix.

21 West, "The Crisis in Black America," in *Prophetic Reflections*, p. 213; "Beyond Multiculturalism and Eurocentrism," in *Prophetic Thought*, pp. 23–4; *Cornel West Reader*, p. 355.

22 West, "The Tragicomic and the Political in Christian Faith" (2002), p. 6.

23 West, "Religion, Politics, Language" (1984), p. 366.

24 West, *Prophesy Deliverance*, p. 16.

25 West, "Spinning Visions" (1994), p. 12.

26 West, *Prophesy Deliverance*, p. 19.

27 Ibid., pp. 18–19.

28 West, *The American Evasion of Philosophy*, p. 229.

29 West, *Restoring Hope*, p. 96.

30 West, "Philosophy and the Funk of Life" (2001), p. 353.

31 West, "Subversive Joy and Revolutionary Patience," p. 162.

32 West, "A Philosophical View of Easter" (1980), p. 24.

33 West, "Subversive Anger, Subversive Joy" interview (1991), pp. 542–3.
34 West, "Present Socio-Political-Economic Movements" (1989), p. 75.
35 West, "On Black Fathering" (1996), pp. 54–5.
36 West, interview with author (1997).
37 Ibid.
38 West, "Conclusion" to symposium on *Ethical Dimensions* (1993), p. 59.
39 West, interview with author (1997).
40 West, "A Philosophical View of Easter," p. 23.
41 Yancy, "Religion and the Mirror of God," in *Cornel West*, p. 122.
42 Ibid., p. 117.
43 West, "Class and State Remain" (1984), p. 43; "Karl Who?" (1983), p. 148; "Christian Theological Mediocrity" (1984), p. 439; review of Rorty's *Philosophy and the Mirror of Nature* (1981–2), p. 185.
44 Dorrien, *Soul in Society*, p. 6.
45 Bennett, "Fitting the Liberation Theme into our Theological Agenda," p. 167.
46 Dorrien, *Reconstructing the Common Good*, p. 10.
47 Dorrien, *Soul in Society*, pp. 42–3.
48 Rauschenbusch, *Christianity and the Social Crisis*, p. 7.
49 West, *American Evasion*, p. 154.
50 Njeri, "Reaching Across the Divide," p. 14.

Chapter 5   Re-conceptualizing Marxism: West's Radicalism

1 West, *The Ethical Dimensions of Marxist Thought*, pp. xx, xxvi, xxvii.
2 West, "Neo-Aristotelianism, Liberalism and Socialism" (1986), p. 81.
3 West, *Prophesy Deliverance*, p. 111; *The Future of American Progressivism*, p. 29.
4 West, *Ethical Dimensions*, p. xxvii.
5 West, "Present Socio-Political-Economic Movements" (1989), p. 77.
6 West, "Neo-Aristotelianism," p. 89.
7 West, interview with author (1997).
8 West, "The Dilemma of the Black Intellectual" (1985), p. 115.
9 Macpherson, *Democratic Theory*, p. 173.
10 West, "CLS and a Liberal Critic" (1988), p. 770; "The Role of Law in Progressive Politics" (1990), pp. 469–70.
11 West, "On the Influence of Lukács," in *Prophetic Reflections*, p. 71; "Race and Social Theory" (1987), p. 80.
12 Rorty, *Achieving our Country*, p. 46.
13 West, "American Radicalism" interview (1995), pp. 28–9.
14 West, "Beyond Eurocentrism and Multiculturalism" interview (1992–3), p. S162.
15 West, *Prophesy Deliverance*, p. 111; *Future of American Progressivism*, p. 29.

16 West, interview in Yancy, *African-American Philosophers* (1998), p. 41.
17 Ibid.
18 West, "Rethinking Marxism" (1987), pp. 55–6.
19 West, "Beyond Multiculturalism and Eurocentrism," in *Prophetic Thought*, p. 17.
20 West, "Harrington's Socialist Vision" (1983), p. 485.
21 Cone cited in White, "Philosopher with a Mission", p. 60.
22 West, "Left Strategies" (1986), p. 41; "Black Theology and Marxist Thought" (1979), p. 559; "Charlie Parker" interview (1991), p. 62.
23 West, "The Prophetic Tradition in Afro-America," in *Prophetic Fragments*, p. 48.
24 West, *Prophesy Deliverance*, p. 119.
25 West, "Race and Social Theory," pp. 82–3.
26 West, "Left Strategies," pp. 42–3.
27 West, *American Evasion*, p. 234.
28 West, "Black Theology and Marxist Thought," p. 560; *Prophesy Deliverance*, pp. 116–17; "Religion and the Left" (1984); "Nihilism in Black America" (1991), p. 221.
29 Williams, *Problems in Materialism and Culture*, pp. 243–6.
30 West, *Breaking Bread*, p. 37.
31 West, "The Crisis in Black America," in *Prophetic Reflections*, p. 212.
32 West, "Religion and the Left," p. 14.
33 West, "Trying to Broaden the Framework" interview (1993), p. 65.
34 West, "Black Politics, Black Leadership" interview (1993), p. 774.
35 West, "Subversive Anger, Subversive Joy" interview (1991), p. 539; *Breaking Bread*, p. 10.
36 West, *Ethical Dimensions*, pp. xiii–xiv; "Conclusion" to symposium on *Ethical Dimensions* (1993), pp. 57–8; "Leaders to Meet an Intellectual Challenge" (1990), p. 37.

Chapter 6   The Multicontextual Public Intellectual

1 Boynton, "The New Intellectuals," p. 53.
2 Flacks, "Making History and Making Theory: Notes on How Intellectuals Seek Relevance," in Lemert (ed.), *Intellectuals and Politics*, p. 13.
3 Bérubé, "Public Academy," p. 75.
4 Bérubé, "Cultural Criticism and the Politics of Selling Out," p. 5.
5 Reed, "What are the Drums Saying, Booker?," p. 32.
6 Marable, "Black Intellectuals in Conflict," p. 39.
7 Bérubé "Public Academy," pp. 78–9.
8 White, "Philosopher With a Mission," p. 62.
9 Cross, "Cornel West Moves North"; Miller, "Gates Forges HU into Black Studies Mecca," p. 2.
10 Wieseltier, "All and Nothing at All," p. 31; Willis cited in Edwards, "Prophet Motive."

11 West, "On the Responsibility of Intellectuals" forum (1992), p. 8.
12 West "Subversive Anger, Subversive Joy" interview (1991), p. 538.
13 West, *The Future of the Race*, p. 71.
14 West, "The Historicist Turn in the Philosophy of Religion" (1985), p. 48.
15 West and hooks, *Breaking Bread*, pp. 23–4.
16 West, "Afterword" to symposium on pragmatism (1990), pp. 1919–20.
17 West, interview with author (1997).
18 West, *Breaking Bread*, p. 29.
19 West, "On Christian Intellectuals" (1984), p. 77.
20 West, "American Radicalism" interview (1995), p. 34.
21 Reed, "What are the Drums Saying, Booker?," p. 35.
22 James, *Transcending the Talented Tenth*, p. 9.
23 West, "The Dilemma of the Black Intellectual" (1985), pp. 122–3.
24 Ibid., p. 117.
25 James, *Transcending the Talented Tenth*, p. 160.
26 West, "The Dilemma of the Black Intellectual," p. 122; *Prophesy Deliverance*, p. 24.
27 West, "The Dilemma of the Black Intellectual," p. 109.
28 Gordon, "Black Intellectuals and Academic Activism," p. 197.
29 West, "On the Responsibility of Intellectuals," p. 5.
30 Cone cited in White, "Philosopher with a Mission," p. 62.
31 Goldberg, *Racial Subjects*, p. 118.
32 West, "Philosophy and the Funk of Life" (2001), p. 354.
33 Ibid., p. 361.
34 West, interview with author (1998).
35 On the "venom" see Monroe, "Cornel Matters," pp. 46–8. Of course this hostility does not emanate entirely from the academy, as the death threats made against him have come from extremist white supremacists.
36 West, cited in Tanenhaus, "The Ivy League's Angry Star," p. 158.
37 West, interview with Smiley (April 2002); Belluck and Steinberg, "Defector Indignant at President of Harvard."
38 West, interview with Smiley (Jan. 2002).
39 West, interview with author (1997).
40 Schuck, "On *Race Matters*," p. 85.
41 West and Moyers, "Subversive Anger" interview, p. 538.

Chapter 7 The Politics of "Conversion": West's "Love Ethic"

1 West, foreword to Abu-Jamal, *Death Blossoms* (1997), p. xii.
2 West, "Nihilism in Black America" (1991), pp. 224–6.
3 West, "In Praise of the Combative Spirit" interview (1996), p. 73.
4 Bellah and Hammond, *Varieties of Civil Religion*, pp. 189–91.
5 West, *Cornel West Reader*, p. 355.

6 West, *Restoring Hope*, pp. 191–3.
7 Brown, *Speaking of Christianity*, pp. 54–9; *Spirituality and Liberation*, pp. 67–72.
8 West, "Nihilism in Black America," p. 223; interview with Stephanson (1988), p. 276.
9 West, "Nihilism in Black America," p. 224.
10 Ibid., pp. 224–5.
11 Yancy, "Critical Thinking May Improve Black Lives."
12 Goldberg, *Racial Subjects*, p. 125.
13 Giroux, *Fugitive Cultures*, p. 43.
14 Dyson, *Race Rules*, pp. 136–7.
15 Steinberg, *Turning Back*, pp. 130–2.
16 Asante, *The Afrocentric Idea*, pp. 5–7.
17 Hadjor, *Another America*, p. 154.
18 Goldberg, *Racial Subjects*, p. 125; Dyson, *Race Rules*, p. 137.
19 West, "Nihilism in Black America," p. 223.
20 West, "Afterword," in Lubiano (ed.), *The House that Race Built*, p. 302.
21 West, "Philosophy and the Funk of Life" (2001), p. 358.
22 West, "Philosophical Faith in Action" interview (1999), p. 50.
23 West, "Left Strategies" (1986), pp. 47–9; "We Socialists," in *Prophetic Reflections*, pp. 240–1.
24 Dyson, *Race Rules*, p. 157.
25 Winant, *Racial Conditions*, p. xiii.
26 West, "West of Righteous" interview (1994), p. 104.
27 West, "Black Politics, Black Leadership" interview (1993), p. 777.
28 West, "Diverse New World" (1992), p. 328.
29 West, foreword to Brettschneider, *The Narrow Bridge* (1996), p. xi.
30 West, Lesley College Speech (1996).
31 Elshtain, *Democracy on Trial*, pp. 30–3.
32 West, "American Radicalism" interview (1995), p. 35.
33 Ackerman, *Social Justice in the Liberal State*, pp. 10–12.
34 West, "Symposium on the Renaissance of Pragmatism" (1990), p. 1925; "Diverse New World," p. 331.
35 West, "Race and Social Justice in America" (1994), p. 39.
36 Mouffe, *Dimensions of Radical Democracy*, p. 12.
37 Mouffe, "Democracy, Power and the Political," in Benhabib (ed.), *Democracy and Difference*, p. 254.
38 West, "Malcolm X and Black Rage" (1992), p. 57.

Chapter 8   Achieving Democracy: Applying the Love Ethic

1 Benhabib, *Critique, Norm, and Utopia*, p. 226.
2 Alves, "Christian Realism," p. 175.
3 Dorrien, "Communitarianism," p. 378.

4 West, "Spinning Visions" (1994), p. 13.
5 Brown, *Speaking of Christianity*, pp. 69–70.
6 West, "Walking the Tightrope" (1997), p. 414.
7 West, interview with author (1998).
8 West, "Walking the Tightrope," p. 413; epilogue to *Jews and Blacks*.
9 West, "Prophetic Alternatives" interview (2000), pp. 270–1.
10 West, *Jews and Blacks*, p. 191.
11 Ibid., p. 212; "Reconstructing the American Left" (1984), p. 14.
12 West, "Black–Jewish Dialogue" (1989), p. 96.
13 Reed, "Black Politics Gone Haywire," pp. 20–2.
14 West, interview with author (1998).
15 Cohen, "Has Cornel West Read His Own Book?"
16 West, "NAACP" (1994), p. A21.
17 West, *The War Against Parents*, pp. 51, 53.
18 Ibid., pp. 88–9.
19 West, Barnes and Noble forum (1998), p. 1.
20 Ibid., p. 5.
21 West, *War Against Parents*, pp. 34, 161.
22 West, "Caring for Crib Lizards" (2001).
23 West, *War Against Parents*, p. 241.
24 Ibid., p. 166.
25 Young, "Cornel West on Gender and Family," in Yancy (ed.), *Cornel West*, p. 186.
26 West, *War Against Parents*, pp. 240–1.
27 Ibid., p. 257.
28 Ibid., pp. 220–5, 263.
29 Elshtain, "A Call to Civil Society."
30 West, *Race Matters*, p. 12.
31 West, *The Future of American Progressivism*, p. 24.
32 Ibid., pp. 62, 70.
33 Carter, *The Culture of Disbelief*, chapter 2.
34 West, interview with author (1998).
35 West, "Philosophy and the Funk of Life" (2001), p. 361.

Conclusion: Creative Tensions

1 West, *Cornel West Reader*, p. xv.
2 West, *The Ethical Dimensions of Marxist Thought*, p. xxviii.
3 West, "Pragmatism and the Sense of the Tragic," in *Keeping Faith*, p. 104.
4 West, *Prophesy Deliverance*, p. 18; *The American Evasion of Philosophy*, p. 233.
5 West, *Prophesy Deliverance*, p. 17.

Bibliography

The following abbreviations are used in the bibliography:

AE   *The American Evasion of Philosophy*
BB   *Breaking Bread*
CWR   *The Cornel West Reader*
ED   *The Ethical Dimensions of Marxist Thought*
KF   *Keeping Faith*
PD   *Prophesy Deliverance*
PF   *Prophetic Fragments*
PR   *Prophetic Reflections*
PT   *Prophetic Thought in Postmodern Times*
RM   *Race Matters*
WP   *The War Against Parents*

Works by West

Books

Prophesy Deliverance! An Afro-American Revolutionary Christianity, Philadelphia: Westminster, 1982.
Theology in the Americas: Detroit 2 Conference Papers (ed. with Caridad Guidote and Margaret Coakley), Maryknoll: Orbis, 1982.
Post-Analytic Philosophy (ed. with John Rajchman), New York: Columbia University Press, 1985.
Prophetic Fragments: Illuminations of the Crisis in American Religion and Culture, Grand Rapids: Eerdmans, 1988.
The American Evasion of Philosophy: A Genealogy of Pragmatism, Madison: University of Wisconsin Press, 1989.

Out There: Marginalization and Contemporary Culture (ed. with Russell Ferguson, Martha Gever, and Trinh Minh-ha), Cambridge: MIT Press, 1990.

The Ethical Dimensions of Marxist Thought, New York: Monthly Review Press, 1991.

Breaking Bread: Insurgent Black Intellectual Life (with bell hooks), Boston: South End, 1991.

Prophetic Thought in Postmodern Times, vol. 1 of *Beyond Eurocentrism and Multiculturalism*, Monroe: Common Courage, 1993.

Prophetic Reflections: Notes on Race and Class in America, vol. 2 of *Beyond Eurocentrism and Multiculturalism*, Monroe: Common Courage, 1993.

Keeping Faith: Philosophy and Race in America, New York: Routledge, 1993.

Race Matters, Boston: Beacon, 1993; rev. edn with epilogue, New York: Vintage, 1994.

James Snead: White Screens, Black Images (ed. with Colin McCabe), New York: Routledge, 1994.

Jews and Blacks: Let the Healing Begin (with Michael Lerner), New York: Putnam, 1995; rev. edn with epilogue subtitled *A Dialogue on Race, Religion, and Culture in America*, New York: Plume-Penguin, 1996.

The Future of the Race (with Henry Louis Gates Jr), New York: Knopf, 1996.

Struggles in the Promised Land: Toward a History of Black–Jewish Relations in the United States (ed. with Jack Salzman), Oxford: Oxford University Press, 1997.

Restoring Hope: Conversations on the Future of Black America (ed. by Kelvin Shawn Sealey), Boston: Beacon, 1997.

The War Against Parents: What We Can Do For America's Beleaguered Moms and Dads (with Sylvia Ann Hewlett), Boston: Houghton Mifflin, 1998.

The Future of American Progressivism: An Initiative for Political and Economic Reform (with Roberto Mangabeira Unger), Boston: Beacon, 1998.

The Courage to Hope: From Black Suffering to Human Redemption (ed. with Quinton Hosford Dixie), Boston: Beacon, 1999.

The Cornel West Reader, New York: Basic Civitas, 1999.

The African-American Century: How Black Americans Have Shaped Our Country (with Henry Louis Gates Jr), New York: Free Press, 2000.

Articles, Chapters, and Forewords

"Philosophy and the Afro-American Experience," *Philosophical Forum*, 9, 2–3 (1977–8), pp. 117–48.

"Black Theology and Marxist Thought," in Gayraud Wilmore and James Cone (eds), *Black Theology: A Documentary History, 1966–79*, Maryknoll: Orbis, 1979.

Rev. of *God Within Process*, by Eulalio Baltazar, *Religious Studies Review*, 5, 1 (1979), p. 69.

"Introduction" and "Schleiermacher's Hermeneutics and the Myth of the Given," *Union Seminary Quarterly Review*, 34, 2 (1979), pp. 67–70, 71–84.

"A Philosophical View of Easter," *Dialog*, 19, 1 (1980), pp. 21–4. Repr. *PF*, pp. 260–6 and *CWR*, pp. 415–20.

Rev. of *A Synoptic Approach to the Riddle of Existence* by Arthur Munk, and *Theology in a New Key*, by Robert McAfee Brown, *Religious Studies Review*, 6, 2 (1980), pp. 129, 132–3.

Rev. of *The Grammar of Faith*, by Paul Holmer, *Union Seminary Quarterly Review*, 35, 3–4 (1980), pp. 279–85. Repr. *PF*, pp. 226–35.

"Socialism, Religion and the Black Struggle," *Religious Socialism*, 4, 4 (1980), pp. 5–8.

"Black Theology and Socialist Thought," *The Witness*, 63, 4 (1980), pp. 16–19.

"Set the Record Straight," *Commonweal*, 107 (Nov. 21, 1980), p. 656.

"The Black Struggle, the Black Church and the U.S. Progressive Movement," in Linda Unger and Kathleen Schultz (eds), *Seeds of a People's Church: Challenge and Promise from the Underside of History*, Detroit: Seeds of a People's Church, 1981.

"The North American Blacks," in Sergio Torres and John Eagleson (eds), *The Challenge of Basic Christian Communities*, Maryknoll: Orbis, 1981.

Rev. of *The Moral Meaning of Revolution*, by Jon Gunnemann, *Journal of Religion*, 61, 2 (1981), pp. 218–19. Repr. *PF*, pp. 84–5.

"Nietzsche's Prefiguration of Postmodern American Philosophy," *Boundary 2*, 9, 3 (1981), pp. 241–69. Repr. *CWR*, pp. 188–210.

Rev. of *Philosophy and the Mirror of Nature*, by Richard Rorty, *Union Seminary Quarterly Review*, 37, 1–2 (1981–2), pp. 179–85.

Rev. of *The Eclipse of Biblical Narrative*, by Hans Frei, *Notre Dame English Journal*, 14, 2 (1982), pp. 151–4. Repr. *PF*, pp. 236–9.

"Lukács: A Reassessment," *Minnesota Review*, 19 (1982), pp. 86–102. Repr. *KF*, pp. 143–64.

"Fredric Jameson's Marxist Hermeneutics," *Boundary 2*, 11, 1–2 (1982–3), pp. 177–200. Repr. *KF*, pp. 165–95 and *CWR*, pp. 231–50.

"Philosophy, Politics, and Power: An Afro-American Perspective," in Leonard Harris (ed.), *Philosophy Born of Struggle*, Dubuque: Kendall Hunt, 1983.

"Black Theology of Liberation as Critique of Capitalist Civilization," *Journal of the Interdenominational Theological Center*, 10, 2 (1983), pp. 67–83.

"Karl Who?" rev. of *A Matter of Hope*, by Nicholas Lash, *Christianity and Crisis*, 43 (April 18, 1983), pp. 148–9. Repr. *PF*, pp. 222–5.

"The Black Church and Socialist Politics," *Third World Socialists*, 1, 2 (1983), pp. 16–19. Repr. *PF*, pp. 67–73.

"Martin Luther as Prophet," *Christianity and Crisis*, 43 (Nov. 28, 1983), pp. 444–5. Repr. *PF*, pp. 257–9.

"Harrington's Socialist Vision," rev. of *The Politics at God's Funeral*, by Michael Harrington, *Christianity and Crisis*, 43 (Dec. 12, 1983), pp. 484–6. Repr. *PF*, pp. 25–9.

"The Paradox of the Afro-American Rebellion," in Sohnya Sayers (ed.),

The Sixties Without Apology, Minneapolis: University of Minnesota Press, 1984. Repr. *KF*, pp. 271–91.

"Winter in Afro-America," *Christianity and Crisis*, 44 (Jan. 23, 1984), pp. 516–17. Repr. *PF*, pp. 35–7.

"Whither Liberation Theology?," rev. of *Faith and Ideologies*, by Juan Luis Segundo, *Commonweal*, 111 (Jan. 27, 1984), pp. 53–7. Repr. *PF*, pp. 197–202 and *CWR*, pp. 393–8.

"Class and State Remain," symposium on *Religion in the Secular City*, by Harvey Cox, *Christianity and Crisis*, 44 (Feb. 20, 1984), pp. 43–4. Repr. *PF*, pp. 212–15.

"Religious Book Week," *Commonweal*, 111 (Feb. 24, 1984), p. 24.

"Red/Green Smokescreen," *Democratic Left*, 12, 2 (1984), p. 15.

"Are We Consuming Us?," rev. of *The Culture of Consumption*, by Richard Wightman Fox and T. J. Jackson Lears, *Christianity and Crisis*, 44 (March 5, 1984), pp. 66–70. Repr. *PF*, pp. 188–92.

"On Christian Intellectuals," *Christianity and Crisis*, 44 (March 19, 1984), pp. 77–8. Repr. *PF*, pp. 271–2.

"Winter in the West," *Religion and Intellectual Life*, 1, 3 (1984), pp. 86–91. Repr. *PF*, pp. 246–9 and *CWR*, pp. 421–4.

"On black–Jewish Relations," *Christianity and Crisis*, 44 (April 30, 1984), pp. 149–50. Repr. *PF*, pp. 171–3.

"In Memory of Marvin Gaye," *Christianity and Crisis*, 44 (June 11, 1984), pp. 220–1. Repr. *PF*, pp. 174–6 and *CWR*, pp. 471–3.

"Religion and the Left: An Introduction," *Monthly Review*, 36, 3 (1984), pp. 9–19. Repr. *PF*, pp. 13–21 and *CWR*, pp. 372–9.

"Black Politics Will Never Be the Same," *Christianity and Crisis*, 44 (Aug. 13, 1984), pp. 302–5.

"Religion, Politics, Language," *Christianity and Crisis*, 44 (Oct. 15, 1984), pp. 366–7. Repr. *PF*, pp. 22–4.

"Christian Theological Mediocrity," *Christianity and Crisis*, 44 (Nov. 26, 1984), pp. 439–40. Repr. *PF*, pp. 195–6.

Rev. of *The Promise of Narrative Theology*, by George Stroup, *Union Seminary Quarterly Review*, 39, 1–2 (1984–5), pp. 141–6. Repr. *PF*, pp. 240–5.

"Reconstructing the American Left: The Challenge of Jesse Jackson," *Social Text*, 11 (1984–5), pp. 3–19.

"The Historicist Turn in Philosophy of Religion," in Leroy Rouner (ed.), *Knowing Religiously*, Notre Dame: University of Notre Dame Press, 1985. Repr. *KF*, pp. 119–34 and *CWR*, pp. 360–71.

"The Politics of American Neo-Pragmatism," in West and Rajchman (eds), *Post-Analytic Philosophy*, New York: Columbia University Press, 1985.

Rev. of *In Memory of Her*, by Elisabeth Schüssler Fiorenza, *Religious Studies Review*, 11, 1 (1985), pp. 1–4. Repr. *PF*, pp. 250–6 and *CWR*, pp. 380–6.

"Realign the Left," *Democratic Left*, 13, 1 (1985), pp. 4–5.

"Not-Always-Perfidious Albion," *Christianity and Crisis*, 45 (Feb. 4, 1985), pp. 5–6. Repr. *PF*, pp. 159–60.

"Violence in America," *Christianity and Crisis*, 45 (April 1, 1985), pp. 104–5. Repr. *PF*, pp. 157–8.

"Sex and Suicide," *Christianity and Crisis*, 45 (June 10, 1985), pp. 222–3. Repr. *PF*, pp. 155–6.

"Contemporary Afro-American Social Thought," *Over Here*, 5, 2 (1985), pp. 11–16. Repr. *PF*, pp. 50–4.

"The Dilemma of the Black Intellectual," *Cultural Critique*, 1 (1985), pp. 109–24. Repr. *KF*, pp. 67–85 and *CWR*, pp. 302–15.

"Faith, Struggle, and Reality," rev. of *Communities of Resistance and Solidarity*, by Sharon Welch, *Christianity and Crisis*, 45 (Oct. 14, 1985), pp. 400–2. Repr. *PF*, pp. 207–11.

"On Visiting South Africa," *Christianity and Crisis*, 45 (Oct. 28, 1985), pp. 412–14. Repr. *PF*, pp. 109–11.

"The British and the Rational" (with Anders Stephanson), rev. of *In the Tracks of Historical Materialism*, by Perry Anderson, *Socialist Review*, 84 (1985), pp. 123–9.

Rev. of *Communists in Harlem During the Depression*, by Mark Naison, *Monthly Review*, 37, 7 (1985), pp. 48–51. Repr. *PF*, pp. 90–3.

Preface to Franz Hinkelammert, *The Ideological Weapons of Death*, Maryknoll: Orbis, 1986. Repr. *PF*, pp. 203–6 and *CWR*, pp. 398–400.

"Neo-Aristotelianism, Liberalism and Socialism: A Christian Perspective," in Bruce Grelle and David Krueger (eds), *Christianity and Capitalism: Perspectives on Religion, Liberalism and the Economy*, Chicago: Center for the Scientific Study of Religion, 1986. Repr. *PF*, pp. 124–36.

"The New Populism: A Black Socialist Christian Critique," in Harry Boyte and Frank Reissman (eds), *The New Populism: The Politics of Empowerment*, Philadelphia: Temple University Press, 1986. Repr. *PF*, pp. 30–4.

Rev. of *Marx's Social Critique of Culture*, by Louis Dupré, *Journal of Religion*, 66, 1 (1986), pp. 85–6. Repr. *PF*, pp. 166–7.

"Left Strategies: A View From Afro-America," *Socialist Review*, 86 (1986), pp. 41–9. Repr. *PF*, pp. 137–43.

"Dispensing with Metaphysics in Religious Thought," *Religion and Intellectual Life* 3, 3 (1986), pp. 53–6. Repr. *PF*, pp. 267–70.

"Unmasking the Black Conservatives," *Christian Century*, 103 (July 16, 1986), pp. 644–8. Repr. *PF*, pp. 55–63.

Rev. of *Religion*, by Leszek Kolakowski, *Old Westbury Review*, 2 (1986), pp. 147–53. Repr. *PF*, pp. 216–21 and *CWR*, pp. 387–92.

"Metaphysics," in Mircea Eliada (ed.), *The Encyclopedia of Religion*, New York: Macmillan, 1987, pp. 485–7.

"Race and Social Theory: Towards a Genealogical Materialist Analysis," in Mike Davis et al., *The Year Left 2*, London: Verso, 1987. Repr. *KF*, pp. 251–70 and *CWR*, pp. 251–63.

Rev. of *Rethinking Marxism*, by Stephen Resnick and Richard Wolff, *Monthly Review*, 38, 2 (1987), pp. 52–6. Repr. *PR*, pp. 177–82.

"Demystifying the New Black Conservatism," *Praxis International*, 7, 2 (1987), pp. 143–51. Repr. *RM*, pp. 73–90.

"Between Dewey and Gramsci: Unger's Emancipatory Experimentalism," *Northwestern University Law Review*, 81, 4 (1987), pp. 941–51.

"Minority Discourse and the Pitfalls of Canon Formation," *Yale Journal of Criticism*, 1, 1 (1987), pp. 193–201. Repr. *KF*, pp. 33–44.

"Marxist Theory and the Specificity of Afro-American Oppression," in Cary Nelson and Lawrence Grossberg (eds), *Marxism and the Interpretation of Culture*, Urbana: University of Illinois Press, 1988.

"Prophetic Theology," in Willis Logan (ed.), *The Kairos Covenant: Standing with South African Christians*, New York: Friendship Press, 1988. Repr. *PF*, pp. 223–33.

"Reassessing the Critical Legal Studies Movement," *Loyola Law Review*, 34 (1988), pp. 265–75. Repr. *KF*, pp. 195–206.

"The Crisis of Black Leadership," *Z Magazine*, 1, 2 (1988), pp. 22–5. Repr. *RM*, pp. 53–70.

"CLS and a Liberal Critic," *Yale Law Journal*, 97, 5 (1988), pp. 757–71. Repr. *KF*, pp. 207–26.

"Black Radicalism and the Marxist Tradition," rev. of *Black Marxism*, by Cedric Robinson, *Monthly Review*, 40, 4 (1988), pp. 51–6. Repr. *PF*, pp. 169–75.

"Present Socio-Political-Economic Movements for Change," in Simon Maimela and Dwight Hopkins (eds), *We Are One Voice: Black Theology in the USA and South Africa*, Braamfontein: Skotaville, 1989. Repr. *PF*, pp. 183–97.

"Black Culture and Postmodernism," in Barbara Kruger and Phil Mariani (eds), *Remaking History*, Seattle: Bay Press, 1989.

Symposium on *Ethics After Babel*, by Jeffrey Stout, *Theology Today*, 46, 1 (1989), pp. 66–8. Repr. *PT*, pp. 175–8.

"Imperatives of Seminary Reform," *Christianity and Crisis*, 49 (April 3, 1989), pp. 101–4.

"Black–Jewish Dialogue: Beyond Rootless Universalism and Ethnic Chauvinism," *Tikkun*, 4, 4 (1989), pp. 95–7.

"Critical Reflections on Art," *Artforum*, 28 (1989), pp. 120–1. Repr. *PF*, pp. 19–24 and *CWR*, pp. 443–6.

"Hegel, Hermeneutics, Politics: A Reply to Charles Taylor," *Cardozo Law Review*, 10, 5–6 (1989), pp. 871–5. Repr. *KF*, pp. 227–34.

"The New Cultural Politics of Difference," in Ferguson, Gever, Minh-ha and West (eds), *Out There*, Cambridge: MIT Press, 1990. Repr. *KF*, pp. 3–32 and *CWR*, pp. 119–39.

"The Religious Foundations of the Thought of Martin Luther King, Jr.," in Peter Albert and Ronald Hoffman (eds), *We Shall Overcome: Martin Luther King, Jr., and the Black Freedom Struggle*, New York: Pantheon, 1990. Repr. in abbreviated form *PF*, pp. 3–12 and *CWR*, pp. 425–34.

"The Role of Law in Progressive Politics," in David Kairys (ed.), *The Politics of Law: A Progressive Critique*, rev. edn, New York: Pantheon, 1990. Repr. *KF*, pp. 235–50 and *CWR*, pp. 269–77.

"Michael Harrington, Socialist," rev. of *Socialism: Past and Future*, by

Michael Harrington, *The Nation*, 250 (Jan. 8, 1990), pp. 59–61. Repr. *PT*, pp. 181–8 and *CWR*, pp. 348–53.

"The Limits of Neopragmatism," *Southern California Law Review*, 63, 1 (1990), pp. 1747–51. Repr. *KF*, pp. 135–42 and *CWR*, pp. 183–7.

"Why I Write for *Tikkun*," *Tikkun*, 5, 5 (1990), pp. 59–60.

"Leaders to Meet an Intellectual Challenge," *The Progressive*, 54, 11 (1990), p. 37.

"Postmodern Culture," in Emory Elliott (ed.), *The Columbia History of the American Novel*, New York: Columbia University Press, 1991. Repr. *PF*, pp. 37–43.

"The Postmodern Crisis of Black Intellectuals," in Lawrence Grossberg et al. (eds), *Cultural Studies*, New York: Routledge, 1991. Repr. *PT*, pp. 87–118.

"Theory, Pragmatisms, and Politics," in Jonathan Arac and Barbara Johnson (eds), *Consequences of Theory*, Baltimore, Johns Hopkins University Press, 1991. Repr. *KF*, pp. 89–106.

"Decentring Europe," *Critical Quarterly*, 33, 1 (1991), pp. 1–19. Repr. *PT*, pp. 119–42.

"Nihilism in Black America," *Dissent*, 38, 2 (1991), pp. 221–6. Repr. *RM*, pp. 17–31.

"The Struggle for America's Soul," rev. of *The Good Society*, by Robert Bellah et al., *New York Times Book Review* (Sept. 15, 1991), p. 13. Repr. *PR*, pp. 199–202.

"Diverse New World," in Paul Berman (ed.), *Debating P.C.: The Controversy over Political Correctness on College Campuses*, New York: Laurel, 1992.

Introduction to William Pipes, *Say Amen, Brother!*, New York: Wayne State University Press, 1992. Repr. *PR*, pp. 31–6.

"Malcolm X and Black Rage," in Joe Wood (ed.), *Malcolm X in Our Own Image*, New York: St Martin's, 1992. Repr. *RM*, pp. 135–51.

"Philosophy and the Urban Underclass," in Bill Lawson (ed.), *The Under-class Question*, Philadelphia: Temple University Press, 1992. Repr. *PT*, pp. 143–58.

"Black Leadership and the Pitfalls of Racial Reasoning," in Toni Morrison (ed.), *Race-ing Justice, En-gendering Power*, New York: Pantheon, 1992. Repr. *RM*, pp. 35–49.

"Black Anti-Semitism and the Rhetoric of Resentment," *Tikkun*, 7, 1 (1992), pp. 15–16.

"Equality and Identity," *American Prospect*, 9 (1992), pp. 119–22. Repr. *RM*, pp. 93–9.

"The Legacy of Raymond Williams," *Social Text*, 30, 3 (1992), pp. 6–8. Repr. *PT*, pp. 171–4.

"Identity: A Matter of Life and Death," *October*, 61 (1992), pp. 20–3. Repr. *PR*, pp. 163–8.

"Learning to Talk of Race," *New York Times Magazine* (Aug. 2, 1992), pp. 24–6. Repr. *RM*, pp. 3–13.

"Beyond Eurocentrism and Multiculturalism," *Modern Philology*, 90 (1992–3), pp. S142–51.

Foreword to Anna Deavere Smith, *Fires in the Mirror: Crown Heights, Brooklyn, and Other Identities*, New York: Doubleday, 1993. Repr. *CWR*, pp. 485–8.

"Horace Pippin's Challenge to Art Criticism," in Judith Stein (ed.), *I Tell My Heart: The Art of Horace Pippin*, Philadelphia: Pennsylvania Academy of the Fine Arts, 1993. Repr. *KF*, pp. 55–66 and *CWR*, pp. 447–55.

Preface to Peter McLaren and Peter Leonard (eds), *Paulo Freire: A Critical Encounter*, New York: Routledge, 1993. Repr. *PT*, pp. 179–80.

"Blacks vs. Jews: The Traps of Tribalism," *Emerge*, 4, 3 (1993), pp. 42–4. Repr. *RM*, pp. 103–16.

"A Reply to Westbrook, Brodsky and Simpson," *Praxis International*, 13, 1 (1993), pp. 46–9.

"Conclusion: The Author Responds" (symposium on *ED*), *Monthly Review*, 45, 2 (1993), pp. 57–60.

Preface to Jim Wallis, *The Soul of Politics*, New York: New Press, 1994.

"The Left After Forty Years," *Dissent*, 41, 1 (1994), pp. 15–16.

"The 80s: Market Culture Run Amok," *Newsweek* (Jan. 3, 1994), pp. 48–9. Repr. *CWR*, pp. 344–7.

"America's Three-Fold Crisis," *Tikkun*, 9, 2 (1994), pp. 41–4.

"Race and Social Justice in America," *Liberal Education*, 80, 3 (1994), pp. 32–9.

"NAACP: Renewing an Old Tradition," *Washington Post* (July 9, 1994), p. A21.

"Spinning Visions," *The Other Side*, 30, 4 (1994), pp. 12–13.

Preface to Jackie Robinson, *I Never Had it Made*, Hopewell: Ecco, 1995. Repr. *CWR*, pp. 536–8.

Preface to Kimberlé Crenshaw et al., *Critical Race Theory: The Key Writings that Formed the Movement*, New York: New Press, 1995.

"Young Blacks, Jews Welcome Chance to Recreate Alliance" (with Michael Lerner), *Northern California Jewish Bulletin* (May 26, 1995). <http://www.elibrary.com>

"Affirmative Action in Context," in George Curry (ed.), *The Affirmative Action Debate*, Reading: Addison-Wesley, 1996. Repr. *CWR*, pp. 495–8.

"On Black Fathering," in Andre Willis (ed.), *Faith of Our Fathers: African-American Men Reflect on Fatherhood*, New York: Dutton, 1996.

Foreword to Marla Brettschneider, *The Narrow Bridge: Jewish Views on Multiculturalism*, New Brunswick: Rutgers University Press, 1996.

Foreword to Jewelle Taylor Gibbs, *Race and Justice: Rodney King and O.J. Simpson in a House Divided*, San Francisco: Jossey-Bass, 1996.

"The Million Man March," with critical response by Michael Walzer, *Dissent*, 43, 1 (1996), p. 97–101.

"Populism and the 1996 Elections," *Tikkun*, 11, 5 (1996), pp. 35–7.

Foreword to Mumia Abu-Jamal, *Death Blossoms: Reflections from a Prisoner of Conscience*, Farmingham: Plough, 1997.

Foreword to Julie Mertus et al., *The Suitcase: Refugee Voices from Bosnia and Croatia*, Berkeley: University of California Press, 1997.

"The Ignoble Paradox of Western Modernity," foreword to Madeleine Burnside, *Spirits of the Passage*, New York: Simon and Schuster, 1997. Repr. *CWR*, pp. 51–4.

Afterword to Wahneema Lubiano (ed.), *The House that Race Built: Black Americans, U.S. Terrain*, New York: Pantheon, 1997.

"Walking the Tightrope: Some Personal Reflections on Blacks and Jews," in Salzman and West, *Struggles in the Promised Land*, Oxford: Oxford University Press, 1997. Repr. *CWR*, pp. 530–5.

Foreword to Herbert Daughtry, *No Monopoly on Suffering: Blacks and Jews in Crown Heights (and Elsewhere)*, Trenton: Africa World Press, 1997.

"Audacious Democrats," in Steven Fraser and Joshua Freeman (eds), *Audacious Democracy: Labor, Intellectuals, and the Social Reconstruction of America*, Boston: Houghton Mifflin, 1997.

Preface to LeAlan Jones and Lloyd Newman, *Our America: Life and Death on the South Side of Chicago*, New York: Washington Square Press, 1997.

"Ethnicity," in Lloyd Boston (ed.), *Men of Color: Fashion, History, Fundamentals*, New York: Artisan, 1998.

Foreword to Richard Newman, *Go Down, Moses: A Celebration of the African American Spiritual*, New York: Clarkson Potter, 1998. Repr. *CWR*, pp. 463–70.

"Progressive Politics and What Lies Ahead" (with Roberto Unger), *The Nation*, 267 (Nov. 23, 1998), pp. 11–15.

Foreword to Marjorie Garber and Rebecca Walkowitz (eds), *One Nation Under God? Religion and American Culture*, New York: Routledge, 1999.

"The Moral Obligations of Living in a Democratic Society," in David Batstone and Eduardo Mendieta (eds), *The Good Citizen*, New York: Routledge, 1999.

"Black Theology and Human Identity," in Dwight Hopkins (ed.), *Black Faith and Public Talk: Critical Essays on James H. Cone's* Black Theology and Black Power, Maryknoll: Orbis, 1999.

Foreword to Drew Leder, *The Soul Knows No Bars: Inmates Reflect on Life, Death, and Hope*, Lanham: Rowman and Littlefield, 2000.

"A Grand Tradition of Struggle," *English Journal*, 89, 6 (2000), pp. 39–44.

Introduction to Malcolm Jarvis with Paul Nichols, *The Other Malcolm – "Shorty" Jarvis*, Jefferson: McFarland, 2001.

"Afterword: Philosophy and the Funk of Life," in George Yancy (ed.), *Cornel West: A Critical Reader*, Oxford: Blackwell, 2001.

"Caring for Crib Lizards" (with Sylvia Ann Hewlett), *The American Prospect*, 12, 1 (2001).
<http://www.prospect.org/print/V12/1/hewlett-s.html>

"Democracy Matters in Race Matters," preface to 2001 edition of *Race Matters*.

Preface to Arvind Sharma (ed.), *Religion in a Secular City: Essays in Honor of Harvey Cox*, Harrisburg: Trinity Press, 2001.

"The Tragicomic and the Political in Christian Faith," preface to twentieth anniversary edition of *Prophesy Deliverance* (2002).

Dialogues and Interviews

Interview with Anders Stephanson in Andrew Ross (ed.), *Universal Abandon: The Politics of Postmodernism*, Minneapolis: University of Minnesota Press, 1988. Repr. *PR*, pp. 81–102 and *CWR*, pp. 278–93.

"Symposium on the Renaissance of Pragmatism in American Legal Thought," with Hilary Putnam and Richard Rorty, *Southern California Law Review*, 63, 6 (1990), pp. 1911–28.

"Subversive Anger, Subversive Joy," with Bill Moyers, *Cross Currents*, 41, 4 (1991), pp. 538–46. Repr. *PF*, pp. 103–12 and *CWR*, pp. 294–301.

"The Political Aftermath of the Gulf War," roundtable with Todd Gitlin, Sheila Tobias, Letty Cottin, and Paul Wellstone, *Tikkun*, 6, 3 (1991), pp. 28–32, 94–5.

"Charlie Parker Didn't Give a Damn," with Marilyn Berlin Snell, *New Perspectives Quarterly*, 8, 3 (1991), pp. 60–3. Repr. *PR*, pp. 9–17.

"Doubting Thomas," roundtable with Kimberlé Crenshaw, Harold Cruse, Peter Gabel, Catherine MacKinnon, and Gary Peller, *Tikkun*, 6, 5 (1991), pp. 23–30.

"A Conversation Between Cornel West and Michael Lerner," in Jack Salzman et al., *Bridges and Boundaries: African Americans and American Jews*, New York: Jewish Museum, 1992.

"Domestic Social Policy After the L.A. Uprising," roundtable with Cynthia Hamilton, Michael Katz, Mickey Kaus, Eric Mann, Lawrence Mead, and Jim Sleeper, *Tikkun*, 7, 4 (1992), pp. 39–44, 74–5.

"Beyond Eurocentrism and Multiculturalism," with Bill Brown, *Modern Philology*, 90 (1992–3), pp. S151–66.

"On the Responsibility of Intellectuals," roundtable with Margaret Burnham, Henry Louis Gates Jr, bell hooks, Glenn Loury, Eugene Rivers, and Anthony Appiah, *Boston Review*, 18, 1 (1993).
<http://www.polisci.mit.edu/bostonreview/BR18.1/responsibility.html>

"Trying to Broaden the Framework: Cornel West Seeks Answers in Black and White," with Dan Wasserman and Mark Feeney, *Boston Globe* (May 16, 1993), p. 65.

"Meeting Race Relations Head-On," *USA Today* (June 22, 1993), p. A11.

"Black Politics, Black Leadership: An Interview with Cornel West," *Christian Century*, 110 (Aug. 11, 1993), pp. 774–7.

"On Architecture?," with Milton Curry and Darell Fields, *Appendx*, 2 (1994).
<http://www.gsd.harvard.edu/~appendx/issue2/west/index.htm>

"West of Righteous," with Anders Stephanson, *Artforum*, 32, 6 (1994), pp. 66–71, 104, 111.

"A Conversation with Cornel West," Sheldon Hackney, *Humanities*, 15, 2 (1994), pp. 4–7.

"Affirmative Reaction: A Conversation with Cornel West on Talent, Tradition, and the Crisis of the Black Male," Henry Louis Gates Jr, *Transition*, 68 (1995), pp. 173–86.

"American Radicalism," with Peter Osborne, *Radical Philosophy*, 71 (1995), pp. 27–38.

"A Conversation with Cornel West," Itabari Njeri, *Los Angeles Times Magazine* (Oct. 22, 1995), pp. 17–20.

"After O.J. and the Farrakhan-led Million Man March: Is Healing Possible? A Dialogue Between Michael Lerner and Cornel West," *Tikkun*, 10, 6 (1995), pp. 12–20.

"Cornel West: In Praise of the Combative Spirit," with Audrey Edwards, *Heart and Soul* (Jan. 31, 1996), p. 73.

"Cornel West Talking About Race Matters," with Kuumba Ferrouillet Kazi, *The Black Collegian*, 24, 1 (1996), pp. 24–35.

"Our Next Race Question: The Uneasiness Between Blacks and Latinos," colloquy with Jorge Klor de Alva and Earl Shorris, *Harper's*, 292, 4 (1996), pp. 55–63. Repr. *CWR*, pp. 499–513.

"How do we Solve Our Leadership Crisis?," with Henry Louis Gates Jr, *Essence*, 27, 2 (1996), pp. 42–4.

"Cornel West on Heterosexism and Transformation," with Vitka Eisen and Mary Kenyatta, *Harvard Educational Review*, 66, 2 (1996), pp. 356–67. Repr. *CWR*, pp. 401–14.

"I'm Ofay, You're Ofay: A Conversation with Noel Ignatiev and William 'Upski' Wimsatt," *Transition*, 73 (1997), pp. 176–98.

Interview with John Nichols, *The Progressive*, 61, 1 (1997), pp. 26–9.

Interview with author, Harvard University, June 11, 1997.

"Black–Brown Relations: Are Alliances Possible?," with Jorge Klor de Alva and Ronald Wakabayashi, *Social Justice*, 24, 2 (1997), pp. 65–83.

"Cornel West," in George Yancy, *African-American Philosophers: 17 Conversations*, New York: Routledge, 1998. Repr. *CWR*, pp. 19–33.

Interview with Henry Louis Gates Jr, *Frontline: The Two Nations of Black America*, Public Broadcasting System (Feb. 13, 1998).
<http://www.pbs.org/wgbh/pages/frontline/shows/race/interviews/west.html>

Interview with author, Cambridge, April 13, 1998.

"Reweaving Webs of Caring," with Bob Kolasky, *IntellectualCapital.com* (May 7, 1998).
<http://www.intellectualcapital.com/issues/98/0507/icinterview.asp>

Barnes and Noble online forum (May 11, 1998).
<http://www.aalbc.com/authors/cornelwestchattext.htm>

"Can These Two Mobilize Parents?," with Stefanie Weiss, *NEA Today*, 17, 1 (1998), p. 58.

"A Symposium on the Life and Work of Sterling Brown," with Chet Lasell, Eleanor Holmes Norton, Paula Giddings, Sterling Stuckey, and Wahneema Lubiano, *Callaloo*, 21, 4 (1998), pp. 1038–74.

"Cornel West Interview," with Ira Hadnot, *Dallas Morning News* (Oct. 11, 1998), p. 1J.

"Philosophical Faith in Action," *Harvard Review of Philosophy*, 7 (1999), pp. 45–55.

"Prophetic Alternatives: A Conversation with Cornel West," in Manning Marable, *Dispatches from the Ivory Tower*, New York: Columbia University Press, 2000.

Interview with Brian Lamb, *Booknotes*, C-SPAN (Feb. 20, 2000).

Interview with author, Cambridge, Feb. 29, 2000.

Interview with Paula Gordon and Bill Russell, *The Paula Gordon Show*, WGUN, Atlanta (Dec. 6, 2000).
    <http://www.paulagordon.com/shows/west/>

"Sketches of a Scholar," with Jessica Green, *Bet.com* (Dec. 31, 2001).
    <http://www.bet.com/articles/0,,c1gb1288–1948,00.html>

Interview with Tavis Smiley, *The Tavis Smiley Show*, National Public Radio (Jan. 7, 2002).
    <http://www.npr.org/programs/tavis/features/2002/jan/020107.west.html>.

Interview with Bill O'Reilly, *The O'Reilly Factor*, Fox News (Jan. 10, 2002).
    <http://www.foxnews.com/story/0,2933,42681,00.html>

Interview with Connie Brod, *In-Depth*, C-SPAN (Jan. 6, 2002).

Interview with Tavis Smiley, *The Tavis Smiley Show*, National Public Radio (April 15, 2002).
    <http://www.npr.org/ramfiles/tavis/20020415.tavis.01.ram>

Lectures

"Commencement Day Address," Wesleyan University, May 30, 1993.
    <http://www.humanity.org/voices/commencements/speeches/index.php?page=west_at_wesleyan>

"On Architecture," Graduate School of Design at Harvard University, 1994.
    <http://www.gsd.harvard.edu/~appendx/issue2/west/index1.htm>

"Class Day Address," Kennedy School of Government at Harvard University, June 7, 1995.
    <http://ksgwww.harvard.edu/~ksgpress/doc3.htm>

"Diversity Day Keynote Speech," Lesley College, Oct. 1996.
    <http://www.lesley.edu/journals/jppp/1/jp3ii2.html>

"The Personal is Political" (with Carol Gilligan), plenary address at Public Education Network Annual Conference, Washington, Nov. 9, 1997.
    <http://www.publiceducation.org/97annual/page-25.htm>

Address at the Black Theology as Public Discourse conference, University of Chicago, April 3, 1998. Video-recording available from C-SPAN.

"America's Night Side," International Press Institute World Congress, Boston, May 2, 2000.
    <http://www.freemedia.at/Boston%20Congress%20Report/boston30.htm>

"Shadow Speech," Shadow Conventions 2000: A Citizens' Intervention in American Politics, Los Angeles, Aug. 13, 2000.
    <http://www.shadowconventions.com/speeches/westspeech.htm>

"Cornel West's Opening Remarks," Coalition of Essential Schools Fall Forum 2000, Providence.
<http://www.essentialschools.org/fforum/2000/speeches/west_00.html>
"Commencement Address," St John's College, Santa Fe, May 20, 2001.
<http://www.sjcsf.edu/cornelwest.htm>

Commentary on West

Allen, Anita, rev. *KF, Ethics*, 105 (1995), pp. 954–5.
Allen, Harry and Barboza, Craig, "Word Up (lift)," *USA Weekend Magazine* (Nov. 18, 2001).
<http://www.usaweekend.com/01_issues/011118/011118music.html>
Allen, Norm, "The Crisis of the Black Religious Intellectual," *Free Inquiry*, 14, 3 (1994), pp. 9–10.
Alston, Kal, "Drum Majors for Justice: Black Public Intellectuals in Contemporary America," *Centennial Review*, 42, 2 (1998), pp. 199–216.
Amin, Samir, "Historical and Ethical Materialism," *Monthly Review*, 45, 2 (1993), pp. 44–56.
Anderson, Jervis, "The Public Intellectual," *New Yorker*, 69 (Jan. 17, 1994), pp. 39–48.
Anderson, Victor, *Beyond Ontological Blackness: An Essay on African American Religious and Cultural Criticism*, New York: Continuum, 1995.
——, "The Wrestle of Christ and Culture in Pragmatic Public Theology," *American Journal of Theology and Philosophy*, 19, 2 (1998), pp. 135–50.
Appiah, Kwame Anthony, "A Prophetic Pragmatism," *The Nation*, 250 (April 9, 1990), pp. 496–8.
Asante, Molefi Kete, *The Afrocentric Idea*, Philadelphia: Temple University Press, 1998.
Bancroft, Nancy, rev. *ED, Journal of Religion*, 72, 4 (1992), pp. 618–19.
Banks, William, *Black Intellectuals: Race and Responsibility in American Life*, New York: Norton, 1996.
Belluck, Pam and Steinberg, Jacques, "Defector Indignant at President of Harvard," *New York Times* (April 16, 2002).
Bernstein, Richard, "The Resurgence of Pragmatism," *Social Research*, 59, 4 (1992), pp. 813–40.
Bérubé, Michael, "Public Academy," *New Yorker*, 70 (Jan. 9, 1995), pp. 73–80.
Beuttler, Bill, "Black, White, and Crimson," *Boston Magazine* (March 2002).
<http://cm.bostonmagazine.com/ArticleDisplay.php?id=70>
Bewaji, J. A. I., rev. *KF, Philosophy of the Social Sciences*, 27, 2 (1997), pp. 212–18.
Bhabha, Homi, "Black and White and Read all Over," *Artforum*, 34, 2 (1995), pp. 16–18.

Booth, Newell, rev. *PD*, *Journal of the American Academy of Religion*, 52, 2 (1984), p. 385.

Bowie, Guillermo, "Ethics and the Indigenization of Marxist Thought," *Monthly Review*, 34, 2 (1993), pp. 37–43.

Bowie, Tanara, rev. *RM*, *St. Petersburg Times* (May 30, 1991), p. 6D.

Bowman, Jim, "A Conference on Racism," *Commonweal*, 121 (Feb. 25, 1994), pp. 6–8.

Boynton, Robert, "The New Intellectuals," *Atlantic Monthly*, 275, 3 (1995), pp. 53–70.

Brick, Howard, rev. *AE*, *Journal of American History*, 79, 2 (1992), p. 687.

Brodsky, Garry, "West's Evasion of Pragmatism," *Praxis International*, 13, 1 (1993), pp. 14–31.

Byerman, Keith, "Hip-Hop Spirituality," *College Literature*, 22, 2 (1995), pp. 134–42.

Calmore, John, "Critical Race Theory, Archie Shepp and Fire Music: Securing an Authentic Intellectual Life in a Multicultural World," *Southern California Law Review*, 65, 5 (1992), pp. 2202–6.

Carruthers, Jacob, "The Fragmented Prophesy and Hybrid Philosophy of Cornel West," in *Intellectual Warfare*, Chicago: Third World Press, 1999.

Cascardi, Anthony, rev. *AE*, *Philosophy and Literature*, 14, 2 (1990), pp. 413–15.

Clark, Kendall, "Criticizing Cornel," *Monkeyfist.com* (Jan. 14, 2002). <http://monkeyfist.com/articles/805>

Cohen, Richard, "Has Cornel West Read His Own Book?," *Washington Post* (June 14, 1994), p. A21.

Coleman, Will, "Cornel West," in Donald Musser and Joseph Price (eds), *A New Handbook of Christian Theologians*, Nashville: Abingdon, 1996.

Collins, Patricia Hill, rev. *BB*, *Signs*, 20, 1 (1994), pp. 176–9.

Copeland, Shawn, rev. *PD*, *Cross Currents*, 33, 1 (1983), pp. 67–71.

Cose, Ellis, "A Prophet With Attitude," *Newsweek* (June 7, 1993), p. 71.

Cotkin, George, "Truth or Consequences," *Reviews in American History*, 18, 4 (1990), pp. 519–24.

Coughlin, Ellen, "Cornel West Matters: The Celebrity Philosopher," *Chronicle of Higher Education*, 39 (Sept. 22, 1993), pp. A8–10.

Cross, Theodore, "Cornel West Moves North," *Journal of Blacks in Higher Education*, 2 (1993).

Davis, Thulani, "Spinning Race at Harvard: The Business Behind the Gates–West Power Play," *Village Voice* (Jan. 16, 2002). <http://www.villagevoice.com/issues/0203/davis.php>

Day, Sherri, "A Professor Who Can Rap the Rap," *New York Times* (May 12, 2001), p. B11.

Dean, William, *The Religious Critic in American Culture*, Albany: SUNY Press, 1994.

DeGenova, Nick, "Gangster Rap and Nihilism in Black America: Some Questions of Life and Death," *Social Text*, 43 (1995), pp. 89–132.

Delaney, Paul, "An Optimist Despite the Evidence," *New York Times Book Review* (May 16, 1993), p. 11.

Delbanco, Andrew, "The Decline of Discourse?," *New York Times Book Review* (April 16, 1995), p. 9.

Doak, Mary, "Cornel West's Challenge to the Catholic Evasion of Black Theology," *Theological Studies*, 63, 1 (2002), pp. 87–106.

Donovan, Rickard, "Cornel West's New Pragmatism," *Cross Currents*, 41, 1 (1991), pp. 98–106.

Dreher, Rod, "Top-Dollar Prof: Bucks Over Blackboards," *National Review* (Jan. 11, 2002). <http://www.nationalreview.com/dreher/dreher011102.shtml>

Dyson, Michael Eric, rev. *PF*, *Theology Today*, 45, 4 (1989), pp. 451–3.

——, *Race Rules: Navigating the Color Line*, New York: Vintage, 1997.

Early, Gerald, "Black Like Them," *New York Times Book Review* (April 24, 1996), pp. 7–8.

——, "The Public Rebuke of a Public Intellectual," *St. Louis Post-Dispatch* (Jan. 13, 2002), p. B3.

Edwards, Brent, "Prophet Motive: The Backlash Against Cornel West," *Feed Magazine* (May 1995). <http://www.feedmag.com/95.05edwards.html>

Elder, Rob, "Prisoner of Hope," *inFlux* (June 1998). <http://influx.uoregon.edu/1998/west/index.html>

Evans, James, "Emergence of Cornel West," *Christianity and Crisis*, 43 (May 16, 1983), pp. 194–6.

Feiden, Douglas, "Whites and Jews Unwelcome as Chavis Summit Convenes," *Forward* (June 16, 1995). <http://www.elibrary.com>

Foster, John Bellamy, "Introduction" to symposium on *ED*, *Monthly Review*, 45, 2 (1993), pp. 8–16.

García, Ismael, rev. *PD*, *Journal of Religion*, 64, 4 (1985), pp. 558–9.

Garey, Anita, rev. *WP*, *Washington Monthly*, 30, 7–8 (1998), pp. 38–40.

Giroux, Henry, "In Living Color: Black, Bruised and Read All Over," in *Channel Surfing: Race Talk and the Destruction of Today's Youth*, Basingstoke: Macmillan, 1997.

Givhan, Robin, "Cornel West, Cloaked in Street Smarts," *Washington Post* (Jan. 25, 2002), p. C2.

Goldberg, David Theo, *Racial Subjects: Writing on Race in America*, New York: Routledge, 1997.

Goodheart, Eugene, "Common Ground," *CLIO*, 23, 1 (1993), pp. 93–6.

Gooding-Williams, Robert, "Evading Narrative Myth, Evading Prophetic Pragmatism," *Massachusetts Review*, 32 (1991–2), pp. 517–41.

——, Rev. *KF*, *Philosophical Review*, 104, 4 (1995), pp. 601–3.

Gordon, Lewis, rev. *RM*, *Political Affairs*, 73, 2 (1994), pp. 34–7.

——, "Black Intellectuals and Academic Activism: Cornel West's 'Dilemmas of the Black Intellectual'," in *Her Majesty's Other Children*, Lanham: Rowman and Littlefield, 1997.

Gray, Herman, "African-American Political Desire and the Seductions of Contemporary Politics," *Cultural Studies*, 7, 3 (1993), pp. 364–73.

Gray, Katti, "Dancing Between Scholarship and Celebrity," *Newsday* (April 22, 2002), p. B2.

Grelle, Bruce, "Christian Political Ethics and Western Marxism," *Journal of Religious Ethics*, 15, 3 (1987), pp. 173–98.

Griffin, David Ray, Beardslee, William, and Holland, Joe, *Varieties of Postmodern Theology*, Albany: SUNY Press, 1989.

Hacker, Andrew, "Diversity and its Dangers," *New York Review of Books*, 40 (Oct. 7, 1993), pp. 21–5.

——, "Goodbye to Affirmative Action?," *New York Review of Books*, 43 (July 11, 1996), pp. 21–9.

Hanchard, Michael, "Cultural Politics and Black Public Intellectuals," *Social Text*, 48 (1996), pp. 95–108.

Hart, William, "Cornel West: Between Rorty's Rock and Hauerwas's Hard Place," *American Journal of Theology and Philosophy*, 19, 2 (1998), pp. 151–72.

Hoffman, Jean, rev. *PD*, *Journal of Ecumenical Studies*, 22, 4 (1985), pp. 805–6.

Holloway, Jonathan Scott, "The Black Intellectual and the 'Crisis Canon' in the Twentieth Century," *Black Scholar*, 31, 1 (2001), pp. 2–13.

Horowitz, David, "Cornel West: No Light in his Attic," *Salon* (Oct. 11, 1999). <http://www.salon.com/news/col/horo/1999/10/11/cornel/index.html>

Hutchinson, Earl Ofari, "Big Babies at Harvard," *Salon* (Jan. 5, 2002). <http://www.salon.com/news/feature/2002/01/05/harvard.html>

Jacoby, Russell, "Pragmatists and Politics," *Dissent*, 37, 3 (1990), pp. 403–5.

Jaggar, Alison, "Moral Justification, Philosophy, and Critical Social Theory," *Monthly Review*, 45, 2 (1993), pp. 17–27.

James, Joy, *Transcending the Talented Tenth: Black Leaders and American Intellectuals*, New York: Routledge, 1997.

Jennings, James, "Re-examining Race Relations in the United States," *Journal of American Ethnic History*, 15, 1 (1995), pp. 56–60.

Johnson, Clarence Sholé, "Cornel West as Existentialist and Pragmatist," in Lewis Gordon (ed.), *Existence in Black: An Anthology of Black Existential Philosophy*, New York: Routledge, 1996.

——, "Cornel West, African American Critical Thought, and the Quest for Social Justice," *Journal of Social Philosophy*, 32, 4 (2001), pp. 547–72.

Johnson, Diane, "My Blue Heaven," *New York Review of Books*, 45 (July 16, 1998), pp. 15–19.

Joseph, Peniel, "In the Post Civil Rights Era," *New Politics*, 5, 4 (1996), pp. 52–4.

Just, Richard, "Go West: A Princetonian Defense of Princeton's New Hire," *The American Prospect* (April 25, 2002). <http://www.prospect.org/webfeatures/2002/04/just-r-04-25.html>

Kakutani, Michiko, "Rage and Reason in the Crisis of Black America," *New York Times* (April 27, 1993), p. B2.

Keller, Catherine and Colombo, J. A., "Two North American Christianities," *Religious Studies Review*, 18, 2 (1992), pp. 103–10.

Kelley, Norman, "Notes on the Niggerati," *New Politics*, 5, 4 (1996), pp. 55–9.

Kilson, Martin, "Wilentz, West, and Black Intellectuals: A Reply," *Dissent*, 43, 1 (1996), pp. 93–4.

King, Richard, rev. *KF, Journal of American Studies*, 29, 1 (1995), pp. 126–7.

Leive, Cynthia, "Parent Power," *Newsday* (May 31, 1998), p. B13.

Leo, John, "Carping in Harvard Yard," *U.S. News and World Report* (Jan. 21, 2002), p. 53.

Lerner, Michael, "The Attack on Cornel West: Racism and Media Cynicism," *Tikkun*, 10, 2 (1995), p. 7.

Lipsitz, George, "Swing Low, Sweet Cadillac: White Supremacy, Antiblack Racism, and the New Historicism," *American Literary History*, 7, 4 (1995), pp. 700–25.

Little, Danielle, "Does Truth Depend Upon the Audience to whom one is Speaking?," *QBR*, 6, 5 (1999), pp. 18–19.

Livingston, Lawrence, "Church Must Address how Race Matters," *Philadelphia Tribune*, (Jan. 28, 1994), p. 1D.

Lott, Eric, "Cornel West in the Hour of Chaos: Culture and Politics in *Race Matters*," *Social Text*, 40 (1994), pp. 39–50.

Loury, Glenn, "Preaching to the Converted," in *One by One from the Inside Out: Essays on Race and Responsibility in America*, New York: Free Press, 1995.

Lyne, John, "The Culture of Inquiry," *Quarterly Journal of Speech*, 76, 2 (1990), pp. 192–209.

McBride, Dwight, "Transdisciplinary Intellectual Practice: Cornel West and the Rhetoric of Race Transcending," *Harvard BlackLetter Law Journal*, 11 (1994), pp. 155–68.

McCabe, J. P., "Social Critics of Color and Normative Approaches to Democracy: Commonalities and Contrasts on Human Development," *Polity*, 29, 2 (1996), pp. 221–45.

McCann, Dennis, "There's Nobody Here But Us Post-Marxists," *Thought*, 62 (1987), pp. 5–12.

McCarraher, Eugene, "Missing: The Vision Thing," *Commonweal*, 127 (May 19, 2000), pp. 25–7.

McCrummen, Stephanie, " A Stormy Exit from Harvard: West's Departure Raises Concerns," *Newsday* (April 27, 2002), p. A38.

McGary, Howard, *Race and Social Justice*, Oxford: Blackwell, 1999.

McLaren, Peter and Dantley, Michael, "Leadership and a Critical Pedagogy of Race: Cornel West, Stuart Hall, and the Prophetic Tradition," *Journal of Negro Education*, 59, 1 (1990), pp. 29–44.

McPhail, Mark Lawrence, "Dessentializing Difference: Transformative Visions in Contemporary Black Thought," *Howard Journal of Communications*, 13, 1 (2002), pp. 77–95.

McWhorter, John, "Bad Rap: Cornel West's Theatrics Reinforce Racist

Stereotypes," *Opinion Journal* (April 20, 2002).
<http://www.opinionjournal.com/extra1/?id=105001956>

Mailloux, Steven (ed.), *Rhetoric, Sophistry, Pragmatism*, Cambridge: Cambridge University Press, 1995.

Marable, Manning, "Black Intellectuals in Conflict," *New Politics*, 5, 3 (1995), pp. 35–40.

Martin, Waldo, "Respect: Whither the Public Intellectual and the Recent Saga of Cornel West," *Tikkun*, 17, 2 (2002), pp. 68–70.

Michael, John, *Anxious Intellects: Academic Professionals, Public Intellectuals, and Enlightenment Values*, Durham: Duke University Press, 2000.

Miller, D. W., "In the Race for the White House, Does Race Matter? Why Harvard's Cornel West Couldn't Save Bill Bradley's Campaign," *Chronicle of Higher Education*, 46 (March 24, 2000), pp. A21–2.

Miller, Richard, "Religion and the American Pubic Intellectual," *Journal of Religious Ethics*, 25, 2 (1997), pp. 369–92.

Miller, Yauw, "Gates Forges HU into Black Studies Mecca," *Bay State Banner* (May 12, 1994). <http://www.elibrary.com>

Milligan, Jeffrey Ayala, "The Idolatry of Multicultural Education: A Prophetic Pragmatic Alternative?," *Multicultural Education*, 6, 3 (1999), pp. 2–5.

Mills, David, "The West Alternative," *Washington Post* (Aug. 8, 1993), p. W14.

Minerbrook, Scott, "A Meeting at the Crossroads," *Emerge*, 6, 7 (1995).

Minow, Martha, "Cornel West Delivers," *Reconstruction*, 1, 2 (1990), pp. 56–62.

Monroe, Sylvester, "Cornel Matters," *Emerge*, 7, 10 (1996), pp. 40–8.

More, Mabogo, rev. *ED*, *South African Journal of Philosophy*, 11, 4 (1992), pp. 115–17.

Morkovsky, Mary Christine, "Philosophies of Liberation," *Laval Théologique et Philosophique*, 54, 3 (1998), pp. 483–90.

Morris, Walter, "West Maligns Black Conservatives," *Christian Century*, 103 (Oct. 8, 1986), pp. 863–4.

Murray, Robert, "Philosophy and Interracial Dialogue," *Philosophical Forum*, 32, 2 (2001), pp. 107–24.

Napier, Winston, "Theocratic Hegemony and the Formation of Cornel West's Prophetic Pragmatism in *The American Evasion of Philosophy*," *Literature and Psychology*, 46, 3 (2000), pp. 1–13.

Negrey, Cynthia, rev. *WP*, *Sociological Focus*, 32, 1 (1999), pp. 115–17.

Neuhaus, Richard John, "The Postmodern Muddle of Cornel West," *First Things*, 56, 10 (1995), pp. 9–10.

Njeri, Itabari, "Reaching Across the Divide," *Los Angeles Times Magazine* (Oct. 22, 1995), pp. 14–15.

Ochs, Peter, "The Sentiment of Pragmatism: From the Pragmatic Maxim to a Pragmatic Faith," *The Monist*, 75, 4 (1992), pp. 551–67.

Oldfield, J. R., "The Fire This Time," *Patterns of Prejudice*, 29, 1 (1995), pp. 85–9.

Painter, Nell Irvin, "A Different Sense of Time," *The Nation*, 262 (May 6, 1996), pp. 38–43.

Paris, Peter, "Neglected Resources in Scholarship," *Religion and American Culture*, 7, 1 (1997), pp. 20–5.

Peters, Cynthia, rev. *WP*, *Z Magazine*, 12, 6 (1999), pp. 58–60.

Peterson, Karen, "Two Parents Work to Write Wrongs," *USA Today* (April 13, 1998), p. 6D.

Pinsker, Sanford, "What's Love, and Candor, Got to do with it?," *Virginia Quarterly Review*, 70, 1 (1994), pp. 174–81.

——, "The Black Intellectuals' Common Fate and Uncommon Problems," *Virginia Quarterly Review*, 70, 2 (1994), pp. 220–38.

Pittman, John, "Postphilosophy, Politics, and 'Race'," in Emmanuel Chukwudi Eze (ed.), *Postcolonial African Philosophy*, Oxford: Blackwell, 1997.

Pratt, Scott, "Philosophy, Criticism, and Social Reform," *Metaphilosophy*, 26, 4 (1995), pp. 337–46.

Puddington, Arch, "Immoderate Moderate," *Commentary*, 96, 2 (1993), pp. 62–4.

Quirk, Michael, "Notes on Prophetic Pragmatism," *Cross Currents*, 44, 4 (1994), pp. 535–9.

Reed, Adolph, Rev. *PD*, *Telos*, 60 (1984), pp. 211–18.

——, "What are the Drums Saying, Booker? The Current Crisis of the Black Intellectual," *Village Voice*, 40 (April 11, 1995), pp. 31–6.

——, "Black Politics Gone Haywire," *The Progressive*, 59, 12 (1995), pp. 20–2.

——, "Protect the Legacy of Debate," *New Politics*, 5, 4 (1996), pp. 60–3.

——, "Defending the Indefensible," *Village Voice*, 41 (April 23, 1996), p. 26.

——, "On Black Intellectuals: Rejoinder to Marable," *New Politics*, 6, 1 (1996), pp. 22–7.

Roberts, Tyler, "Michael Walzer and the Critical Connections," *Journal of Religious Ethics*, 22, 2 (1994), pp. 333–53.

Romano, Carlin, "Philosopher Express," *Philadelphia Inquirer* (June 23, 1993), p. F1.

Rorty, Richard, "The Professor and the Prophet," *Transition*, 52 (1991), pp. 70–8.

Russell, Dick, *Black Genius and the American Experience*, New York: Carroll and Graff, 1998.

Sanders, Mark, "Responding to Contemporary Crisis," *Callaloo*, 17, 2 (1994), pp. 645–50.

Sanoff, Alvin, "Cornel West: A Theology for the Streets," *U.S. News and World Report*, (Dec. 28, 1992), p. 94.

Schuck, Peter, "On *Race Matters*," *Reconstruction*, 2, 3 (1994), pp. 84–9.

Selle, Robert, rev. *WP*, *World and I*, 14, 1 (1999), p. 272.

Seymour, Gene, "Cornel West Matters," *Newsday* (Jan. 17, 1994), p. 34.

Simpson, Lorenzo, "Evading Theology and Tragedy?: Reading Cornel West," *Praxis International*, 13, 1 (1993), pp. 32–45.

Somerick, Nancy, rev. *RM*, *Public Relations Review*, 20, 2 (1994), pp. 211–12.

Steele, Meili, "Exile or Rootedness: The Politics of Difference in Edward

Said and Cornel West," in *Critical Confrontations: Literary Theories in Dialogue*, Columbia: University of South Carolina Press, 1997.

Steele, Shelby, "White Guilt = Black Power," *Wall Street Journal* (Jan. 8, 2002).

Steinberg, Stephen, *Turning Back: The Retreat from Racial Justice in American Thought and Policy*, Boston: Beacon, 1995.

Stewart, David, rev. *WP*, *Theology Today*, 56, 4 (2000), pp. 606–7.

Sundquist, Eric, "The Talented Tenth," *Commentary*, 102, 1 (1996), pp. 60–2.

Tanenhaus, Sam, "The Ivy League's Angry Star," *Vanity Fair* (June 2002), pp. 152–60.

Torres, Carlos Alberto, "Democracy, Education, and Multiculturalism: Dilemmas of Citizenship in a Global World," *Comparative Education Review*, 42, 4 (1998), pp. 421–47.

Trescott, Jacqueline, "Beyond Academics: Harvard's Dream Team Has Salvaged Black Studies," *Emerge*, 10, 5 (1999), p. 38.

Van Leeuwen, Mary Stewart, "Parenting and Politics: Giving New Shape to 'Family Values'," *Christian Century*, 115 (July 29, 1998), pp. 719–21.

Walsh, Joan, "America's War on Children," *Salon* (April 1998). <http://www.salonmagazine.com/mwt/feature/1998/04/cov_23feature.html>

Warren, Nagueyalti, "Cornel West," in Jessie Carney Smith (ed.), *Black Heroes of the 20th Century*, Detroit: Visible Ink Press, 1998.

Watley, William, rev. *PD*, *Theology Today*, 40, 3 (1983), pp. 374–7.

Weisberg, Jacob, "Bill Bradley's Naomi Wolf," *Slate.com* (Nov. 15, 1999). <http://slate.msn.com/?id=1003998>

West, Charles, rev. *ED*, *Theology Today*, 49, 3 (1992), p. 439.

Westbrook, Robert, "Democratic Evasions: Cornel West and the Politics of Pragmatism," *Praxis International*, 13, 1 (1993), pp. 1–13.

White, Jack, "Philosopher with a Mission," *Time* (June 7, 1993), pp. 60–2.

Wiener, Jon, "Jews, Blacks, TNR," *The Nation*, 260 (March 27, 1995), p. 404.

Wieseltier, Leon, "All and Nothing at All: The Unreal World of Cornel West," *New Republic*, 212 (March 6, 1995), pp. 31–6.

Wilentz, Sean, "Race, Celebrity, and the Intellectuals," *Dissent*, 42, 3 (1995), pp. 293–9.

——, "Sean Wilentz Responds," *Dissent*, 43, 1 (1996), pp. 95–7.

Williams, Delores, rev. *RM*, *Theology Today*, 51, 1 (1994), pp. 158–62.

Williams, Robert, rev. *PD*, *Horizons*, 12, 1 (1985), pp. 189–91.

Wilson, Robin and Smallwood, Scott, "Battle of Wills at Harvard," *Chronicle of Higher Education* (Jan. 18, 2002), p. A8.

Wood, Mark David, *Cornel West and the Politics of Prophetic Pragmatism*, Urbana: University of Illinois Press, 2000.

——, "Religious Studies as Critical Organic Intellectual Practice," *Journal of the American Academy of Religion*, 69, 1 (2001), pp. 129–62.

Yancy, George, "Critical Thinking May Improve Black Lives," *Philadelphia Tribune* (March 2, 1995).

——, "George Yancy Talks Theology, Philosophy," *Philadelphia Tribune* (April 7, 1995).

——, "This Million Man March is Not Going to be a Picnic," *Philadelphia Tribune* (Sept. 12, 1995).

——, (ed.), *Cornel West: A Critical Reader*, Oxford: Blackwell, 2001.

Young, Robert, "Keeping Faith and Losing Politics," *Minnesota Review*, 41, 2 (1995), pp. 288–91.

——, "The Linguistic Turn, Materialism and Race: Toward an Aesthetics of Crisis," *Callaloo*, 24, 1 (2001), pp. 334–45.

Zisman, Paul, rev. *AE*, *Educational Studies*, 23, 2 (1992), pp. 208–13.

Other Works

Ackerman, Bruce, *Social Justice in the Liberal State*, New Haven: Yale University Press, 1980.

Alves, Rubem, "Christian Realism: Ideology of the Establishment," *Christianity and Crisis*, 33 (Sept. 17, 1973), pp. 173–6.

Anderson, Victor, *Pragmatic Theology: Negotiating the Intersections of an American Philosophy of Religion and Public Theology*, Albany, SUNY Press, 1998.

Aronowitz, Stanley, *The Death and Rebirth of American Radicalism*, New York: Routledge, 1996.

Batstone, David et al., *Liberation Theologies, Postmodernity, and the Americas*, New York: Routledge, 1997.

Bell, Derrick, *Faces at the Bottom of the Well: The Permanence of Racism*, New York: Basic, 1992.

Bellah, Robert et al., *Habits of the Heart: Individualism and Commitment in American Life*, rev. edn, Berkeley: University of California Press, 1996.

Bellah, Robert and Hammond, Philip, *Varieties of Civil Religion*, New York: Harper and Row, 1980.

Benhabib, Seyla, *Critique, Norm, and Utopia: A Study of the Foundations of Critical Theory*, New York: Columbia University Press, 1986.

——, (ed.), *Democracy and Difference: Contesting the Boundaries of the Political*, Princeton: Princeton University Press, 1996.

Bennett, John, "Fitting the Liberation Theme Into Our Theological Agenda," *Christianity and Crisis*, 37 (July 18, 1977), pp. 167–9.

Bernstein, Richard, *Beyond Objectivism and Relativism*, Oxford: Blackwell, 1983.

Bérubé, Michael, *Public Access: Literary Theory and American Cultural Politics*, London: Verso, 1994.

——, "Cultural Criticism and the Politics of Selling Out," *Electronic Book Review*, 2 (1996). <http://www.altx.com/ebr/ebr2/2berube.htm>

Bloom, Allan, *The Closing of the American Mind*, New York: Simon and Schuster, 1987.

Bounds, Elizabeth, *Coming Together/Coming Apart: Religion, Community, and Modernity*, New York: Routledge, 1997.

Boxx, William and Quinlivan, Gary (eds), *Public Morality, Civic Virtue, and the Problem of Modern Liberalism*, Grand Rapids: Eerdmans, 2000.

Brown, Robert McAfee, *Spirituality and Liberation*, London: Spire, 1988.

——, *Reclaiming the Bible: Words for the Nineties*, Louisville: Westminster, 1994.

——, *Speaking of Christianity: Practical Compassion, Social Justice, and Other Wonders*, Louisville: Westminster, 1997.

Cady, Linell, *Religion, Theology and American Public Life*, Albany: SUNY Press, 1993.

Carter, Stephen, *The Culture of Disbelief: How American Law and Politics Trivialize Religious Devotion*, New York: Anchor, 1993.

Cladis, Mark, "Mild-Mannered Pragmatism and Religious Truth," *Journal of the American Academy of Religion*, 60, 1 (1992), pp. 19–33.

Cone, James, *A Black Theology of Liberation*, rev. edn, Maryknoll: Orbis, 1986.

——, *Black Theology and Black Power*, twentieth anniversary edition, Maryknoll: Orbis, 1990.

Cook, Anthony, *The Least of These: Race, Law, and Religion in American Culture*, New York: Routledge, 1997.

Cox, Harvey, "Radical Hope and Empirical Possibility," *Christianity and Crisis*, 28 (May 13, 1968), pp. 97–8.

Crouch, Stanley, *The All-American Skin Game, or, The Decoy of Race*, New York: Pantheon, 1995.

Dickstein, Morris (ed.), *The Revival of Pragmatism*, Durham: Duke University Press, 1998.

Diggins, John Patrick, *The Rise and Fall of the American Left*, New York: Norton, 1992.

——, *The Promise of Pragmatism*, Chicago: University of Chicago Press, 1994.

Dorrien, Gary, *Reconstructing the Common Good: Theology and the Social Order*, Maryknoll: Orbis, 1990.

——, *Soul in Society: The Making and Renewal of Social Christianity*, Minneapolis: Fortress, 1995.

——, "Communitarianism, Christian Realism, and the Crisis of Progressive Christianity," *Cross Currents*, 47, 3 (1997), pp. 364–78.

Du Bois, W. E. B., *The Souls of Black Folk: Essays and Sketches*, Chicago: A. C. McClurg, 1903.

Dyson, Michael Eric, "Martin Luther King, Jr.: The Evil of Racism and the Recovery of Moral Vision," *Union Seminary Quarterly Review*, 44, 1 (1990), pp. 85–99.

——, *Reflecting Black: African-American Cultural Criticism*, Minneapolis: University of Minnesota Press, 1993.

——, *Between God and Gangsta Rap*, Oxford: Oxford University Press, 1996.

Elshtain, Jean Bethke, *Democracy on Trial*, Concord: Anansi, 1993.

——, "A Call to Civil Society," *Society*, 36, 5 (1999), pp. 11–19.

Feagin, Joe and Vera, Hernán, *White Racism*, New York: Routledge, 1995.

Festenstein, Matthew, *Pragmatism and Political Theory from Dewey to Rorty*, Cambridge: Polity, 1997.

Fowler, Robert Booth, *Enduring Liberalism: American Political Thought Since the 1960s*, Lawrence: University of Kansas Press, 1999.

Frankenberry, Nancy, "Pragmatism, Truth, and Objectivity," *Soundings*, 74, 3 (1991), pp. 509–24.

Fraser, Nancy, *Justice Interruptus: Critical Reflections on the "Post-Socialist" Condition*, New York: Routledge, 1997.

Giddens, Anthony, *Beyond Left and Right: The Future of Radical Politics*, Cambridge: Polity, 1994.

Giroux, Henry, *Fugitive Cultures: Race, Violence and Youth*, New York: Routledge, 1996.

Goldberg, David Theo, *Racist Culture: Philosophy and the Politics of Meaning*, Oxford: Blackwell, 1993.

——, (ed.), *Multiculturalism: A Critical Reader*, Oxford: Blackwell, 1994.

Gooding-Williams, Robert (ed.), *Reading Rodney King, Reading Urban Uprising*, New York: Routledge, 1993.

Gutiérrez, Gustavo, *A Theology of Liberation: History, Politics, and Salvation*, Maryknoll: Orbis, 1973.

Gutmann, Amy (ed.), *Multiculturalism and "The Politics of Recognition,"* Princeton: Princeton University Press, 1992.

——, and Thompson, Dennis, *Democracy and Disagreement*, Cambridge: Harvard University Press, 1996.

Hadjor, Kofi Buenor, *Another America: The Politics of Race and Blame*, Boston: South End, 1995.

Harris, James Henry, "Practicing Liberation in the Black Church," *Christian Century*, 103 (June 13, 1990), pp. 599–604.

Hauerwas, Stanley, *A Better Hope: Resources for a Church Confronting Capitalism, Democracy, and Postmodernity*, Grand Rapids: Brazos, 2000.

Hopkins, Dwight (ed.), *Black Faith and Public Talk*, Maryknoll: Orbis, 1999.

Jacoby, Russell, *The Last Intellectuals: American Culture in the Age of Academe*, New York: Basic, 1987.

Jennings, Jeremy, and Kemp-Welch, Anthony, *Intellectuals in Politics*, London: Routledge, 1997.

King, Martin Luther, *Stride Toward Freedom: The Montgomery Story*, New York: Harper and Row, 1958.

Kraemer, Hendrik, *The Theology of the Laity*, London: Lutterworth, 1958.

Laclau, Ernesto and Mouffe, Chantal, *Hegemony and Socialist Strategy: Towards a Radical Democratic Politics*, London: Verso, 1985.

Lemert, Charles (ed.), *Intellectuals and Politics: Social Theory in a Changing World*, London: Sage, 1991.

Lentricchia, Frank, *Criticism and Social Change*, Chicago: University of Chicago Press, 1983.

Leonard, Stephen, *Critical Theory in Political Practice*, Princeton: Princeton University Press, 1990.

McGovern, Arthur, *Liberation Theology and its Critics*, Maryknoll: Orbis, 1989.

Macpherson, C. B., *Democratic Theory: Essays in Retrieval*, Oxford: Clarendon, 1973.

Marable, Manning, *Beyond Black and White: Transforming African-American Politics*, London: Verso, 1995.

——, *Black Liberation in Conservative America*, Boston: South End, 1997.

Mouffe, Chantal (ed.), *Dimensions of Radical Democracy: Pluralism, Citizenship, Community*, London: Verso, 1992.

——, *The Return of the Political*, London: Verso, 1993.

Nicholson, Linda and Seidman, Steven (eds), *Social Postmodernism: Beyond Identity Politics*, Cambridge: Cambridge University Press, 1995.

Niebuhr, Reinhold, *Moral Man and Immoral Society: A Study in Ethics and Politics*, New York: Scribner, 1932.

O'Meally, Robert (ed.), *The Jazz Cadence of American Culture*, New York: Columbia University Press, 1998.

Pittman, John (ed.), *African-American Perspectives and Philosophical Traditions*, New York: Routledge, 1997.

Pottenger, John, *The Political Theory of Liberation Theology*, Albany: State University of New York Press, 1989.

Ransby, Barbara, "The Black Poor and the Politics of Expendability," *Race and Class*, 38, 2 (1996), pp. 1–11.

Rauschenbusch, Walter, *Christianity and the Social Crisis*, New York: Macmillan, 1907.

——, *Christianizing the Social Order*, New York: Macmillan, 1912.

——, *A Theology for the Social Gospel*, New York: Macmillan, 1917.

Reynolds, Charles and Norman, Ralph (eds), *Community in America: The Challenge of Habits of the Heart*, Berkeley: University of California Press, 1988.

Robbins, Bruce, *Secular Vocations: Intellectuals, Professionalism, Culture*, London: Verso, 1993.

Rorty, Richard, *Contingency, Irony, and Solidarity*, Cambridge: Cambridge University Press, 1989.

——, "On Intellectuals in Politics," *Dissent*, 38, 4 (1991), pp. 483–90.

——, *Achieving our Country: Leftist Thought in Twentieth-Century America*, Cambridge: Harvard University Press, 1998.

Rouner, Leroy, *Civil Religion and Political Theology*, Notre Dame: University of Notre Dame Press, 1986.

Sandel, Michael, *Democracy's Discontent: America in Search of a Public Philosophy*, Cambridge: Harvard University Press, 1996.

Sanks, Howland, "Liberation Theology and the Social Gospel: Variations on a Theme," *Theological Studies*, 41, 4 (1980), pp. 668–82.

Schlesinger, Arthur, *The Disuniting of America: Reflections on a Multicultural Society*, New York: Norton, 1992.

Shriver, Donald, *An Ethic for Enemies: Forgiveness in Politics*, Oxford: Oxford University Press, 1995.

Sigmund, Paul, *Liberation Theology at the Crossroads: Democracy or Revolution?* Oxford: Oxford University Press, 1990.

Squires, Judith (ed.), *Principled Positions: Postmodernism and the Rediscovery of Value*, London: Lawrence and Wishart, 1993.

Steinberg, Stephen (ed.), *Race and Ethnicity in the United States: Issues and Debates*, Oxford: Blackwell, 2000.

Sturm, Douglas, "Martin Luther King, Jr., as Democratic Socialist," *Journal of Religious Ethics*, 18, 2 (1990), pp. 79–106.

Taylor, Charles, *Sources of the Self: The Making of the Modern Identity*, Cambridge: Cambridge University Press, 1989.

Trend, David (ed.), *Radical Democracy: Identity, Citizenship, and the State*, New York: Routledge, 1996.

Wallis, Jim, *The Call to Conversion: Recovering the Gospel for These Times*, San Francisco: Harper, 1981.

Walzer, Michael, *The Company of Critics: Social Criticism and Political Commitment in the Twentieth Century*, New York: Basic, 1988.

Westbrook, Robert, *John Dewey and American Democracy*, Ithaca: Cornell University Press, 1991.

Williams, Preston, "An Analysis of the Conception of Love and its Influence on Justice in the Thought of Martin Luther King, Jr.," *Journal of Religious Ethics*, 18, 2 (1990), pp. 15–31.

Williams, Raymond, *Problems in Materialism and Culture*, London: Verso, 1980.

Winant, Howard, *Racial Conditions: Politics, Theory, Comparisons*, Minneapolis: University of Minnesota Press, 1994.

Young, Iris Marion, "Difference as a Resource for Democratic Communication," in James Bohman and William Rehg (eds), *Deliberative Democracy: Essays on Reason and Politics*, Cambridge: MIT Press, 1997.

Index